NEW YORK

Publisher: Aileen Lau
Editor: Catherine Khoo
Design/DTP: Sares Kanapathy
                              Sarina Afandie
Illustrations: Shirley Eu-Wong
Cover Artwork: Susan Harmer
Maps: Annie Yeo

 Published in the United States by
PRENTICE HALL GENERAL REFERENCE
15 Columbus Circle
New York, New York, 10023

Copyright © Sun Tree Publishing Ltd
1994

All rights reserved,
including the right of reproduction in whole or in part in any form.

PRENTICE HALL is a registered trademark and colophon is a trademark of
Prentice-Hall, Inc.

ISBN 0-671-87900-6

Titles in the series:
Alaska - American Southwest - Australia - Bali - California - Canada - Caribbean - China -
England - Florida - France - Germany - Greece - Hawaii - India - Indonesia - Italy - Ireland -
Japan - Kenya - Malaysia - Mexico - Nepal - New England - New York - Pacific Northwest
USA - Singapore - Spain - Thailand - Turkey - Vietnam

USA MAINLAND SPECIAL SALES
Bulk purchases (10+copies) of the Travel Bugs series are available at special discounts for
corporate use. The publishers can produce custom publications for corporate clients to be
used as premiums or for sales promotion. Copies can be produced with custom cover
imprints. For more information write to Special Sales, Prentice Hall Travel, Paramount
Communications Building, 15th floor, 15 Columbus Circle, New York, NY 10023.

Printed in Singapore

NEW YORK

Text by Sean Sheehan

With contributions from
Catherine Khoo
Morten Strange

Editor
Catherine Khoo

Prentice Hall Travel

New York   London   Toronto   Sydney   Tokyo   Singapore

C O N T E N T S

C O N T E N T S

C O N T E N T S

C O N T E N T S

grand, but the

The city may be

people of the Big Apple provide the dynamism.

In the concrete jungle,

appreciation is

greater for greenery and

flowers, in parks or window boxes.

From the

quintessence of art

to culture to the latest revues to hit the world, New York has it all.

Welcome to New York! The most exciting and glamorous city in the world and one where the conventional American expression – "Have a nice day"– has never sounded so trite and inadequate. Niceness is a concept that cannot convey the energy and provocation that the city offers, the sheer frisson of being there, and the bewildering mix of emotions that the visitor will experience. The first impression is often one of speed, the unwavering pace of a city that never rests or slows down which in 1938 led Cecil Beaton to think that the average street pace was around 40 miles an hour. In the nearly 60 years that have passed since that observation was made the tempo has increased and the vibrancy of the people is more dynamic than ever.

New York is a city that never sleeps!

Colorful & Complex

Not people – but peoples. No community on the planet has such a diverse and diverting complexion.

New York compels with the ambience of the rich and famous.

Even fellow Americans visiting from other parts of the United States are as surprised by this as everyone else is. It is not merely the presence of the United Nations Building that gives New York its international character, it is also the daily lives of millions of people whose cultural affinities embrace not only the American way of life but also the life of the Caribbean, South America, Africa, Asia and Europe. This is an essential part of the city's colorful and complex makeup which means that New York offers the food, music, theatre, dance – and shopping – of the whole world. New York is a "world city", this is its *raison d'etre*, its core of identity and its guarantee of a future. And New York with all its rich manifestations are there for visitors to explore and enjoy.

City of Contradictions

There is a contradiction at the heart of New York that cannot be extricated from its fascinating appeal. It is a city that has thrived on welcoming the oppressed and the dispossessed. The Statue of Liberty stands as its potent symbol of freedom and emancipation, and New York maintains this proud commitment to personal liberty. People are drawn to live and work here because the opportunities are real ones. This is where everyone is invited to try their hand at whatever they want to do – get rich, explore their own self, begin a new life – and it

Having a ball of a time!

is this open invitation that drives the dynamics of the city and gives it a magnetic, captivating appeal. Many people do succeed, some become millionaires, others just satisfied and happy. John Lennon was a multimillionaire before he ever set foot on Manhattan so it was not the lure of money that led him to declare that New York was the city in which he should have been born.

But, John Lennon died in Manhattan and his premature death represents the other, less attractive, side of the city. New York is also a city beset with social problems that cannot be ignored. The drug addiction that runs rampant through the streets leads to crime, poverty produces homeless beggars, and the beautiful and the rich share the same small island as the deprived and poor. Lou Reed, the city's poet and erstwhile conscience, speaks of the "Statue of Bigotry" which too is part of life in the city!

Yet this contradiction between wealth and poverty indicates the tremendous opportunities for personal and material progress that run alongside human failures is a perversely fascinating dialectic. It accounts for the shifts in feeling that most visitors experience; from love to loathing, from fear to fascination. It cannot be any other way for this is part of the magic of a city where the weird and the wonderful co-exist.

The American writer John Steinbeck expressed it well: "New York is an ugly city, a dirty city. Its climate is a scandal, its politics are used to frighten children, its traffic is madness, its competition is murderous. But there is one thing about it – once you have lived in New York and it has become your home, no place else is good enough."

Touring the City

Where do you start exploring New York? The city's topographical divisions are legion and while some make geographical sense – Uptown, Downtown – some are merely obscure – SoHo, Tribeca – and others portend distinctions – Lower East Side, Upper East side – the crucial significance of which is not made clear in the names.

Bethesda Plaza in Central Park.

Begin in the heart of the city with a street that helps define New York, Fifth Avenue, and go from there to some of the buildings and places that no one leaves the city without seeing. And even if the city was your home it would take a lifetime to explore all the sights and attractions. Hence, the major problem that confronts any visitor is how to use the short time available to best effect. If time is short a tour has its advantages: there are scores to choose from; they are available in five languages, and range from 20-minute helicopter rides to eight-hour programs that include most of the classic sights. One of the best trips is the three-hour Circle Line cruise around Manhattan, which passes under bridges and past landmarks like the Statue of Liberty, the United Nations as well as the Bronx borough.

City tours are often tantalising because the atmosphere of the city lies within one's reach but can never be fully experienced until one steps out onto the pavement without a tour guide. Parts of the city must be explored on foot: the stalls and restaurants of Chinatown, the shops of Fifth Avenue, the bars and clubs of Greenwich Village, the arty pretensions of SoHo, evening time around Times Square, daytime in Central Park, a working day around Wall Street... these are just some of the locations where New York works its magic, not due to some spectacular sight being seen or visited but because of the symbiosis between the human land-

Fast Facts

Area: 779 sq km (30 sq miles), the five boroughs of Bronx, Brooklyn, Manhattan, Queens & Staten Island.

Population: According to the 1990 census, 7,323,000 in the five boroughs, but there are at least one million illegal residents in the city.

Government: The elected mayor of the city has extensive executive powers. The Board of Estimate decides on policy and consists of the mayor and the five borough presidents. The present mayor is David Dinkins, a member of the Democrat party which traditionally controls the city.

Religion: Christian, mainly made up of various Protestant denominations, Catholics and Greek Orthodox. There is a significant Judaic congregation and Islam is also represented.

People: There is no ethnic majority. People of African, Irish, Italian and East European descent have been joined by Puerto Ricans, Dominicans, Chinese, Greeks and Indians. Recent arrivals include refugees from South-east Asia, Central and South America.

Economy: Major world financial center with Stock Exchange in Wall Street; advertising; the media; publishing; textiles; light industry.

Language: English is the main language but the ethnic mix means many other languages are also spoken. Spanish is the chief second language.

Currency: The US dollar ($)

State Flower: Rose

State Bird: Bluebird

License Plate : Dark blue on white, with red stripes and red Statue of Liberty.

A happy New York patriot.

scape and the physical surroundings. The result is a series of photographic images that stays in the visitor's mind long after he flies home. The image may be that of Lower Manhattan seen from halfway across Brooklyn Bridge while city secretaries whisk past seemingly oblivious to the joggers and roller-skaters speeding by, or the ice skaters in Central Park with the Manhattan skyline rising up behind them in a block along Central Park South, or a stretched Lincoln waiting outside Bloomingdale's while the steam rises around it from a manhole.

Lovers of art cannot leave New York without a visit to the glorious Metropolitan Museum of Art, a museum so extraordinarily rich in its art and artefacts that you will always keep returning, or the equally enticing wacky Guggenheim with its unique collection of modern art housed in Frank Lloyd Wright's architectural masterpiece and the Cloisters Museum, located in the northwest corner of Manhattan which houses an astonishing collection of medieval art, providing the visitor with one of the strangest experiences the city has to offer.

Architectural Experiences

The intoxicating views from the top of the Empire State Building make it obvious that the buildings in New York constitute the most visually spectacular art form ever created. Certain structures – often made even more familiar by the movies – demand to be seen and to be gazed at in wonder. The art deco splendor of the Chrysler Building on Lexington Avenue and 42nd Street is one of the most evocative... but every visitor discovers his own personal favorite. It might be the spiritual charms of the Cathedral of St John the Divine, the heady materialism of Trump Tower, or the pure elegance of the World Trade Center, but every walk around the city brings a new building into focus and a new reaction from the gazer.

Borough Browsing

Sometimes the canyons created by the thin streets between skyscrapers prove claustrophobic and it is time to escape. Manhattanites know this experience only too well and have made provision for playful unwinding. The city without Central Park is unthinkable but there are also other excursions to be made – via bridge, tunnel or subway – to the outer boroughs. Manhattan is only one of New York City's five boroughs. Each borough boasts its own unique attractions. A stroll through Brooklyn Heights is a rare treat and calms the spirit after a hectic morning across the East River. The notoriety of the Bronx should not deter anyone from relaxing in the New York Botanical Gardens and a ferry ride across to Staten Island, the most isolated of the boroughs, is another classic experience not easily forgotten.

The annual Macy's parade brings cheer and colour to the grand avenues of New York City.

Not everything can or will be seen. It is not necessary because the thrill of being in New York is not measured by the number of places visited or sights seen. Some of the most memorable moments will come from chance encounters with other people, snippets of conversation overheard on the subway, the private tingle of excitement to be enjoyed by just walking past Grand Central Station or being in Macy's department store.

New York will provide scores of different experiences and conflicting impressions. It is a city to be enjoyed, to get exhausted in, to become exasperated by. It's a city to be in and a trip not easily forgotten.

Threthe earliest New Yorkers were the Native American *Algonquin* tribes. There were several different groups of them living in what is now Manhattan, fishing the Hudson River, hunting reindeer and wild turkeys and growing maize, beans and tobacco along the banks of the river. They had lived this settled life for thousands of years before the first white man set eyes on the continent of America. The Algonquin bore no animosity towards the strangers who made their way upriver in 1524, and the newcomers were sufficiently intent on their own mission to allow the strong river currents to dissuade them from even stepping foot on the land. These newcomers were French explorers, led by the Italian Giovanni da Verrazano, who were searching for the elusive North West Passage that could link the Atlantic with the Indian spice lands. It would be almost another century before any European actually touched Manhattan soil.

The statue of George Washington looking over Wall Street.

An old print of the Brooklyn Bridge over the East River, 1883.

Henry Hudson

Henry Hudson, an Englishman working for the Dutch, was also searching for the legendary North West Passage when he sailed up the river that would later carry his name. The year was 1609 and this time his men disembarked and made contact with the inhabitants. The Algonquin thought that they were meeting the Supreme Being and were duly

getting the ship icebound and questioned his ability to bring them home safely; the rebels set Hudson, his son and a few supporters adrift on the icy waters in a small boat, and they were never to be seen again.

The First Dutch Settlers

The Dutch trading post prospered and in 1624 the first settlers arrived. Altogether 30 families initially set up home on what is now Governor's Island, later moving to the much larger and more inviting island of Manhattan. They named their settlement New Amsterdam and the story of how their governor, Peter Minuit, purchased the entire island of Manhattan from the natives for a few trinkets has gone down in history as the first and best of the many lucrative deals that would be struck for New York real estate. The whole truth, however, is that the Indians who negotiated with Minuit neither owned or even lived on Manhattan! So, who were the real entrepreneurs?

These first Dutch settlers and those who joined them were a very different set of people from the other early settlers who arrived on America's shores to escape famine or religious persecution. The Dutch were hoping to establish a major trading post and they succeeded beyond their wildest dreams. So prosperous was the pace of development on the flat salt marshes of the south that by 1644 New Amsterdam opened up as a

respectful. Word soon reached Holland that the native Americans would trade their valuable mink, beaver and otter furs. Soon after a Dutch trading post was established. Henry Hudson returned to New York in 1610, this time flying the British flag, but he arrived in winter and the cold weather precipitated a mutiny amongst his crew. They blamed him for

An unhurried Central Park in 1861.

trading post to other merchants including English merchant traders who settled in the Dutch colony.

The Dutch were a thorn in the side of the British who coveted the commercial enclave created by the Dutch West India Company. Ironically, the Dutch colonists were also aggravated by their own authorities. Their discontent was particularly focused on the authoritarian policies of the Company governor, Peter Stuyvesant. He ruled for 17 dicta-

ain's other possessions in North America, though not for long...

Life Under the British

Under British rule New York's reputation as a city of low morals and high alcohol content flourished, one governor even spent most of his time walking about the city dressed as a woman! Dissatisfaction grew amongst those who wanted more for their rapidly expanding city. Meanwhile the rest of the American colonies experienced a move toward independence. This movement was not lost on the hardy and enterprising folk of New York who deeply resented the way the British were attempting to rake in extra revenue by way of punitive measures such as the Stamp Act of 1765. The Act levied a tax on all papers required for official business in the American colonies and it was the first direct tax imposed without the consent of the colonial assemblies. New York's street-fighting Sons of Liberty engaged in a number of provocative and symbolic acts, like the melting down of a statue of George III. Matters reached a head in 1770 when British soldiers killed one of the members of the Sons of Liberty. In retrospect this encounter, called "The Battle of Golden Hill," has been claimed as the first fatality of the American Revolution. It occurred only weeks before the Boston Massacre, which is the more generally recognised first act of bloodshed committed during the War

torial years until 1664 when the British king, Charles II, granted the territory to his own brother the Duke of York.

British warships blockaded the colony but the colonists were not inclined to die fighting for Stuyvesant and New Amsterdam became New York without a drop of blood being shed! The expanding colony was added to Brit-

Brooklyn Bridge and Manhattan at dusk.

of Independence.

General George Washington

The British interest in holding New York was purely a strategic one, and the 20,000 or so people living in old Dutch and newer English dwellings on the tip of Manhattan were not the key players. In 1776 the British commander, General Howe, with 200 ships and over 30,000 men under his command was able to force his enemy, led by General George Washington, to retreat north to a small Dutch settlement called Harlem. Washington was again forced to retreat and suffered heavy losses at the Battle of White Plains (fought in what is now the Bronx) losing a third of his 4,000 men.

For the next seven years, New York remained a British garrison town while rebel prisoners starved to death in prison ships moored on the Hudson River. The city was not relieved until after the formal surrender of the British in 1783 after which Washington was able to march in a triumphant victory parade from Harlem southwards to Manhattan literally reversing the course of his earlier retreat. He announced to the crowd that "I am not only retiring from all public employments, but am retiring within myself." He had spoken too soon, for New York had became the capital of the new American nation and it was in the new capital, in 1789, that Washington was inaugurated as the first President of the United States. New York would not remain the capital city but it rapidly became the largest and most important city in the fledgling United States.

Economic Expansion

A major factor that helped propel New York's economy was the opening of the Erie Canal in 1825. The canal connected the city with the Great Lakes and the Mid-West. The port of New York quickly established itself as the center of maritime trade along the length of the east coast. Any entrepreneur planning to market his products in the expanding communities of the American heartlands worked through New York. And as the port expanded, so too did employment opportunities, for not only was there work to be had in the docks but a slowly increasing number of factories were being established in the city area. All of this precipitated a great wave of immigration from Europe and beyond.

An American Indian.

The American Dream

The immigrants came in their thousands, then in millions, as the great American Dream found its way into the hearts and minds of poor Irish peasants who had little to lose by leaving a country that exported all its wealth to Britain. By 1848, they were joined by thou-

sands of Germans who were also fleeing a repressive system. They were soon followed by Italian peasants and Eastern European Jews. New York was the first port of call and while many new immigrants moved on westwards, the city became the permanent home for hundreds of thousands of exiles.

Imagine how they stood there,
what they stood with
that their possessions may
become our power.

Cardboard. Iron. Their
hardships parcelled in them.
Patience. Fortitude.
Long-suffering
in the bruise-coloured dusk

Fiorello LaGuardia

It takes a special kind of person to get elected, let alone reelected, as mayor of New York and Fiorello LaGuardia was special enough to manage the feat three times in succession. He had flair and panache and the citizens of the city took him to their hearts, delighted by both his politics and his sense of humor – and the ability to mix the two, as when city employers and a coal union were endlessly arguing to no avail. LaGuardia simply had the heating turned off in their negotiating room! When a newspaper strike deprived children of their favorite cartoon stories, LaGuardia broadcasted them from the radio himself. In another famous incident, a group of Nazis wanted to visit the city so, instead of trying to have them banned, he provided them with a Jewish police escort.

But LaGuardia was a lot more than just a colorful extrovert. Born into a mixed Jewish and Italian family, he was brought up in the streets of East Harlem and acquired a proficiency in five languages besides English. As a young man struggling to pay his way through law school, LaGuardia's linguistic skills earned him money as an interpreter on Ellis Island, helping to process the naturalisation papers for immigrants who often couldn't speak a single word of English.

His political career began in 1916 when he entered Congress as a Republican and he quickly established a reputation for his razor sharp wit and progressive policies. As well as possessing a quick wit, his sound grasp of administration and economics enabled him to rebuild a city's morale that had been shattered by the Wall Street crash of 1929.

With the help of President Roosevelt's New Deal he was able to secure massive loans for municipal building projects that remained untainted by allegations of corruption. Thousands of acres of new parks were created and important new bridges were completed, like the two connecting Queens with the Bronx – the Henry Hudson and the Triborough.

LaGuardia was not just considered immune to corruption; he actively sought out the criminal element and one of his first dramatic acts as mayor was to order the arrest of Lucky Luciano, one of the city's most notorious gangsters, and there followed a purge of the police force.

LaGuardia was in office as mayor of New York for twelve years following the Great Depression and when he retired, due to ill-health in 1945, his departure was genuinely missed. He remains the most popular leader the city has ever had and, while having an airport named after a politician is no big deal, making a musical about one of its mayors is not something many cities get around to. But Broadway hosted *Fiorello*, Italian for (Little Flower) and LaGuardia's affectionate nickname became the title of a musical that celebrated the politician that citizens really did respect.

of the New World.

And all the old songs.
And nothing to lose.

(Eavan Boland: *The Emigrant Irish*)

However, what awaited the immigrants was no paradise on earth. New York was overcrowded and under administered and those who stayed joined the pool of cheap disposable labor living in overcrowded and unsanitary conditions. Between 1818 and 1840 the city suffered from yellow fever and cholera epidemics caused by the enormous strain placed on water supplies and sewage systems. When the economy took one of its periodic downturns as it did in 1837, unemployment spiralled in a matter of weeks. Food riots by the dispossessed were not uncommon and more than

The Statue of Liberty was presented in the commemoration of the centennial anniversary of American independence.

once troops appeared on the streets to guard buildings. At the same time, though, there were fabulous opportunities for those who had a share of luck and some capital. When the American Civil War began in 1861 there were an estimated 600 millionaires living in New York City!

The Civil War

The outbreak of civil war produced mixed reactions amongst New York's population. For many of the recently arrived immigrants, the civil war meant little and a conflict over the rights of black slaves living in the unknown southern states was not an issue that directly touched them. Fernando Wood, the mayor, and city leader of the Democratic Party, had as his power base the numerically large and decidedly anti-war, immigrant community. At first Wood came out against the war, then declared his support for the South and at one stage was even proclaiming the notion that New York should secede from the Union.

On the other hand, Abraham Lincoln was rousing the consciences of the Northerners by turning the war into a moral crusade against injustice. His famously influential "Might makes Right" speech was delivered from the Cooper Union Building in 1860. Although the bulk of the actual fighting took place far away from the city (when the war finally got underway), New York became an important center for progressive opposition to the practice of slavery.

The Conscription Act

Attitudes to the war exploded into violence when the Conscription Act became law in 1863. Anger was aroused not so much at the prospect of imminent conscription but at one particular clause in the Act. This clause allowed the normally compulsory military service to be deferred by the payment of $300/-, a sum sufficiently large at the time to mean that only the rich could buy themselves out of the fighting. New Yorkers took to the streets in protest and four days of large scale rioting erupted. Over a thousand people lay dead when the Draft Riots finally came to an end. Two years later the city also bore witness to another victim of the civil war when the body of Abraham Lincoln lay in state in City Hall and well over 100,000 mourners queued to pay their last respects to this great American leader.

Reconstruction & "Boss" Tweed

While many parts of the war-torn country struggled to adjust to peace, New York, which had only suffered a loss of life and property during the Draft Riots, was now well poised to lead the post-war expansion. Major building works, like the Brooklyn Bridge, Central Park and the Metropolitan Museum, got under way and millions of dollars was there to be made by speculators. Anyone in a position to allocate contracts was open to massive corruption. One man in particular, William Marcy Tweed, emerged as the kingpin in any important financial deal involving municipal services.

For six years "Boss" Tweed controlled the Democratic Party machine and illicit money poured into his pockets and those of his henchmen (including New York's mayor) from wealthy contractors who were greedy to secure lucrative deals.

He earned an estimated $200 million whilst being buoyed up by the political support that was craftily engineered by his willingness to speed up the immigration process for thousands of new arrivals. In his own way, Tweed became a hero of sorts amongst the poor, who applauded his soaking of the rich. The stories of his audacious scams became legendary.

In 1871, after his antics were repeatedly exposed by the newspapers, he eventually found himself facing a court investigation and decided to leave the country. Traveling through Central America, Cuba and then Europe, he was finally caught in Spain and returned to face imprisonment. The newspapers which helped to put him there were delighted to point out that he would spend the remaining years of his life in a prison that he himself had commissioned and received bribes for.

An Ethnic Melting Pot

Prohibition & The Wall Street Crash

In the two decades before and after the turn of the century there were further waves of immigration. The year 1907 saw an unprecedented 1.25 million immigrants arrive in New York and the ethnic topography of the city began to take shape. This was the era that created Chinatown and the Italian community. Numbers were further swelled by the influx of more Jews from eastern Europe, African-Americans from the southern states flocked to Harlem in the north of Manhattan while the Lower East Side became an ethnic melting pot. Poverty acted as a glue helping to bond together the disparate cultures that struggled to survive amidst appalling overcrowding and torturingly long working hours.

Out of the squalor, New York started to emerge as the biggest city on the face of the earth and, despite the low wages and poor conditions, thousands more arrived each week. On any one day over 2,000 people passed through Ellis Island, the first port of call for new citizens.

The 1920s recorded a number of significant events. Immigration laws were passed to stop any further floods of visitors and the infamous Prohibition laws were introduced in an attempt to forbid the manufacture, sale and transportation of all alcoholic drinks in the United States. Nowhere was the attempt a more complete flop than in New York City where countless illegal drinking clubs (known as speakeasies) mushroomed in every corner of the city and drinking became more fun than ever before. The manufacture and distribution of the illicit brews fostered an era of gangsterism that has been immortalised in film. Prohibition came to an end in 1929. Unfortunately the criminal gangs did not disappear as quickly as the speakeasies.

The 1920s witnessed the flowering of a hedonistic lifestyle that went hand-in-hand with the carefree dismissal of Prohibition laws. It was a creative pe-

New York Gangsters

Gangsters and gangsterism began with simple protection rackets whereby the proprietors of shops and businesses paid a weekly sum – a kind of insurance premium — against damage to their premises. Revenue collected in this way was then used to finance loan sharking operations and the purchase of fruit machines that were then rented out to clubs and bars. Prostitution rackets were another source of reliable income to gangs who sported names like the "Dead Rabbits," the "Five Pointers" and the "Red Onions."

When Prohibition attempted to outlaw the sale of liquor anywhere the gangs suddenly found a new and very lucrative source of income. The stakes were high enough to tempt gang leaders to cross the traditionally respected territories that different mobs had carved out for themselves. Gradually a few mobsters rose to prominence. This was the era of legendary bosses like Dutch Schultz, Legs Diamond and Abe Reles. When they were not trying to assassinate each other they formed corporate enterprises and met in the backroom of Midnight Rose's Candy Store in Livonia Avenue. It was here that Murder Inc. held its board meetings and discussed various proposals. Murder Inc. was a business which would, in return for a negotiated payment, carry out the execution of any named individual. Albert Anastasia, who at 19 years of age had been on Death Row in Sing Sing prison, was elected to head the operation. After his release from prison on a technicality he had risen through the ranks and when informed of his promotion as head of operations for Murder Inc, he had enquired if he had any choice in the matter. "You can accept the job and its responsibilites or you can go to the cemetery," he was told. He accepted the position.

Anastasia and his team of contract killers were eventually exposed by Burton Turkus, the chief assistant to New York's District Attorney William O'Dwyer. In 1940 Turkus nailed "Kid Twister" Reles, who had once boasted of killing eleven men. In return for immunity he became an informer and sent four gangsters to Death Row. Turkus himself could not be bribed and for this reason he earned himself the nickname of "Mr Arsenic."

The most infamous gangster of all was Al Capone who started off as a small time leader of a Brooklyn mob. It was only after he offended another gangster that Capone's boss decided to look after his protege by sending him off to Chicago for safety. The rest is history...

riod in all sorts of ways, perhaps best summed up by the style of jazz music that swept through the clubs and bars of the city. Jazz, with its insouciance, improvisation and its disregard of convention, explored musical extremes. It became a fitting tribute to New York's insistence that hard work deserved lots of play. Opportunities for play were unbounded, from gambling clubs and showgirls to family weekends at Coney Island and visits to Midget City where hundreds of dwarfs cavorted for the pleasure of city dwellers. Each spectacle was fringed with a edge of hysteria, as shown by the bizarre funeral procession of Rudolph Valentino in 1926. It was only a matter of time before the bubble finally burst.

The crash came in 1929 and the six year economic depression that followed led to 25 percent unemployment. Shanty towns sprang up in the center of Central Park to collect the human fallout. The only relief was provided by the enlightened rule of Mayor Fiorello LaGuardia (see box story) who did everything possible to revamp the city's economy and restore a sense of civic pride. Using President Roosevelt's New Deal Program, he pumped thousands of dollars into the creation of jobs in the city.

But, it took another world war to reassert New York's preeminence. As thousands of American GIs spent their leave carousing in Times Square, in the recesses of nearby Columbia University Robert Oppenheimer and his team of scientists were secretly working on the "Manhattan Project," which reached its deadly fruition in August 1945 when atomic bombs were dropped on Hiroshima and Nagasaki to herald in the end of the First World War.

The Post-War Period

The end of the war signalled the beginning of another stage in the city's momentous history. In 1945, La Guardia stepped down and was replaced by Wiliam O'Dwyer under whose authority the building boom of those years created much of the plate glass skyscraper image that is so well known today. In 1950, O'Dwyer went into exile to escape prosecution for his links with gangsters. As white middle-class families vacated the city, their numbers were replaced by a new wave of immigrants from Puerto Rico. Urban tension spilled over into race riots in 1964 and the city staggered from one financial crisis to another. In 1975, New York was about to declare itself bankrupt. Ignored by the central government it was finally bailed out by two of the city's largest unions. Tight planning controls were set on the city's administration and once the central government realised that the city was seriously trying to balance its budgets, huge loans made possible the continuation of the city's services. Nevertheless, thousands of the city's workers lost their jobs, ironically some of them being the people whose pension funds had been used to bail out the city's finances in its time of crisis.

In 1978 Ed Koch was elected mayor. He was determined to smash crime, keep the unions in check and keep a tight control on the city's spending, thereby bringing investors back to the city. The huge federal loans were paid back ahead of schedule, another construction boom began in 1985, and there was a budget surplus – the city had spent less money than it earned! But, if New York now looks shinier, cleaner – and is a safer place – the poor have benefitted the least. The austerity of the 1990s has only made their position worse and the city's urban poverty is one of the major problems facing the current mayor, African-American David Dinkins. His first term of office has been moderately successful and the pressures are mounting by the New York community to tackle the racial problems, the city's economic problems, create more jobs, further reduce the threat of crime and solve the problem of the homeless. If he only succeeds halfway, he will usurp Le Guardia's reputation as the greatest mayor the city has ever seen.

Government

The foundations of the city's government go back to the late 18th century when a social organisation was formed by immigrants, known as Tammany. It soon developed into a powerful political machine that ran New York. Tammany Hall, which once stood on the corner of Frankfort Street and Park Row, became synonymous with three features of the city's government: municipal corruption, the Irish connection and the Democratic Party. The local government worked through a system that elected a number of constituency bosses. Each boss worked using fair means and foul to secure the allegiance of the voters in his constituency.

The home where Roosevelt was born.

Throughout the 19th century the Irish were the dominant immigrant group and politicians eagerly cultivated their support. The party machine was financed by payoffs from business interests anxious to

Helping The Homeless

The homeless camping in Central Park.

No one can be in New York for very long without being made aware of the problem of homelessness. Sooner or later the plight of a homeless individual will be brought to your attention. It may be the slumped figure of a man or woman on the pavement with a cardboard placard outlining his or her life story. It may be less passive than that when a person addresses you and your fellow passengers on a subway train and asks for assistance. The individuals who speak to you on the train may be homeless persons themselves or they may be working for an organisation which helps those without a place to sleep that night.

The people who do this are invariably genuine and, if they are working for a homeless group, they will bear an identification tag authenticating their role. If you are out early in the morning you will come across the homeless – a sleeping figure on a park bench or curled up on a pavement over a subway grate where the heat rises – and however much distaste one might initially feel, the reality is that thousands of New Yorkers are in this situation every night and not all are drug abusers! Some will be alarmingly ordinary folk who have unexpectedly found themselves unemployed, only to discover that the system they once worked for has completely discarded them.

For most of the year, the problem is not a fatal one, but come the notorious bitter cold of one New York winter and there are inevitable casualities. The police turn out a vagrant from a subway station only to discover his corpse on the sidewalk the following morning. In a city that houses some of the wealthiest people on earth, where the Statue of Liberty proudly welcomes the poor and huddled masses, it remains an uncomfortable truth that as many 10,000 people do not have a place to sleep in.

To be fair, the city has recognised the problem. In 1979, court action was taken on behalf of the homeless. The judicial decision which resulted stated that New York had a legal obligation to provide for their homeless. This decision was accepted by City Hall. The result was the construction of large-scale bunkers consisting of hundreds of bunk beds that offered a free night's lodging to the dispossessed. To the unfortunate inmates, who slept under the gaze of bright lights which are kept on all night (in the interests of security), this came as a mixed blessing. Equally unsatisfactory were the welfare hotels that hired out rooms to the homeless and then claimed rents from City Hall for their apparently solicitious endeavours. The annual bill approached $100 million and neigborhoods adjacent to the welfare hotels felt threatened and intimidated.

City Hall continues to battle with a problem that cannot be ignored. Smaller accommodation centers have been set up around the city and queues of ragged people waiting in line outside a building testify to their dependence on soup kitchens that offer them their only hot meal for the day.

secure contacts or avoid bureaucratic constraints. And, while the kind of wholesale corruption that was once taken for granted is no longer tolerated, the city's connection with the Democratic Party is still a strong and influential one with over two-thirds of the electorate regularly voting Democratic. The mayor's position has also traditionally been filled by a Democrat.

Mayor's Position

Tammany Hall no longer stands but the post of mayor, once a Tammany stronghold, continues to wield enormous political power and prestige. A wide range of important positions, from the head of the police department to senior administrative posts, come directly under the mayor's control and no other individual enjoys the same executive sweep as he does when it comes to crucial budgeting decisions.

A mayor is elected for a four-year term. He usually keeps his position by being reelected. He also works with the City Council, made up of elected politicians. Running a city as large and as complex as New York, both in terms of economics and politics, is more demanding a task than that faced by many

national governments. There will continue to be startling challenges, dramatic failures and enduring successes.

During the second half of the 1960s, and for most of the 1970s, the task of governing New York, a city seemingly beyond redemption, was a thankless task. Race riots and strikes compounded severe underlying economic stress brought about by a diminishing tax revenue, which was mainly caused by the exodus of middle-class families and corporations to the suburbs and beyond.

By 1975, the city was teetering on the edge of bankruptcy, unable to deliver public payrolls, and the central government in Washington adamantly refused the tab.

Confidence Restored

What saved the city was last-minute fund-raising by two big trade unions and Big MAC (Municipal Assistance Corporation), the latter being a hastily formed group that borrowed millions of dollars for the city on the strict understanding that not a cent would be wasted or misspent.

Confidence was gradually restored, especially due to the election of a new

Ed Koch, the mayor who restored New York's confidence.

adding to the general sense of fiscal well-being by pouring into the Big Apple. Transatlantic fares had dramatically dropped, the downward spiral of the dollar helped to balance the city budgets, and the new expansionist spirit was summed up by the addition of the ostentatious Trump Tower to the Manhattan skyline.

David Dinkins

The 1980s saw a fitting farewell to the excesses and inequalities of the Reaganite 1980s and New York also came to earth with a bump after the stock market crashed in October 1987. Acknowledging the new mood of sobri-

mayor who was determined to avoid earlier financial catastrophes. The new city boss was Ed Koch, who was first elected in 1978 and, like LaGuardia, born and bred in the locality, he projected a theatrical sense of self-confidence as he buzzed around the city in his helicopter and was able to retort criticisms with his barbed wit which won admiration from streetwise and apolitical New Yorkers. "How am I doing?" became one of his favorite catchphrases when he knew the answer had to be a favorable one, and allegations of shady Tammany-style deals in his administration never managed to ruffle his poise or his hold on power.

By 1985 the city was actually scoring a budget surplus, and tourists were

David Dinkins was his successor.

Roosevelt Island

Getting there is really half the fun. A horizontal cable car runs between the island and 60th Street at Second Avenue and for US$1.60 you can literally get an uplifting experience as the tram rises alongside the Queensborough Bridge and crosses the East River. The journey can also be accomplished by train but this offers little attraction apart from the fairly unique experience of arriving at a spotlessly clean and modern New York subway station.

Roosevelt Island is two miles long and only 800 feet wide and is home to about 80,000 residents. The Canarsie Indian name for the island was "Minnahannock" which when roughly translated means "It's nice to be on the island." This sentiment still holds good, especially if you just want to experience the sensation of leaving Manhattan behind albeit for a short while. From the island's promenade you can enjoy delightful views of the crowded metropolis across the water and as the Circle Line tourist ferries regularly ply past, it is easy to feel that you are outside of it all, a mere observer on a nearby island.

Dutch hog farmers bought the island in 1637 and it passed through various hands before New York City purchased it for US$32,000 in 1882. The authorities turned the place into "Welfare Island," as it came to be known, by building a smallpox hospital, prison and psychiatric institution.

Not surprisingly, this had the effect of keeping most people away from the place and most of those who did find themselves on the island were not there voluntarily! Boss Tweed was incarcerated in the penitentiary in 1873 as was Mae West some years later after being arrested for her part in the lewd play "*Sex*". One famous visitor who did arrive voluntarily was Charles Dickens who came to inspect the smallpox hospital to compare its conditions with those of England's hospitals. He also visited the **Chapel of the Holy Shepherd**, in the middle of the modern shopping precinct, where the bell was rung each morning to awaken the inmates of the nearby alms houses.

Today, the island has two functioning hospitals for the chronically ill and there are as many motorised wheelchairs on the roads as there are cars! The old smallpox hospital at the southern end of the island is closed off, but at night it is lit up with floodlights and looks like a palace. The main residential area is at the other end of the island where building work began in the 1970s, following the plans laid down by the prestigious team of Philip Johnson and John Burgee.

From the tram plaza turn right on the main road and walk along the riverfront, past the subway station, to the main shopping area where there are a couple of restaurants. The **Roosevelt Island Operations Corporation**, at 91 Main Street, has walking guides but it is difficult to get lost and there is an island bus that you can charter for US$0.10 a ride which will return you to either of the stations. Be sure to walk over to the Queens side of the island if you want to see a grim view of the borough's coastline.

ety, Ed Koch finally exiled and was replaced by the altogether different David Dinkins in 1990. It was the first time that an African-American politician managed to climb to the top of New York's greasy pole of office. Puerto Ricans and African-Americans, who have traditionally been portrayed as confront-

Keeping The Big Apple Clean

An enormous amount of garbage accumulates in New York everyday: over 30 tons of rubbish in the subway alone, and 35,000 tons of garbage from homes and stores. Over 20 years ago it was calculated that there was more trash floating down the Hudson than the combined waste of London, Paris and Tokyo. Every year about four million tires are discarded and because environmental restrictions have raised the cost of disposing them they have become fixtures of the city's landscape in poorer neighborhoods. They are piled higgledy-piggledy in vacant lots or accumulated under elevated highways looking like giant doughnuts baking in the sun.

Where does all the garbage end up? For years most of it has been deposited on the Fresh Kills Landfill on Staten Island. This same landfill now gives the island the unenvied distinction of housing the world's largest man-made structure. By 1973 there used to be at least one landfill in each borough but four of the borough authorities found good reasons for closing each of their landfills down and shifting their garbage to Staten Island. Brooklyn came up with the most original excuse; as their landfill situated near Kennedy airport, grew higher and higher, there was an increasing danger that the hordes of seagulls feeding off the top would cross the flightpaths of planes, get sucked into the propellers and stall the engines.

Fresh Kills is now the only landfill in the city and it is growing at the rate of 75 feet a day. At first glance, the landfill actually looks clean, but dead sea gulls line the sides of the highway and the stench of garbage fills the air. Not surprisingly, the residents are becoming more and more alarmed at having to suffer the health and environmental side-effects and the city is desperate to find an alternative. A vast incineration plant is being planned and recycling projects are now being introduced in all the boroughs. The alternative has been nightmarishly spelled out by the Commission of Sanitation: "We are doomed to face an ecological nightmare of New York buried under its own garbage."

A related problem is that of supplying the city with the one and a half billion gallons of water that are required on a daily basis. The bulk of the water flows from the mountain rivers in the Catskills and beyond. Giant reservoirs hold the water and divert it into tunnels that flow down to the metropolis. Although this system was constructed in the early 20th century, incredibly enough it has still managed to cope with the ever-increasing demands of the burgeoning populace. A vast new reservoir and tunnelling system has been in continuous construction since 1970 and is likely to continue well into the 21st century.

However, there are no equally ambitious plans to deal with the disposal of the city's sewerage and waste is still directly pumped into the Hudson and the sea. The city is kept reasonably clean but the rivers and sea are deeply polluted and swimming in them poses serious health hazards!

ing one another in a slum alleyway, combined their electorate voting power to vote for a politician who could help them. During the 1980s, when Trump Tower stood as a palpable icon of how the very rich could wallow in luxury, the poor kept getting even poorer. The infant mortality rate in Harlem, for instance, was equal to that of any Third World country, and the urban squalor and high unemployment rate is ironical for a city that boasts the United Nations headquarters.

But there is a danger of falling into journalistic cliches when describing the problems faced by New York's government. The city is not an apocalyptic nightmare and, believe it or not, there

A less tidier section of East Village awaiting improvement.

are signs of improvement. Mayor Dinkins' administration has risen to the challenge of dealing with the depressing media image of the city and is keen to point out that many, many other American cities have a far higher crime rate than the Big Apple. A "Safe Streets Safe City" campaign has been launched with a modest modicum of success and the increase in the number of policement on street patrol has resulted in a decrease in the number of rape victims and subway crimes.

New York has a history of deep troughs and ecstatic highs and somehow manages to keep going and reinventing itself. The 1980s, with its dangerous cocktail of high living for the powerful few and cynical indifference to the poor, came to an explosive end with the stock market crash of 1987 and therace riots of 1992.

The present mayor is probably more in tune with the needs of the people than anyone in that office since LaGuardia and there is a grim determination to ride out the contemporary depression and come out stronger.

New immigrants continue to flock to the city, the American Dream has not died and it is difficult to imagine New York losing its magnetic pull on tourists and citizens alike. The charisma remains, its pool of talent eddies but never runs dry. In the end, while there is undoubtedly an element of chaos, the other side of the same coin always reveals a self-renewing dynamism.

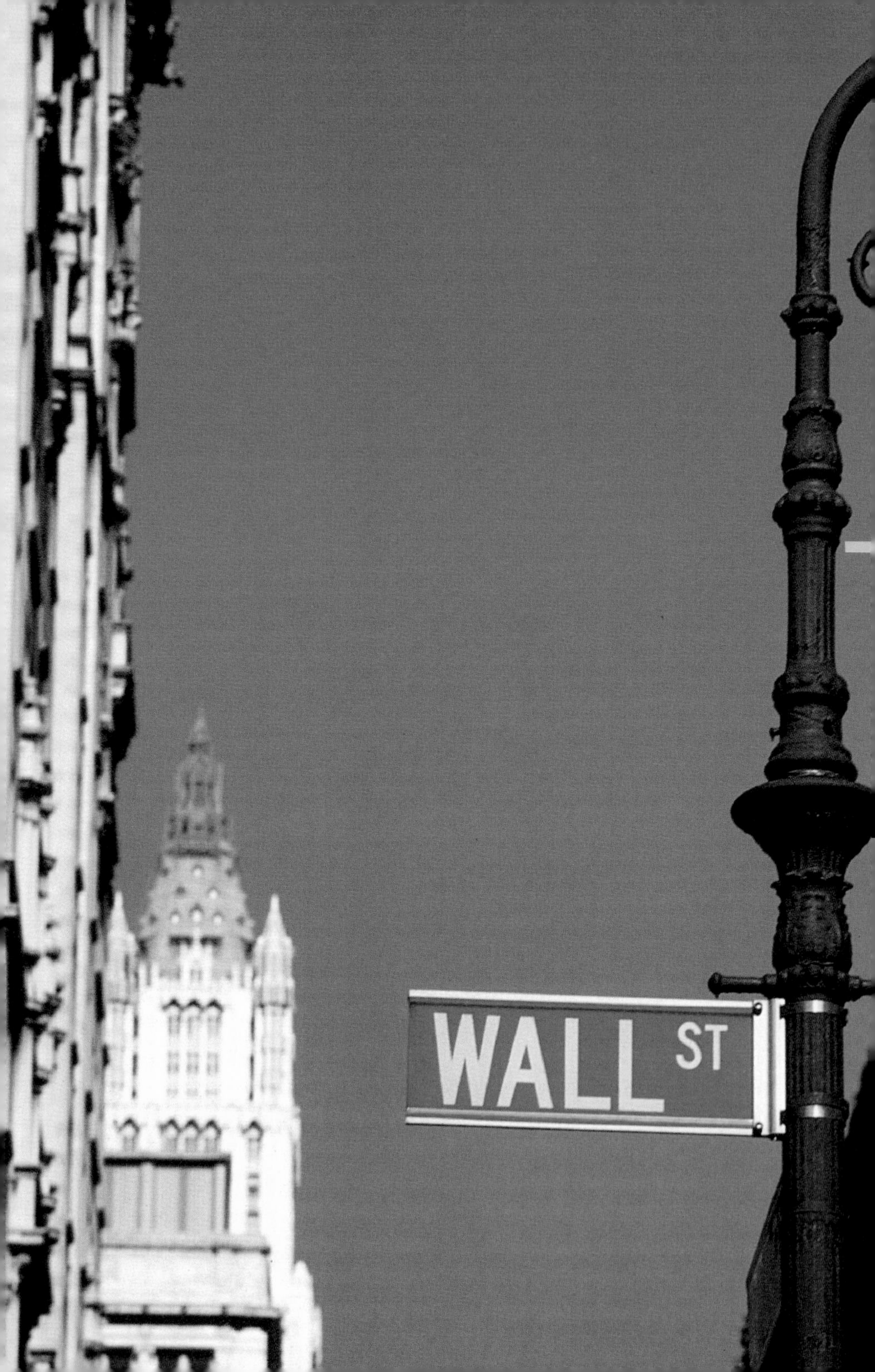
WALL ST

I f the very worst fears about a collapse of the American economic order were ever to be realised, the opening scenarios would unfold in New York. The politicians and the President himself may reside in Washington DC but, it is indisputably New York that functions at the economic heart of American capitalism. It has been estimated that half of the *world's* capital comes from investments originating in New York with Wall Street at the epicenter. Everything between City Hall and the southern tip of Manhattan is Wall Street, the street itself being one of the city's very few anticlimaxes, but Wall Street is also a state of mind. It is the economic consciousness, but never the conscience; it is the place where the American economy thinks itself through periodic highs and lows.

Wall Street, home to financial institutions and stockbroking homes.

Sometimes the highs are really high, as in those six or seven years during the presidency of Ronald R e a g a n which gave rise to the non-pejorative use of the term

31

The lavish interior of a boutique, one of the many fabulous stores to be found in New York.

Reaganomics; and Wall Street celebrated by making more money than ever before. Everyone knew about the catastrophic low of 1928 but this was regarded as ancient history. Until, that is, October 19th, 1987.

Black Monday

On Black Monday, October 19th, the Dow Jones average fell by a heart-stopping 508.32 points. The fall of over 20 percent sent tremors around the globe – the London stock exchange dropped by over 10 percent, Frankfurt 7.1 percent, Hong Kong 11.1 percent, even the mighty Japanese economy could not ride the storm and fell 2.3 percent in a single day.

An apocalyptic tone was clearly discernible in the deadly serious comments. An eminent city economist and academic compared it to a nuclear explosion – "Once you have seen it, you know it can happen again. The world has changed." If nothing else, it provided tangible proof of the power of the New York financial scene.

In retrospect the underlying causes for the 1987 crash seem clear enough. The economic engine went into overdrive and where it stayed for far too long.

Applying the brakes was out of the question as the accelerator was stuck but it was only after the event that this became apparent. Before the Big Bang,

New Yorkers believe in living life to the full. Christmas lights still sparkle bright despite a downturn in the economy.

investment banking was attractive and its glamor was synonymous with New York.

There had long been signs of the inevitable *hubris* and of course it was in New York that these were to be observed. One after another brash New York City investment bankers and bondsmen were arrested, charged and convicted for violation of securities laws and obstruction of justice, and in a short time the most powerful investment bank on Wall Street collapsed. The end of the junk bonds era should have been a warning; the giddy recklessness of the 1980s was over, but it took Black Monday for the message to permanently sink in.

The consequences of the 1987 crash have been felt the world over. But, the aftermath for New York was particularly bitter. Slightly less than 100,000 employed in white collar jobs associated with the financial services sector lost their jobs. The result was a consequent drop in purchasing power that contributed to an undercurrent of nervousness that surfaced as a massive loss of confidence in consumer spending. House prices fell and redundancies occurred as the multiplier effect rippled through the economy. A full recovery has still not taken place and the visitor to New York will benefit from this in incidental ways.

Restaurants, for example, soon felt the effect of their customers' tightening of belts and a competitive setting of fixed prices for dinners as well as lunch

New York City attractions like the South St. Seaport attract locals as well as tourists.

began to become common. *Nouvelle cuisine*, which has been affecting the presentation and content of all sorts of food, began to be seen as symptomatic of the financial rip-offs that had brought Wall Street to its knees.

New York Survives

As traumatic as Black Monday and its aftermath have been, New York survived. No sooner were investors picking up the pieces of their broken financial lives then the lure of opportunities in the new eastern Europe began to cheer some hearts.

The big corporations began to adjust to the new set of realities, trimming their budgets accordingly and started to devise new identities to suit the changing circumstances.

A good example is advertising, which remains one of the mainstays of the New York money scene. Virtually every advertisement agency worth its name has located a major branch if not its head office in the city, although the days when a Madison Avenue address was a mandatory part of the image have long since gone.

Nowadays, an advertising agency does not merely handle the media presentation of a product or a company, instead a total package is offered, from product design right through to the color of the shelf in which the product will eventually be displayed.

Economic Powerhouse

New York remains the economic power-house of the United States because this is where all the important decisions are made. It remains the undisputed capital of American finance, with the headquarters of every major bank and insurance company being located here.

It is no coincidence that Citicorp, one of the world's leading banks (with assets now approaching US$300 billion), should have one of America's most architecturally confident buildings. Or that Metropolitan Life, the top insurance company in the United States, should dominate Park Avenue with its name emblazoned in giant letters across the top of the former Pan Am building.

New York is the publishing center of the United States and one in five of the leading 500 publishing giants houses its base in Manhattan. These facts alone account for the hordes of commuters that flood into the city everyday, the 250,000 white collar workers who disappear into the Rockefeller Center and are at their desks and computer screens by 9:00 am, and the fact that the Wall

Street area has to stagger its lunch breaks otherwise the density of humans per square foot of pavement would prove life-threatening!

But there is more stoking the New York economy than the major corporations. For every company that counts its employees in the hundreds, there are 50 times as many that employ less than a hundred workers each and know each employee by name. This too accounts for the faceless thousands who queue up in the delicatessans each morning for their breakfast takeaways.

Role Of Real Estate

But, power is not measured in numbers and the magnitude of New York's economic wealth is more clearly demonstrated by looking at the role of real estate in the city. Even in a small town or village this is the best indicator of the local power vectors and it is the same for the Big Apple. Successful developers measure the profits of their million-dollar investments by 500 percent or more.

Nowadays even the *Village Voice*, once a bastion of anti-establishment

The 1928 Wall Street Crash

The New York
Stock Exchange,
mother of all bourses.

serve Bank at five percent interest and then lending it out at double that rate.

By the spring of 1928, over four million shares were changing hands in a single day and by Thanksgiving and the election of President Herbert Hoover, everyone's optimism about the state of the market was confirmed. Hoover more or less declared that at current prices, shares were a bargain. Unfortunately many ordinary people misunderstood this as the green light being given to them to invest their own money. In 1929 the madness continued to escalate.

The most momentary loss of confidence would necessarily induce some brokers to sell at a cheaper rate in order to settle their debts. But once this happened, and it apparently started with shares in General Motors being quickly sold off, the very momentum that had fuelled the market was thrown into reverse gear. It began for real on Black Thursday, October 24th, and five days later some 16 million shares were traded. The Stock Exchange collapsed with a loss of over $100 million, which was an absolutely staggering amount of money at that time.

Thousands of small investors lost their life savings. On Black Thursday, 11 speculators committed suicide and in the following month, two men with a joint back account, now empty, jumped hand-in-hand from the Ritz. The Great Depression had begun and, although rooftop suicides were not as common as legend has it, massive unemployment set in across America and then Europe. The human misery was immense and the international consequences profound.

The year 1928 was a boom year on Wall Street. Investors and traders had never had it so good and there seemed no end to their making of ever-increasing profits. On paper it was a simple: buy shares on one day, wait a day or a week or a month for the market to rise, and then sell the same shares at a handsome profit. It was perfectly legal and all that was needed was continued confidence in the market, and when that confidence went unquestioned the element of risk receded into the background. Unfortunately as the risk factor decreased the greed factor increased, and a hidden agenda was at work; stoked up confidence and pushed the market higher and higher, for on that path lay unbounded riches. Never mind if the market did not really justify the constant climbing, think only of today and the incredible dividends that were to be had.

The Stock Exchange system as it worked during the 1920s almost invited the kind of greed that was finally to bring everything tumbling down. A speculator could buy shares by having to come up with only a small percentage of the actual cash value of the shares. This enabled the shares to be transferred to his name and on the strength of his possession of these same shares, money could be borrowed from a bank which was then used to pay off the outstanding balance. The banks were happy to collude with this as they were raking it in by themselves borrowing from the Federal Re-

Pavement economy.

dissent, has initiated a "Real Estates Options" supplement that fronts as "a guide to the architectural and historical treasures" but which is financed by property advertisements.

Sometimes there are blips, as when Leona Helmsley, the wife of the property magnate Harry Helmsley (whose eponymous building nudges the Met Life on Park Avenue), serves a prison sentence for tax evasion, and when such a thing occurs there seems to be a collective surge of evasion and feelings of guilt.

In the summer of 1993 the judiciary pointed out the unfairness of twice denying Leona Helmsley parole, the unspoken truth being that other notables are admired, and their property deals highlighted in the press, for benefitting

in the same way. It has not gone unnoticed that the Catholic Church is one of the city's biggest landlords and that its profits accrue according to the same principles that dictate the commercial dealings of a Donald Trump. Real estate is a big business that affects the lives of thousands of New Yorkers – you only have to see the property section of the ludicrously hefty *New York Times* every Sunday to realise this – yet it functions as monopolistically as possible. Of the more than 10,000 real estate brokers in the city, about 10 percent of them handle 90 percent of the business.

A New York gangster was once asked why he robbed banks and he replied, "That's where the money is." He could have been describing his own city!

New York has dramatic shifts in temperatures which dictate the best and worst times to visit the great metropolis.

Winter Descends

From the beginning of December, and lasting for three to four months, winter descends with a vengeance and even visitors accustomed to cold winters will be taken aback at the ferocity of a snow blizzard tearing its way through the city. To say that the wind carries a bite is not a metaphor to be taken lightly and if you plan to visit New York at this time of the year, then come prepared with a coat, scarf, gloves and as many layers of clothes as you can comfortably manage. Disembarking in winter without adequate protection against rain, wind and snow will result in a miserable start to any trip. Snow

After a heavy snowfall on Park Avenue.

Geography & Climate

Cooling off in Central Park during the sweltering summer.

blizzards can suddenly hit and unexpectedly. In March 1993, the worst of the winter weather brought the airport to a standstill and ground the city to a halt. Extreme winter weather does not run uninterrupted for four months or more. In-between the freezing cold days, which usually stretch between January and February, there are brisk, refreshing cold spells when the sky is bright and clear. Heavy snowfalls, of four inches or more, are a rarity. Much more common are light snowfalls that are easily tolerated and often very enjoyable.

The warm glow of autumn in the country.

Hot & Humid Summers

During the summer, which lasts from June through August, the heat and humidity can be as hostile as the winter cold. Air-conditioning blasts away and a visitor traveling on foot has to become acclimatized to sudden changes of temperature, from the cold drafts of department stores to the sweltering steaminess of street pavements. Having said that, the months of July and August present no special challenge to those coming from tropical climes and a thunderous downpour of rain is often a welcome relief.

The best time to visit New York is from April to May and between September and November. Carrying an umbrella in spring will prove handy for sudden showers. A real bonus for these two months is that neither the heating nor the air-conditioning in buildings is set at extremes.

The month of September is like a second spring to New Yorkers and there is a palpable sense of life regenerating itself as people celebrate the Labor Day weekend. A new sports season draws in the crowds and the month also sees the beginning of a new season of theater and art shows.

A Sense Of Geography

A sense of the geography of New York is something that one needs to acquire before even setting foot off a plane – it certainly will not emerge on the streets and sidewalks! New York City is a part of New York state.

There are also two other bordering states: New Jersey to the west and Connecticut to the northeast. Of the five boroughs that make up the city, four are located on islands and are only connected to the mainland by a complex network of tunnels and bridges.

The Hudson River flows southwards into the Atlantic Ocean and in doing so separates the island of Manhattan from the mainland state of New Jersey. Manhattan is 13 miles long and, at the most, only two and a half miles wide.

Yet, it is in these scant 23 square miles that you will spend most of your time.

However, finding your way about this relatively small area can be a demanding business.

Average Temperatures

Maximum Temperatures

	Jan	Feb	Mar	Apr	May	Jun	Jul	Aug	Sep	Oct	Nov	Dec
Centigrade	39	40	48	61	71	81	85	83	77	67	54	40
Fahrenheit	4	5	8	16	21	27	29	20	25	19	12	5

Minimum Temperature

	Jan	Feb	Mar	Apr	May	Jun	Jul	Aug	Sep	Oct	Nov	Dec
Centigrade	26	27	34	44	53	63	68	66	60	51	41	30
Fahrenheit	-3	-3	1	6	11	17	18	19	16	10	5	-1

Orientation

The word "street", when prefixed by a number refers to the east-west axis in Manhattan. For instance, West and East 14th Street, is the same long street which stretches from the Hudson River on one side right across to the East River on the other side. If a street sports a regular name, like Henry or Canal Street, it will be situated in Downtown Manhattan which is where the early colonists first settled and where they named their streets in the same manner as they would have done in the Old World. As Manhattan expanded northwards, logic dictated a more mathematical nomenclature and numbers soon replaced words.

The north-south axis has avenues instead of streets but a numbering system is again employed – most of the time. The nearest avenue to the East River is First Avenue and the nearest to the Hudson River is Twelfth Avenue. In-between Third and Fifth Avenue there are three wildcard avenues with their own names: Lexington, Park and Madison Avenues. Broadway is like an avenue, in that it runs from the north to the south, but it does not run in a straight line and cuts across the normally rigid grid system.

Manhattan has a threefold division into Downtown, Midtown and Upper Manhattan. The Downtown area extends as far north as 14th Street (although some people claim the boundary is 23rd Street), the area stretches from there till Central Park. Once north of Central Park you are in Upper Manhattan. The subway system understands downtown to mean anywhere south of the station you are in and uptown is anywhere northwards.

Streets and avenues, uptown and downtown – it may all look reassuringly logical on a map but it is so easy to get confused when you actually travel on foot. Take on a neighbourhood at a time, familiarise yourself with the route to and from your hotel and avoid trying to cover too much ground in one day. The Circle Line Ferry, which departs from Pier 83 on 12th Avenue at 42nd Street, is an excellent way to travel around the whole island of Manhattan. You can listen to the commentary with a map in-hand which is yet another useful orientation exercise.

Mastering the subway and bus routes takes a bit of time but this is the way millions of New Yorkers travel and once you have a couple of routes under your belt you will feel a lot better. A route worth remembering is the 6-line that plys up and down between the Upper East Side and Chinatown.

On the other side of the island, the C-line connects Greenwich Village and the Financial District with Columbia University in Upper West Manhattan. Using the subway late at night is not recommended but buses are fine and, while they crawl along during the day, they are fast, safe and efficient at night.

The infamous subway system that has become, in the filmmaker's iconography at least, a visual synonym for urban decay and anti-social behavior also runs underground. This is a little out-of-date as the graffiti-ridden carriages have all but disappeared and thousands of uniformed and plain-clothes policemen patrol the stations and trains. Taking the subway remains the fastest and most efficient way of getting about. It is generally quite safe during the day. Traveling underground is not exactly wholesome, but the performance of buskers offers some compensation.

First attempts at deciphering the network maps of the subway system is rather like trying to crack an elaborate code. For starters, you have to seek out the "S" displayed on a globe which signals a street entrance to a subway station. A basic recall of the city's geography is essential in order to decide whether you are planning to travel uptown or downtown. Different turnstiles access the different directions and there are no maps to aid you on the platforms.

Staten Island

Staten Island, to the southwest of Man-

hattan, is the least explored borough of New York although everyone makes a perfunctory visit there because of the spectacular views afforded by a trip on

Winter descends with a vengeance in Long Island.

the wonderfully inexpensive Staten Island ferry leaving Manhattan. The island also has a bridge connection to one of New York's other four boroughs – Brooklyn. Brooklyn would be the fourth largest city in the United States if it were independent.

Brooklyn

Brooklyn is connected to Manhattan by three bridges that cross the East River, the waterway that divides Manhattan from Brooklyn and Queens which together make up the western end of Long Island.

The East River, is not really a river in the strict geographical sense of the word, although it certainly looks like one when walking across the Brooklyn Bridge! The walk across the bridge is a hugely enjoyable orientation exercise, which also offers glorious views of the island in the background. The view from the **Esplanade** on Brooklyn, which the locals call **The Promenade**, offers one of the best wide-angled views of the Manhattan skyline.

Bronx

The Bronx is the only borough that forms part of the American mainland. It also stands out from the other four in a number of ways. It has a fearsome reputation for violence and urban dereliction that are so far removed from its homely beginnings in the mid-17th century when a Dutch (or Swedish) family purchased a large tract of farming land here.

The family's name was Bronck and this area remained a rural backwater until well into the 20th century. Even today, the borough's public parks occupy ten times more space than the original 500 acres purchased by the Bronck family.

Unfortunately, this is just one of the borough's many attractive features that the average New Yorker usually ignores. Admittedly, the South Bronx is dangerous territory and a no-go area for tourists but fortunately the major attractions, like the zoo and the botanical gardens, are safely located north of here.

A stroll through the streets that are home to the city's largest Italian community is relatively safe, and relaxing compared to the concrete and glass of Manhattan.

Beneath The Surface

There is also another landscape that exists below the streets and underneath the skyscrapers of New York. At the innermost level is a bedrock of schist that dates back over 200 million years ago, and it is the solidity and density of this layer that supports the closely packed skyscrapers.

Above this rock but beneath street level there is a network of tunnels, pipes and cables so incredibly complicated that the subway system map seems simple by comparison. In fact, no comprehensive mapping has ever been attempted and it still not uncommon for engineers to stumble across segments of systems that no one has known of!

Given its density, New York's capacity for creating pollution is frightening.

The carbon monoxide being pumped out of the millions of the cars is only one aspect of this. Electricity, gas, water and sewerage circulates through the city every minute of the day and night is well distributed by the subterranean network. A constant reminder that the system is bursting at the seams can be heard, when you listen to the steam escaping from manhole covers, or when utility teams are hard at work repairing yet another burst water pipe.

Flora and Fauna

One of the best reasons for leaving Manhattan is to visit the **Bronx Zoo** which houses one of the largest collection of animals and has gone to great efforts to erode criticisms directed against the concept of an urban zoo. Some 4,000 animals roam over 250 acres, helping to fulfil the zoo's ambition of recreating all the major plant ecologies. For instance, in the "Wild Asia" section of the zoo, the Bengali Express monorail brings visitors fairly close to elephants and tigers who move around freely in their 40 acres of territory. In the "World of Birds," where there is no need for protection, you can move as close to the 500 dazzlingly-coloured birds as they will allow. Most of the simulated environments have been cleverly constructed – not just for the benefit of visitors. In the "Himalayan

Flowering plants in The Cloisters.

47

The Bronx Zoo houses one of the largest collection of animals
within its 250 acres.

Birding in New York

Red shouldered Hawk.

Birdwatching in New York? Yes, it does sound like some kind of bad joke when you envisage the skyscrapers, fancy avenues and slums, until you think of ... of course, Central Park! Central Park is the main birding location in the Big Apple and generally New York City is better equipped than most other large cities for watching birds. In fact more bird species have been spotted here (currently 410) than in all of Great Britain!

Central Park

With its 350 hectares of greenery, Central Park is by far the most important natural oasis in the concrete jungle of Manhattan. The park is much visited by locals and visiting birders and has an impressive checklist of 250 species (the one-day record is 101 different birds seen). The "Ramble" between 72nd and 79th Street opposite the American Museum of Natural History is regarded as the best spot from which to go birding.

It is especially good during spring and fall when many migratory birds visit, as New York is in the middle of a major migratory artery funneling millions of individual species back and forth between breeding grounds in the north and wintering sites in the south. In fact, many smaller birds get confused by the tall buildings and bright lights of Manhattan and end up taking a rest in the denser parts of the Park. The "Ramble" is especially good for warblers, vireos and flycatchers; in fact some secretive songbirds like the Mourning Warbler and Lincoln's Sparrow can be better spotted here than in most other places because of the relative light undergrowth.

The migration seasons here are actually quite broad and almost overlap, with spring movements starting in late-February, peaking in late-April to late-May and lasting till June. Then in late July the fall migration stretches from October to November.

During the spring and summer many resident birds like woodpeckers, chikadees, wrens, thrushes, blackbirds and finches can be found in the park. Before the outbreak of winter (from November to February) when sub-zero conditions prevail, most of these birds retreat with the passage migrants southwards.

What is left behind are a few hardy species most of which are not native American. Just like New York used to be the major landing port for human immigrants from Europe, the city has also acted as an entry point for avian newcomers.

The House Sparrow which arrived in 1850 now dominates the urban areas coast-to-coast from Canada to Mexico. The European Starling which was introduced into Central Park in 1890, now inhabits most of the continent, forming massive flocks numbering tens of thousands during evening roosts.

The Reservoir at 90th Street is also worth checking during winter. It is a well-known haunt for waterbirds like ducks, loons, grebes and gulls. Rare species are often spotted around here.

Common Cardinal.

American Robin.

Starling.

good during the fall migratory season when shorebirds, ducks and gulls congregate here. Access into the reserve is controlled but you can obtain an entry permit at the gate. Land birds also stop by and there are large resident populations of herons and rails – a total of 312 species have been seen here alone, some in large numbers. The **Jacob Riis** and **Forest Park** are both near Jamaica Bay and are good places to spot landbirds like jays, thrushes, tanagers and shrikes, often including rarities.

And despite its reputation for run-down residential and industrial quarters the Bronx actually boasts some of the best parks in New York; the **Van Cortlandt Park** near 242nd Street is larger than Central Park! **Pelham Bay Park** on Long Island is mainly a coastal habitat with many different freshwater and saltwater wetlands and surrounding woodlands which create an ideal habitat for all kinds of birds ranging from forest species to pelagic Great Cormorants perched on offshore rocks.

Up-State

The vast variety of habitats is the main reason why New York has such a rich avifauna. This area of the East Coast acts as a transitional zone between the Spruce Belt reaching down from the north and the Eastern Forest spreading up from down south. Many northern birds reach the southern limit of their distribution in New York. In fact, for some southern species this is their northern limit!

From the treeless peaks of the Adirondack Mountains to the lowlands of the Hudson River Valley, New York State sports a patchwork of habitats comprising coniferous forests, deciduous woodlands, farmlands and wetlands. Each habitat holds a slightly different birdlife and this diversity is exactly what makes birding in New York so exciting. Incidentally, apart from the UK, the density of birdwatchers in this area is higher than anywhere else in the world. The birders are well organized and the bird life thoroughly documented.

For further information start by consulting some of the sources below.

Around The City

Each of the other major boroughs within Metropolitan New York City all have their green breathing spaces. In the city that never sleeps you still need an occasional reminder that the world is more than glass and concrete and that we humans are not the only inhabitants.

In Brooklyn, visit **Prospect Park** and the nearby **Botanic Garden**, a walk through this large area, including a stop at **Lookout Hill** will reveal numerous small passerines and raptors (especially from the hawk family).

The famous **Jamaica Bay Wildlife Refuge** is part of Queens, largely a man-made wetland area of ponds and tidal mudflat. It is especially

Common Grackle.

More Information

In New York City call the birding hotline at tel: (212) 832 6523 for the latest taped information on where to see the best birds. Around the state there are similar services available in Long Island tel: (212) 979 3070, Albany tel: (518) 439 8080, Buffalo tel: (716) 896 1271, Rochester tel: (716) 461 9593 and at Syracuse tel: (315) 682 7039. The main US ornithological society, The National Audubon Society, has its headquarters in New York at 700 Broadway, NY 10003; their magazine *American Birds* is packed with relevant information.

To help you identify the different bird species, there are several fine fieldguides available on the American market. Roger Tory Peterson's *A Field Guide to Eastern Birds,* revised countless times, covers New York and is legendary amongst the birding community. Today, many birders use *Birds of North America,* published by the National Geographic Society because it illustrates all birds found in the United States in one user-friendly volume.

For specific information on New York birds, consult *Birds of New York State* by John Bull, and to find out where to go to find the best birding locations there is no better guide than *Where to Find Birds in New York State: Top 500 Sites* by Susan Roney Drennan.

Highlands World," some of the rocks are artificially heated from the inside so as to provide warm resting places for prowling snow leopards.

Central Park Zoo

And even without leaving Manhattan, wildlife can be also be appreciated at the recently renovated **Central Park Zoo**. Before 1988, when renovation work was completed, what existed was a convincing argument for the abolition of zoos. However what has slowly emerged is a carefully managed program that makes sensitive use of only five acres. There are no big animals cramped and confined like prisoners, and everything is divided into three climatic zones – tropic, temperate and polar – with the minimum of caging.

Central Park has plenty of other attractions apart from its small zoo. It is

Polar bear in the Central Park zoo.

into autumn before a canopy of leaves begins to carpet the walkways.

"Wildman" Brill

big enough (almost 850 acres) to support an indigenous flora and fauna that thrives in the middle of what is otherwise an incredibly urbanised and artificial community. Without the park, the dozen or so ornithology clubs in Manhattan would have little reason to exist, and cynics point out that without Central Park, Manhattanites would not know what grass and trees look like! That is going too far, but the park does register the passing of the seasons in a way that is not apparent elsewhere in the city. Winter ice provides ski slopes for young people armed with sledges and the pools and lakes are transformed into skating rinks. Spring brings hosts of daffodils and cherry blossoms and summer soon follows with banks of tulips and rhododendrons. Squirrels are hard at work in the autumn and the forest of trees undergo their splendid changes of color weeks later than they normally would in the "real" countryside. The reason is that the surrounding towers of concrete offer a form of protection against the forces of nature and it is well

A living testimony to the flora and fauna of Central Park is to be found in "Wildman" Steve Brill who conducts tours through the park, pointing out sights that a jogger would rarely notice. The tours do not just take you to the trees where woodpeckers are customarily found but also includes bushes whose berries are almost instantly fatal and mushrooms which if eaten would necessitate a rush to the nearest hospital. "Wildman" who is now in his 40s fostered his interest in plants during a childhood in Queens when Greek neighbors told him about edible grape leaves that could be found in a local park. He became a professional food gatherer and now earns a living by conducting "edible" tours of city parks. His knowledge is wide-ranging and impressive: "Indians used black walnut to dye clothing... tea from the hawthorn tree can help to treat heart diseases... white snakeroot is poisonous and if eaten by cows, this deadly poison is excreted through their milk and passed to humans which is how Abraham Lincoln's

Brooklyn Botanical Gardens.

mother was killed!" Over 18,000 people have accompanied "Wildman" on his tours, which created headlines in 1986 when park officials signed for one of his tours incognito and clamped handcuffs on him after he picked and ate a dandelion. The picking of plants in Central Park is prohibited. The media gleefully carried his promise "not to eat all of Central Park" and the embarrassed authorities dropped the charge.

Gardens & Parks

New York's other parks are tiny in comparison to Central Park but in their own small way they too provide moments of tranquility. **Bowling Green**, tucked

away in the heart of the financial district, has two claims to fame; it was the city's first park and is the only circular one. Here, and in nearby **Battery Park**, office workers munch their sandwiches while seated in the shadows of the skyscrapers.

Outside Manhattan, the **Brooklyn Botanic Garden** is a haven of bucolic bliss. In some ways it is more relaxing than Central Park because there is less here to distract the visitor. There is a "Rose Garden", a "Japanese Garden" and a delightful "Shakespeare Garden" (which is filled with plants and flowers that were featured in Shakespeare's plays). There is also a garden for the visually impaired where the emphasis is on the cultivation of fragrances. A visit

Gremlins & "Vilelife" in the City

The film *Gremlins II* (the first was not set in New York) tells the hilarious and occasionally frightening story of how nasty little creatures took over one of Manhattan's premier skyscrapers and wreak havoc on all. When the movie was released in 1990, one reviewer half-jokingly said that creatures as vile as the movie's gremlins could indeed be found crawling up from the sewers and into the pipes of a plush apartment block. The reviewer may also have had in mind the earlier *Ghostbusters* film which did feature vile creatures – paranormal ones this time – festering away in dark corners of the city's subway system and sewerage pipes.

The reality behind the fiction is that so much garbage is thrown away by visitors in Central Park that the rats there are known to grow to an extra large size as a result – over 17 inches from nose to tail and every attempt made to exterminate them so far has failed. In 1988, park authorities set about trying to attract barn owls to the park – a family of barn owls will devour up to 18 rats in one night – but not enough barn owls were attracted to seriously threaten the domain of the rats.

New York is also home to thousands of species of insects and over 50 different types of reptiles, including two species of lizard. Every now and then, there is a reported sighting of something larger, but the man-eating alligator that haunts the sewers is a mythical creature created out of an urban imagination fuelled by stress and fear. What is real though is the cockroach, and enough of them exist to prove far more terrifying than the odd alligator or two. There is simply too much food and too much garbage in the city to forever eradicate this household pest and every home in New Yorker sports some kind of poison or gadget designed to deter them.

The good news is that New York attracts some very pleasant and interesting forms of wildlife. A pair of peregrine falcons were found nesting on top of Riverside Church and harmless bats have made homes on the underside of the Brooklyn Bridge for as long as people can remember. And height has proven no barrier to the wildlife of the city for mice and ants have been found on top of the World Trade Center. Did they get to the top by the elevators or that incredibly long journey all by themselves? Who knows …

to the Botanic Garden makes a perfect complement to the culture-rich contents of the nearby Brooklyn Museum.

The same neighborhood is also home to another park that was designed by Olmsted and Vaux. **Prospect Park** is considered by many (including the designers themselves) to be a better showcase of their talent than Central Park. It is more relaxing, with less traffic and Brooklyn's fauna probably prefers it as well! People come here to collect the nuts from the gingko tree, a tree native to China which is now found along many of the city's sidewalks.

The gingko is unusual for a number of reasons: the nuts are highly edible though the smell before roasting is repugnant and the tree itself is dioecious (it can bear either male or female flowers). Most important of all, to ensure its survival in a city like New York, it seems immune to polluted air.

People

Everyone knows that New York is multiracial but just how rich the ethnic mix actually is can come as a surprise to someone who has not spent time in the city.

Take Harlem for instance. While the popular image – a neighborhood peopled by black Americans – is historically true it fails to do justice to the vibrant mix of races and cultures that make up today's Harlem. The neighborhood has distinct sub-districts where Blacks are the majority, others clearly Hispanic and even there the streets can be broken down into clearly definable quarters where people from the island of Dominica predominate. Terms like Black or Hispanic are generic labels for clusters of different nationalities. Officially there are two million Hispanics, probably nearer to three if all the illegal immigrants, consisting of Puerto Ricans, Colombians, San Salvadoreans, Argentineans and others

New Yorker all decked out in costume and opinion.

57

The yellow cabs whizzing around the city are often driven
by foreign cab drivers.

were taken into account. Black residents include black Americans, as well as people from Ethiopia, Senegal, Haiti, Ivory Coast and Jamaicans. And this is just one neighborhood in one of the five boroughs!

Melting Pot

The 1990 census came up with Pacific Islanders, 27,000 Native Americans and a residual 852,714 people regarded as racially unclassifiable. The figures disguise an intoxicating brew when it is realised that Caucasians include families who grow up speaking Greek, Turkish, Italian, Hebrew, Maltese, German and a host of Eastern European tongues.

The Asian residents of New York include Indians, Pakistanis, Bangladeshis and Chinese-speaking people who hail from China, Taiwan, Korea, Malaysia, Indonesia, Vietnam, Cambodia, Laos and Thailand.

In the telephone directory there are five columns of names under Ng and if all of them got together, it would be unlikely that they would even share a common dialect.

Thomas E Dewey, the Governor of New York State for 12 years, commented that "New York isn't a melting pot. It's a boiling pot." And, it is true that occasionally the volatile mixture boils over into open conflict and violence, not just between black and white but between gangs and groups belonging to the same

Policewomen in East Village.

ethnic class.

On the other hand, a good case could be made out for claiming that no other city in the world has dealt with its racial and ethnic differences so valiantly, honestly and successfully.

The conflicting values that beset the race problem in New York are well illustrated by the recent Leonard Jeffries case. Jeffries, a black university professor, made a speech referring to a Jewish and Mafia conspiracy to denigrate blacks in the movies. This upset the Jewish community, stirred up racial discontent, and resulted in his sacking. In 1993, he successfully argued that this was a violation of his right to free speech and the court awarded him US$400,000 in damages.

Freedom?

The right to freedom of expression is at the heart of the American consciousness and is practiced to its hilt in New York. For the last two years gays have protested at the annual Saint Patrick's Day celebrations because the organisers have denied them the right to march under a gay banner.

The city politicians, who are firmly committed to a policy of non-discrimination on grounds of race, religion or sexual orientation, cannot be seen to endorse their exclusion. On the other hand, the politicians do not want to antagonise the significant Irish vote, however conservative they may be, and

Who's Typical ?

It is far easier to describe the stereotypical New Yorker. His name is Riley, six feet tall and he is a policeman. His parents are both Irish who emigrated well before the age of 20 in order to escape rural poverty and seek a new life on the other side of the Atlantic. Riley is a Catholic, conservative in his thinking but contentious and impatient. He looks down on immigrants from Puerto Rico – forgetting that his parents once shared a similar plight – whilst at the same time admitting that he respects the Koreans because they embody a work ethics he was brought up to admire.

Riley probably does exist but he is not typical. If he lives in Manhattan he has a 61-percent chance of being white; in the Bronx 47 percent, Brooklyn 57-percent, Queens 71-percent, and Staten Island 89 - percent.

The typical New Yorker could be Edgar Raac, born and bred in Brooklyn from Ecuadorean parents. He has had a machine gun held to his head, he has been threatened with guns and knives and holds a more dangerous job than most policemen. He drives a cab around the city and has been doing so for only six months and he knows that 19 taxi drivers have been murdered in that same time. That is eight more than the number of US marines killed in Operation Desert Storm and 18 more than the number of policemen killed in the city over the six months. Raac earns about $15,000 a year.

Then again, the typical New Yorker might be an Indian newsagent, a Jewish deli waiter, a Chilean short-order cook or a Korean greengrocer. He or she will speak and understand English but may well be more comfortable with Spanish or Cantonese. The smartly dressed young men and women who work in the Midtown skyscrapers and who *look* typical may well live in the furthest suburbs of Queens or the eastern side of Long Island. Manhattanites like to refer to the commuters as B&Ts (Bridge and Tunnel) because their long journeys to and from work is seen to detract from the task of really living in the city.

What about the legendary rudeness of New Yorkers and their apparently congenital inability to be polite? They might be curt and impatient at times, and the one-liner comment does seem to be a trademark, especially in public situations where it seems they would gladly take on the role of the brusque urbanite. An English tourist waiting patiently to be served at an empty counter in Macy's department store notices that the staff manning a nearby counter are serving no one yet they remain indifferent to his plight. Humming and tapping on the counter produces no response and finally losing patience, he enquires, "Excuse me, but why am I not being served?", the answer is simple: "You're not being served sir because there's no one there." But for every incident like that there are likely to be more instances of New Yorkers being courteous and considerate to visitors. Abrupt answers are often a pose and when consideration is shown to them it is often amply returned.

The typical New Yorker does not exist. What does still exist is the typical movie image of the New Yorker, the short wheezing and balding Brooklyn taxi driver who has little in common with Edgar Raac, who really does exist!

they juggle their conflicting loyalties with a finesse that only seasoned politicians can master.

The unattractive side to an overly simplistic notion of freedom is that it includes the right to be desperately poor and even homeless.

A source of fascination, and trepidation, for any newcomer to the city is the dramatically sudden transition from an area of unashamed comfort and wealth to one of bleak deprivation and haunting poverty. The Upper East Side, the archetypal haven of the rich and beautiful that is so often portrayed in Woody Allen films, borders on the Puerto

Students in Greenwich Village.

Rican slums of lower East Harlem, with only a block or two separating them. The respective residents of these two areas have little reason or inclination to mix.

The invisible boundary is crossed when visitors inadvertently stray a block off course and find themselves in a different world.

The average New Yorker is well-off compared to the average American, earning a higher wage, saving more and is less likely to remain permanently unemployed.

New York's Korean community have proven enterprising and industrious.

The Worm In The Apple

Sociologists have speculated on the impact on New York's crime rate if drugs were legalised. No one doubts the link between street crime and the drug user's need to feed his or her habit. It contributes to the fact that while the city is by no means the most dangerous in America, mugging is a crime that strikes New Yorkers more often than the citizens of any other city. Mugging is the quintessential New York crime and its terrifying mixture of robbery and assault strikes fear and anxiety among residents and tourists.

New Yorkers live with these realities; indeed they are not allowed to for-

get them because the newspapers analyse crimes and their statistics in the same way that the *Wall Street Journal* reports on economic trends. The fear of crime creates a tangible tension that is an inescapable part of the New York experience.

It partly accounts for the defensive body language that is so apparent on the subway – no one ever stares, gestures are kept to an absolute minimum by all except the young. Even the slightest body contact produces an apology – and the darkness and gloominess of the subway is designed to produce a sense of vulnerability. It is no wonder that subway crime lies deep in the psyche of every New Yorker. A journey by bus reveals a more relaxed and less taut side

Famous New York Women

America's first-born saint, **Elizabeth Ann Seton**, was brought up in the city where she was born in 1774. New York was also home to **Leona Helmsley**, the queen of the Helmsley empire and wife to one of the country's richest men, imprisoned for income tax fraud. Apart from such illustrious saints and sinners, many notable women have achieved fame in the city, though being famous has never guaranteed happiness. **Billy Holiday's** life and experiences in New York is a tragic illustration of this fact.

Billy Holiday was not born in the city but her mother moved to New York to look for work after the end of the World War I. Billy grew up in Harlem. After her mother fell ill young Billy began to look for work in speakeasies and her exceptional singing voice was soon noticed. While she quickly rose to fame as a blues singer, her personal life was marred by a succession of unhappy relationships. She turned to drink and drugs to escape and while her reputation as a singer soared to new heights, her decline into alcohol and drug addiction was equally rapid. Laying in a hospital bed in 1959, she was arrested for possession of heroin and placed under police guard while she lapsed into a coma from which she never woke.

The life of an equally famous black singer, **Ella Fitzgerald**, shared some similarities with that of Billy Holiday but fortunately with a happier ending. Her family also came to the big city looking for employment and the young singer grew up in the Bronx. Like her tragic counterpart she first achieved fame in the clubs of Harlem but her personal life was not dogged by the misfortune and exploitation that destroyed Billy Holiday. She has become the world's most famous female jazz singer, with more than a thousand songs to her credit. Graduate students write doctoral theses' on her unique contribution to jazz music. And her response to all this fame? "I sure get all shook up when folks start theorising about my singing. I just tell 'em to sit back and relax. Yeah, that's it, relax. I just sing as I feel, man."

On the contemporary scene, **Muriel Siebert** continues to challenge the male dominated business world since becoming the first woman to gain membership to the New York Stock Exchange. Her counterpart in the world of magazine publishing, **Gloria Steinem**, is still contributing to *Ms* magazine which she founded in 1971. In the world of the arts there are many famous New York women. Back in the 1920s **Peggy Guggenheim** began collecting art treasures which she later donated to the art gallery founded by her extremely rich uncle. In the process she played decisive roles in the lives of people like Samuel Beckett and Jackson Pollack. It was also a woman who saved the New York City Opera from bankruptcy – the opera singer **Beverly Sills** from Brooklyn, who managed to follow her successful singing career with her new profession as a financial wizard.

to the urban traveler and the visitor should experience the contrast just to appreciate how artificial the subway syndrome is.

The Good News

The good news is that urban paranoia is just that – paranoia. Even on a subway ride the tension relaxes when humor is allowed to express itself. Often the voice of the train guard announcing the stations and line connections is so muffled or delivered with such painful boredom that it is inaudible. But then one train will have a guard with a soul who, when the train doors fail to close properly because someone is keeping it open to allow a late entry, gently admonishes: "It would be nice if you removed your foot from the door." Just to be extra nice

Ethnic Social Clubs

New York has always been a city of immigrants. From the very beginning, when the Dutch arrived and the English came not long after, when they shared the land with French and Scandinavian settlers as well as African slaves and native Indians, New York has a unique cultural mix that thhe word "melting pot" does not vividly describe.

Perhaps this cultural mix is best exemplified by the existence of ethnic social clubs.

Above the entrance to the **Club Deportivo Dominicano**, one of the many Dominican social clubs peppered across Upper Manhattan's Washington Heights, a sign reads: *Bienvenido A Tu Segunda* (Welcome to Your Second Home). The city's many ethnic social clubs have been providing a second "home" to diverse groups of immigrants for well over a century.

In fact, some of them, like the **Irish Ancient Order of Hibernians**, trace their foundations back to the first wave of immigration in the 1840s and 1850s.

For years the clubs have been functioning with little official recognition or even awareness of their existence. A tragic event that occurred on the night of March 25, 1990, changed all this when 87 New Yorkers were killed when the **Bronx Happy Land Social Club** was set alight by an arsonist.

Most of those who died were Latinos, largely Honduran immigrants. In the subsequent investigation the extensive network of ethnic social clubs was revealed. Nearly 600 such clubs were ordered closed because of their illegal locations in buildings that did not meet fire and building codes.

A commission was set up to look into the role these clubs played in the lives of immigrants. Their importance has now been officially recognised by City Hall with many of the closed clubs now being registered and reopening in new premises.

The various clubs offer a fascinating insight into the city's cultural melting pot. A host of community centers known to its members as *casitas de madea* (little wooden houses) are constructed by Puerto Ricans on vacant city lots in the vernacular style of their island's domestic architecture.

They are small wooden shacks with an open verandah, once common in the rural and urban shantytowns of Puerto Rico and now to be found in East Harlem, the Lower East Side and the South Bronx.

From another part of the world, the **Asanteman Association of America** was founded in New York in 1982 and serves the 15,000 Asanti people of Ghana who live in the city. They elect a "king" after candidates contesting for this honor make their case before a council who will then cast their votes. The king remains in office for three years.

There is no rule about the leader coming from a divine family, recent kings have included a refrigerator repair man and a plumber. Following West African judicial tradition, the king is often asked to settle personal, marital and business disputes. In a city where lawyers' fees are extremely high, this is a highly pragmatic service.

The **Castel del Golfo Social Club** provides its Sicilian members with premises for card-playing, sponsors a children's soccer team and celebrates the annual feast of *Madonna di Soccorso*.

Sometimes a club is formed with a highly specific purpose, like the **Stuyvesant Heights Senior Citizen Center**, which was formed in 1975 by Brooklyn's senior citizens who share a love for southern African-American quilting. They meet once a week to quilt traditional patterns, a skill handed down from their southern mothers and grandmothers.

Sometimes the clubs have a commercial as well as a social purpose. For instance, the **Korean Produce Association** was founded in 1973 to promote Korean business relations, fight against anti-Korean discrimination and provide economic assistance to established greengrocers. The association organises the Annual Korean Harvest & Folklore Festival in Flushing Meadows, Queens and celebrates *Choo-Seok* (autumn moon), the traditional Korean harvest festival.

This is one of the very few occasions when Korean-American merchants take a day off work, as they usually work up to 18 hours a day, seven days a week.

Contemplating moves in the park.

he might later add: "Your heart may have been in the right place but your foot wasn't."

New Yorkers are aware of street crime and the AIDS epidemic, and take sensible precautions, but they do not live in a permanent state of fear and anxiety. The number of crimes for 1992 have now dropped for two years in a row: car thefts are down by 9.3 percent; robberies are down by 7.4 percent and burglaries have decreased by 7.5 percent.

The good news is that the vast majority of people in the city are hardworking folk who work to pay rent, buy groceries and have some money left over to enjoy the good things in life. What makes them special? They are often larger than life characters, or at least they seem to be so because talking quietly does not come easy to them and the visitor has no choice but to share their conversation.

They sound sardonic but are rarely sarcastic; they laugh exuberantly but curse vociferously when something upsets them; they cling precariously to the ideal of an individual's freedom but often appear remarkably conformist.

The *New York Times* is the daily bible for many and if the paper slams a new play, for instance, or praises a new restaurant, then the play sinks into oblivion and the food review will be photocopied, enlarged to the maximum and plastered across the restaurant window for the next three to four years.

Learning The Lingo – A Guide To The Language Of New York

No matter where you learnt to speak English, if you have never been to New York before, be prepared for a linguistic culture shock. Many New Yorkers tend to speak fast and run a string of familiar words together with a nasal drawl that can be at first disconcerting. Fellow Americans from outside the city like to exaggerate the accent and portray cab drivers as saying "you wanna go to toity-toid and toid?" (which means "do you want to go to 33rd Street and Third Avenue?"), but no one really speaks like this.

What may come as a surprise is the fact that English is often spoken as a second language in many parts of New York. Department stores and hotels may create the comfortable impression that English is universally spoken and understood but this is an illusion. In many smaller shops and food places, be prepared for looks of incomprehension when English is spoken too quickly or with an unfamiliar accent. Spanish is commonly heard in all parts of the city and is used on the street, on television and in shops.

Another disconcerting aspect of language use in New York is the unpredictability of it all. A complete stranger will be disarmingly polite and apologise if they step in front of you on the street and a request for information may be met by a courteous display of friendliness and consideration. However in the next minute you might meet a shop assistant who will seem abrupt to the point of rudeness when asked a simple question and fellow pedestrians who curse loudly if you get in their way.

Everyday Words & Expressions

B & Ts: Acronym for Bridge and Tunnel people, that is, those who commute to Manhattan. The term is often used dismissively by those who live within Manhattan.
Bagel & a "schmear": A cream cheese spread.
Bill: Banknote.
Check: In a restaurant the word refers to the bill.
Drugstore: Chemist.
Condo: The abbreviated form of condominium, an individual apartment within a building.
Diaper: Nappy.
Four-lane highway: Dual carriageway.
Gas/Gasoline: Petrol.
Hood: The bonnet of a car.
Pants: Trousers.
Restroom/Bathroom/Washroom/Comfort Room/John: All five terms are used interchangeably to mean a toilet.
Rez: Abbreviation for a restaurant reservation.
Seltzer: Non-flavored carbonated drink.
Slice: Piece of pizza.
Sneakers: Tennis shoes.
Soda: Flavored carbonated drink.
Stand-on-line: Queue up.
Stoop: A platform with steps at the entrance to a house.
Sunny side-up: Eggs fried one side only, as

Be Yourself

Yet every statement about New Yorkers is likely to be contradicted. They are conformist in many respects but in a city approaching a population of ten million how can one generalise about their social attitudes?

And, if many are conformists this is

certainly not the impression that the city makes on the first time visitor.

Bewildering, absurd, manic – yes, but not conformist. Where else can the following happen? A man can walk out of his apartment dressed in a remarkably realistic Batman costume, presumably on his way to a fancy dress party, only to find his key get jammed in the car door.

opposed to being turned over and done on both sides.

Vacation: Holiday

In a city that is made up of so many different cultural and ethnic groups it is not surprising that the English has been infused with a variety of argot and slang expressions. Slang is ephemeral by nature and what was highly fashionable last year can quickly fossilise and lose currency. Another problem for the visitor is not just knowing the right slang to use but knowing how and when to use it. The list below will help you to understand what is being said.

Chill out: Relax.
Clover hole: An Irish bar.
Dinkies: A couple with a dual income and no children.
Doggie: A $10 banknote.
Flaky: Usually referring to a state of mind or personality and the meaning can stretch from mentally unstable, at one extreme, to just mildly eccentric.
Funky: Eccentric or odd in an interesting way
Off the wall: As with the word **flaky**, the meaning can range from insane to just odd.
Schmuck: An offensive person.
Talk Turkey: To speak honestly.
WASP: Acronym for White Anglo-Saxon Protestant.
Wussy: A weak-minded person.
Yuppie: Young urban professional.

Two teenagers jiving to the sound of rap songs on the corner wander over to help, later joined by a passing pedestrian, and eventually the door is opened. Batman waves his thanks and drives off, the pedestrians resume their business, and no one ever feels the need to comment on the driver's appearance. This can and really does happen.

New Yorkers will impress themselves

on the visitor not by being read about in books or magazines, nor through the countless movies that feature the city and its citizens, but by chance encounters and passing conversations.

A day may pass when journalistic clichés about New Yorkers seem to be borne out – they rush past, hostilely indifferent to everyone except for the occasional rude snarl at a motorist who failed to give way – but when an opportunity presents itself the mask drops and people emerge.

The writer once spent a day in Manhattan carrying around two large fishing rods which proved a remarkable catalyst for social intercourse. A taxi driver who had not left the city for 20 years recounted his childhood trips to the countryside; an elderly man on Roosevelt Island remembered the day he caught an eel in the river and a curious and puzzled woman stopped to ask what the rods were going to be used for.

The truth is that many New Yorkers consciously or unconsciously present an image of themselves that has been projected and fostered by the media. They *enjoy* the distinction of being perceived as the ultimate urban dwellers of the ultimate world city.

Why not? Given an environment so jammed with different cultures, conflicting value systems, an unforgivable mix of the idle rich and the desperately poor with most people somewhere between the two extremes – the New Yorker has good reason to feel special.

I

n a city as multi-ethnic as New York virtually every religious faith is represented and most of the religions have adherents from more than one country.

Catholic: In Name & Nature

The main Roman Catholic church in Brooklyn deals with the international complexion of its celebrants by holding services in 26 languages, including Creole, Armenian, Old Slavonic and Maltese. But, Catholicism is only one of the Christian denominations in New York, a city that holds the country's largest population of church-attending Christians. If you consider the total number of adherents of all the different churches that exist in the state, the number reaches nearly nine million, which is more than any other state in the United States. In

■ ■ ■ ■ ■ ■ ■

Mass at St Bartholomew's on Christmas eve.

St Patrick's Cathedral.

New York City alone there are some 500 churches and synagogues.

Traditionally, the Roman Catholic church has exerted more than just a spiritual force among its congregation and is generally reckoned to constitute a political force, one that goes back to the early days when Irish immigrants controlled City Hall. Even today seven out of every nine priests in New York are of Irish descent.

The Roman Catholic church also claims the numerically largest congregation amongst the non-white residents

Temple Emanuel.

of Harlem although many blacks belong to Baptist, Episcopalian (the American name for the Anglican church) and Lutheran churches.

Living The Faith

A visit to a Baptist church service in Harlem is one of the highlights of any visit to New York (see box on Black Gospel Style). Just one visit will make obvious the close relationship between pastor and flock in a church that has historically close links with the African-American.

In the 19th century many churches did not have a problem reconciling their Christian doctrines with the practice of slavery – the Baptist church was courageous enough to do so. Many Baptist ministers were leading the struggle for the abolition of slavery and in the 20th century they emerged as prominent figures in the civil rights campaigns of the 1960s.

This tradition of confronting the social problems of its parishioners is still evident today in the Saint Paul Community Baptist Church in Brooklyn. Under the pastoral leadership of Reverend Johnny Ray Youngblood, the church has successfully replaced the area's brothels and numbers joints with a school and affordable housing.

Dealing head-on with social realities also means the church entrance is guarded with an electronic surveillance

Black Gospel Style

Children's choir in the Metropolitan Baptist Church, Harlem.

The best possible reason for visiting Harlem is for the opportunity it provides to experience the Black Gospel style of a Baptist church service. Quite unlike any other church service in terms of its combination of prayer, song and music, it represents a very special experience even for those with little or no religious faith of their own. Many of the songs that are belted out can be traced back to the days of slavery. For example the hymn "My Eyes have Seen the Glory of the Lord," with its celebratory chorus of "Glory, Glory Hallelujah" was sung by black Unionist troops as they marched through the southern towns at the end of the civil war to announce the formal abolition of slavery. The tragic conditions of the slave trade also help to explain the plaintive melancholy that pervades so many of these songs and hymns. However, at the same time, the pathos is transcended by a zealous faith and abiding optimism that cannot fail to uplift the spirits of anyone attending a service.

A typical service will consist of two preachers, male and female, flanked by two choirs each consisting of six to a dozen singers dressed in white cotton gowns with colored stashes. The choirs are predominantly female but will differ in their style of singing. One choir might excel at European hymns delivered in an operatic manner, while another might be mainline Black Gospel, characterised by hand movements and a rhythmic swaying. Both choirs will have musical backing in the form of an organ, a piano and a tambourine. All choir members (individually or in unison) will interject the words of the preacher with murmurs of assent and expressions of devotional confirmation.

A Sunday service will last for up to three hours but visitors usually attend at the beginning and leave after about an hour. The service begins with short readings from the bible by each of the preachers, whose powerful and oratorical way of delivering their words is spellbinding to observe and listen to. It is very reminiscent of the rhetorical style of Martin Luther King or Jessie Jackson, both of whom started out as Baptist preachers. After the bible readings, the Lord's Prayer is delivered by the preacher with each phrase being repeated in a musical chant by the two choirs together. After this a member of the congregation (someone renowned for his fine voice) will be called upon to offer a hymn. It will usually be one of the old Black hymns, like "Look Where He Brought Me From," that can easily transport the listener back to another time and place.

A number of tour companies organise a Harlem Gospel tour. Gray Line (tel: 397 2600) have a regular Sunday morning trip while Harlem Spirituals (tel: 757 0245) conduct a tour Sunday and Wednesday. Both trips last for about four hours, take in many of Harlem's sights, and cost about $30. Fears about your personal safety should not, however, deter you from hopping on the M2 bus and getting off at 128th Steet and Seventh Avenue for the Sunday 11:00 am service at the Metropolitan Baptist Church (tel: 663 8990).

system and the parking lot sports a chain-link fence topped by razor wire.

Inside the church, the heads of the parishioners bob in African *kufi* hats and Jamaican dreadlocks that reach down to the shoulders of their pinstripe suits as Reverend Youngblood reads from the bible to his 5,000-strong congregation.

Judaism

New York has the largest Jewish community in the world and half of the city's synagogues are located in Brooklyn. The borough is also home to one of the world's most fascinating sects, the Satmar Hasidim of Williamsburg. Hasidic Jews are the most orthodox of all.

By comparison Reformed Jews seem to be members of a different religion altogether! The former is an extremely hierarchical sect within Judaism and at the top comes the *rebbe* (the Hasidic rendering of rabbi), followed by the *Talmidei Hacamim* who busy themselves with the study of scripture, then comes the *Balebatishe Yiden*, who are primarily involved in business ventures and finally the *Yiden*.

The gradations in rank are reflected in the dress of the male Hasidic Jew. The *Yiden* looks like a typical Orthodox Jew;

a dark suit with the *yarmulke* (skullcap worn by Jewish males) and the black *homburg* (a man's felt hat) on the head. The higher ranks grow a beard and sidelocks while the *rebbe*, in full sartorial dress, wears a wide-brimmed sable hat, a long silk coat with back pockets, breeches above a white hose and sports special slippers on his feet.

Their extreme orthodoxy makes itself felt in dietary laws, for whatever is consumed must be *glat kosher* (the food have to be prepared not only according to the usual *kosher* laws; cleaned and purified according to Jewish ordinances, but personally supervised by a Hasidic Jew who has been approved of by an experienced *rebbe*). Clothing worn by a Hasidic Jew cannot contain a combination of linen and wool. This taboo was based on a single prohibition found in only two sentences in the bible. There is even a garment factory in Brooklyn dedicated to unseaming clothes for the purpose of checking for possible contaminated material.

The Satmat Hasidim of Williamsburg does not approve of the state of Israel and rejects Zionism as a political force that usurps what is strictly a spiritual dimension.

TITUS 2:13
LOOKING FOR THAT BLESSED HOPE AND THE

A Buddhist shrine in Chinatown.

They have been compared to the Amish folk of Pennsylvania, who have turned their back on the modern world and all its sinful manifestations, but a shop located in West 47th Street near Sixth Avenue negates the comparison. The 47th St Photo, one of Manhattan's biggest and best suppliers of electronics, is owned and run by the *Balebatishe Yiden!*

New York but they are not the only ones. Greek Orthodox churches, Buddhist temples, Hindu and Sikh temples, Islamic mosques, and a whole host of Protestant sects – Methodist, Seventh Day Adventist, Lutheran, and Episcopal Zion – all have churches dotted across all five boroughs and throughout the state. No matter what the religion being practised the congregation is likely to be mixed.

A Greek Orthodox church will certainly have a majority of Greeks but many of the city's Russians and Romanians will also attend services. A Buddhist temple will draw celebrants from all the Southeast Asian countries including white middle-class New Yorkers who find the belief system more congenial than the ones they were brought up in, and the mosques will include Pakistanis, Turks and African-American Muslims. And sooner or later, at some street corner or other, the visitor will stumble across some of the city's more bizarre religious groups.

One such group, who are currently making their presence felt in Midtown Manhattan with the aid of megaphones and posters, consists of militant-looking young men who claim that the African-Americans are the lost tribe of Israel, the true Jews of the world. Their main speaker has the same right to be heard as Cardinal O'Connor of the Roman Catholic church – the American Constitution says so – and the average New Yorker, whatever church they may subscribe to, respects this right.

Other Faiths

Catholic and Baptist churches and Jewish synagogues make up a sizeable majority of the religious buildings in

Festivals

I t should come as no surprise to learn, in a city that defines itself by way of its multi-cultural identity, that festivals are many in number and varied in style. What they hold in common is a propensity to use part of Fifth Avenue as the venue for their parades.

One of the exceptions is the Chinese New Year festivities, the first major event after Christmas, as the firecrackling and lion dances are centered around Mott Street in Chinatown. For most of the others, though, whether it be the Greek Independence Day Parade or the Gay Pride March, a section of Fifth Avenue is the preferred route for the floats, bands, dancers and celebrants.

The 44-day long Festival of Light in the Wintergarden is a must in your itinerary.

When Irish Eyes Are Smiling

Over 40 million Americans claim Irish descent so it is not surprising that Ireland's Saint Patrick's Day which falls on March 17th, is also celebrated

Macy's parade has become a major festival for New York City.

in New York. What is slightly more surprising is the fact that it is easily the city's grandest and most colorful celebration and has more razzmatazz than anything ever mounted in Ireland on the same day. During the weekend closest to March 17th, New York literally paints itself green and there is a tremendous outpouring of Irish nationalist sentiment. The city has a number of well-established Irish bars and they are packed to overcrowding. Traditional Irish music is played everywhere and visitors will notice zealots proudly dis-

much a family affair. To enjoy a good view of the march it is essential to arrive in plenty of time. A place worth making for is **Saint Patrick's Cathedral**, where the Bishop of New York meets the Gaelic bands.

For the last few of years, an element of controversy has crept into what is otherwise pure carnival. Gay rights activists who have been denied the opportunity to officially contribute to the parade have responded by staging an unofficial demonstration. By the end of the day, recrimination and counter-recrimination is lost in the general enthusiasm that has been fuelled by the drinking of generous amounts of Guinness®.

Independence Day

Fifth Avenue is also the venue for many other festivals and parades. America's **Independence Day** is always celebrated by a parade with marching bands and in the evening the skies over lower Manhattan bursts into color as Macy's firework displays explode into action. All of the city's boroughs will have organised celebrations to mark the day that the foundation document of the United States of America was adopted by the country's fledgling Congress.

Ninth Avenue Festival

One celebration that does not involve Fifth Avenue is the **Ninth Avenue Festi-**

playing a sprig of the three-leaved, green shamrock pinned to their clothes. The shamrock is flown in from Ireland just for the festival. If you can not wear the real plant, a plastic substitute is the next best thing.

On the day of the parade itself, Fifth Avenue is absolutely packed with participants and spectators and it is very

Scarecrows and pumpkins on Halloween Day.

val that takes place each May. It is a food festival – a gastronomical extravaganza, and every restaurant and cafe situated along the route will display its delicacies to tempt the pedestrian.

The cuisine, by simply reflecting the different cultures that cook and eat in the city and by responding to the fact that visitors want to eat and move on, turns the event into a specialist, international fast food festival. Just turn up with an empty stomach at Ninth Avenue and 36th Street and work your way along to 59th Street.

have booked your tickets over a month in advance, the only chance of securing a ticket is by way of the returns which are sold on the same day as the performance. Returns are frequently available so it is always worth turning up at the Lincoln Center to see what is available.

Jazzy Heights

Jazz was not born in New York but this is where it has settled and the **Jazz Festival** in June is its greatest celebration. The city is proud of its jazz festival and has good reason for feeling this way.

The festival is not simply grafted onto the city by sponsors looking for a location that boasts a big market. This is one of those events where business companies fall over backwards to host the event. But the month only distills and highlights the kind of music that has always lain at the heart and soul of the city.

The origins of jazz can be traced back to the capital city of Mississippi, New Orleans. It was only during the 1920s that this magical music first traveled north to New York where it has been nurtured ever since and remains as closely identified with the city as "The Beatles" to Liverpool and Mozart to Salzburg.

The festival has something to suit every budget, from free lunchtime shows in the parks and clubs to prestigious events staged in the big concert halls

Film Fest

Every year, from mid-September to early October, New York plays host to one of the major international film festivals. The prestigious **New York Film Festival** regularly features over 20 new American and European films and unless you

that attract international stars from all corners of the globe. No one form of jazz dominates the event and the visitor can seek out something special or just sample the variety. It is all here, from Dixieland and fusion to hard bop, be-bop and the avant-garde. Whatever the size of the venue, the atmosphere is wonderfully atmospheric and the audiences soak it up. Just relax and observe the studied nonchalance of the other players when their gyrating saxophonist takes off on an extended solo and the crowd urges him on and on... Small clubs would never dream of extending their premises, although they could easily fill up a space three times larger. The enforced intimacy is something to be enjoyed rather than endured.

Salsa Festival

Mainstream jazz in New York has encouraged many musical offshoots and hybrids and one of these, salsa music, holds a festival of its own every autumn. Salsa music represents a cross between traditional jazz and the dance rhythms of African and Latin music. The September **Salsa Festival** is a golden opportu-

nity to savor this sound. But, the best musical treat of all is when jazz and salsa musicians come together to fuse their music through improvisation. Such jam sessions are well worth seeking out.

Classical Scene

Aficionados of classical music are not left out of the festival scene and throughout the summer months regular events are scheduled for both indoor and outdoor performances. The **Mostly Mozart Festival** always begins with a free outdoor show and then moves on to the 2,700-seater **Avery Fisher Hall**. The program features a main Mozart item, with supporting items from other composers. This Festival has an admirable policy of keeping ticket prices as low as possible.

Undoubtedly, the most prestigious offerings of classical music are the concerts given by the **New York Philharmonic** in Central Park. The Philharmonic is normally in residence at the Avery Fisher Hall from September to May and a glance at the limousines and chauffeur-driven cars that draw up outside will give you some idea of the price

Calender Of Events

January/February: **Chinese New Year.** The timing of these ten days of celebration vary according to the annual cycle of the moon. During the Chinese New Year season, Chinatown is packed with people and dragon parades.

March: **St Patrick's Day.** A grand parade down Fifth Avenue is held on March 17th.

April: **Easter Celebrations.** Department stores compete with extravagant flower shows and on Easter Sunday, Fifth Avenue hosts yet another parade.

May: **Ninth Avenue Festival.** A street food festival.
Greek Independence Day Parade. In the middle of the month the city's Greek population mounts a parade with marching bands, ethnic costumes and colorful floats.

June: **Festival of St Anthony.** Little Italy, in Lower Manhattan, comes alive for nearly two weeks with street stalls over-flowing with tempting fast food, prepared Italian style. A somber daytime procession brings the festival to a close.
Puerto Rican Day. A celebration held to honor San Juan. It brings New York's sizeable Puerto Rican population onto Fifth Avenue above 59th Street.
Cultural Events. Throughout the month a wonderful variety of music, drama and dance events held in the parks and major buildings like the Rockefeller and World Trade Center.
Gay Pride March. The last Sunday in the month brings another colorful parade onto the streets. This one winds its way from Columbus Circle to Greenwich Village.

July: **Fiestas de Loiza Aldea.** During the second weekend of the month a Puerto Rican religious festival which begins at the Church of San Pueblo at Lexington Avenue and 117th Street brings together separate groups of men, women and children who carry statues of Saint James to Ward's Island where music, food and dance soon take over.

Independence Day. On the 4th of the month festivities break out in all the boroughs. The harbor area often attracts colorful ships and at night, fireworks light up the sky over the East River.

July/August: **New York Philharmonic Concerts** bring the parks to life with their free shows.

September: **Festival San Gennaro.** This is the second Italian event of the year and again the emphasis is on food, augmented by street stalls featuring clever little games of chance. An impressive nighttime procession which marches along Mulberry Street brings the festival to an end.

Steuben Day Parade. A modest but high-spirited reminder that Germans are a part of the city's ethnic makeup. The parade down Fifth Avenue is usually held in the middle of the month and is named after Baron von Steuben. The Prussian general fought alongside George Washington at the battle of Valley Forge, contributing to America's victory in the War of Independence.

September/October: **New York Film Festival.** For three non-stop weeks new films are shown every afternoon and evening.

October: **Columbus Day Parade.** This parade, held around the 12th of the month, attracts one of the city's biggest crowds. The area around Fifth Avenue, from 44th to 72nd Street, comes alive with celebrants of all nationalities. The number of marching bands and colorful floats is only matched by the resplendence of the St Patrick's Day Parade.

November: **New York City Marathon.** A very motley collection of over 20,000 runners wind their way for 26.3 miles through all five boroughs.

December: **Christmas Celebrations.** The month starts with tree-lighting ceremonies and ends with the hugh **New Year's Eve** bash held in Times Square.

of a ticket. On the other hand, throughout the summer, the same orchestra performs for free in **Central Park** and other outdoor locations and it is one of the highlights of the festival season.

Without Central Park, the festival calendar would miss more than just the Philharmonic. The park is also home to summer's **Shakespeare Festival** when two plays are performed at the outdoor "Delacorte Theatre" and at the "Sheep Meadow" the Metropolitan Opera holds on its own summer programs. Both the music and the drama is absolutely free, and tickets are given out on the day of performance, on a strict basis of one ticket per person. Bringing your own food for a picnic is all part of the fun.

New York rarely celebrates in a small way and **Easter** is no exception. A special easter egg display is mounted at the **Ukrainian Museum** and this exhibition of *pysanky* (delicately-painted eggs) is easily the most artistic expression of the egg painting craze that descends upon the city in the fortnight leading up to Easter Sunday.

Special egg dying kits are on sale everywhere as schools and families apply their design talents to hard-boiled eggs. A colorful selection of such eggs can be seen in Central Park on Easter Saturday when egg-rolling competitions take over the park's Great Lawn.

At this time of the year, bouquets of flowers take over many of the department stores and no one does it more colorfully than Macy's. Even the tiny "Channel Gardens" in the **Rockefeller**

Center host a magnificent display of Easter lilies.

Easter Parade

The climax to the Easter celebrations is the **Fifth Avenue Easter Parade**, a fairly unique event in that this is not a highly

Channel Gardens in Rockefeller Center at Christmas.

organised affair. There is no order of procession and no sponsored 60-foot egg on the back of a lorry with bunny girls bursting out of it. Instead, there is an equally flamboyant and exuberant celebration by whole families who have chosen to spend weeks preparing for this day. They turn out in incredible Easter costumes, some hired and some painstakingly homemade, replete with video recorders and cameras.

It is a sight well worth seeing and all the activity takes place between 49th and 59th Street.

Celebrate the end of the year and the beginning of a new one in Times Square.

Christmas Celebrations

Christmas celebrations are announced by the tree-lighting ceremonies that take place around the city early in the month. One of the most elegant of these occasions occurs in the "**Channel Gardens**", where the lilies have been replaced by fir trees and the sunken plaza is transformed into a ice rink. A huge tree overshadowing the rink, and the lighting up at night, always attracts a big crowd. Once this is over, the cue is given for a score of other trees around the city to blaze into multicolored displays and Christmas fever begins in earnest. From now till December 24th every department store (both within and outside) located along Fifth Avenue competes for the consumer's attention with explosions of color and animated displays. The most expensively produced displays in the United States are on show and for the two Sundays before Christmas, the area of Fifth Avenue between 34th Street and 57th Street is turned into a pedestrian mall for most of the day. The streets becomes a magnet for artists and entertainers. This is Christmas at its most frenzied and intense.

New Year's Eve

The end of the year is celebrated in traditional style in **Times Square** where, as the last seconds of the old year tick by,

The Chinese usher in the new year with lion dances and
a great bang of firecrackers.

a giant Big Apple makes its way down a flag pole outside Times Square. If not deafened by the sound of cheering carousers, shrieking whistles will be heard from the harbor area and if you really enter into the spirit of the occasion you can enjoy the hugs and handshakes of complete strangers.

Thanksgiving

Thanksgiving was originally a harvest festival which was held to commemorate the end of summer's labor in the fields for the first farmers who arrived on Manhattan. However across America, Thanksgiving has developed into a major family festival that in some ways is more intimate and private than Christmas, mainly because it lacks the commercial hullabaloo. Families, who might not necessarily come together at Christmas, would never miss the Thanksgiving reunion. The visitor to the city is not always in a position to appreciate this family bonding that takes place over the last weekend in November. The last Thursday of the month is always a public holiday and business grinds to a halt over the ensuing weekend.

The public celebration of Thanksgiving is traditionally organised by Macy's department store on Thursdays. This is the time when you can see those giant, helium-filled cartoon characters lumbering down Central Park West to Columbus Circle.

I n New York, culture, what is often thought of as the province of the intellectual in other cities, is less exclusive. Everyone, highbrow, lowbrow or in-between is accommodated. A visit to the ballet will require a degree of formal dress and will cost some money – orchestra seats for the American Ballet Theater are priced at US$65, while a visit to a jazz club, requires equally *de rigueur* dress but could cost less than half that amount for an entire evening. Or you could stand in the street and watch a mime artist for the loose change in your pocket.

Most artistic venues will have a ticketing system that covers a range of budgets, so this is not the main problem facing a visitor thinking about where to go and what to see. No, the problem is that of making a choice. There is too much to see in too little time and the bewildering range of possibilities can induce a paralysis of the will. Think

Nighttime neons of Broadway theatres and restaurants.

about what interests you – "high" culture or "popular" culture, music, dance or cinema, comedy or tragedy – make a decision and buy the tickets.

Broadway On and Off

The real Broadway consists of about 20 theaters which offer a dazzling array of musicals, comedies and dramas. The productions are always very expensive and replete with stunning sets and costumes. This partly accounts for the high prices of tickets. Another factor contributing to the cost will often be the big-name actors and actresses who play leading roles. Hollywood stars are attracted to the idea of proving themselves in front of a live audience and the theater companies want the celebrities to attract audiences.

Apart from Broadway, there is also **Off-Broadway** which refers to those smaller theaters, mainly located in the Greenwich Village area, which mount productions that hope to make it to the big league. Sometimes the shows run longer than anything on Broadway itself. At the **Sullivan Street Theater**, for instance, a family musical called *The Fantasticks* has been running for 35 years! Seeing an off-Broadway show used to be a hit-and-miss affair but it has become an increasingly conventional and safe choice for an evening's entertainment. The sensible approach entails investing a dollar or two for a copy of the *Village Post* or the weekend *New York Times* to see which shows attract the most attention. There will be more variety than Broadway shows, including straight drama, revues, comedies, musicals and one-person shows. Ticket prices average US$25 and half-price seats are also available from the TKTS Booth in Times Square.

It is not uncommon to hear the comment that there is an inverse proportion between Broadway shows and genuine artistic intent. Broadway's motives, it is said, are purely commercial and art does not just take second place, in fact it does not even enter the equation. If this strikes a chord with you, then abandon the neon lights of Times Square and head for an **Off-Off Broadway** production. These are avant-garde performances – happenings or events – that take place in all sorts of venues, including theaters and in return for a reasonable investment you will enjoy, or perhaps endure, an assault upon your artistic sensibilities. The subject matter may be an adaptation of an 18th-century Irish love poem, a comedy staged in Spanish, a comedy of manners, or an Agatha Christie murder mystery. Fortunately, many of these shows have a heavy dose of humor and are frequently hugely enjoyable, like a current show about Hollywood stars trapped in a room with two gay florists and a macho gunman! Again, it is best to consult the newspapers and magazines for reviews and recommendations. For a show to be listed as Off-Off Broadway it has to take place in a venue with

Theter Works!

A Broadway show always beckons despite the prophecies of doom that periodically threaten to bring the whole phenomenon crashing down. The American recession that began in the late 1980s, and which still has not lifted, has certainly affected other major art forms, yet Broadway's theaters remain strangely immune to the general trend. Shows like *Miss Saigon* and *Les Miserables* continue to sell out on every night of the year and there is always the expectation that another monster hit is just waiting in the shadows. People remember that on the night of May 21st, 1975, the low-key Newman Theater had the critics reeling at the press opening of *A Chorus Line*. The *New Yorker* columnist compared his experience to being at the first performance of Beethoven's Eroica Symphony or to the first basketball fans witnessing Hank Luisetti of Stanford taking a *one-handed shot*! After a few months at the Newman, *A Chorus Line* moved to the Schubert Theater on Broadway where it ran for 15 years with well over 6,000 performances. Not only did it gross millions of dollars and win numerous awards, the show also achieved a rare emotional bonding with its audience. This was Broadway at its best – a show that managed to reflect the needs and anxieties of ordinary people, not to mention the fact that for the first time the sensibilities of gays were reflected in a major Broadway hit. The show endures as a reminder of what a popular musical can achieve.

Very few theaters are actually located on Broadway itself, a street that runs the whole gamut of New York from the grim haunts of the West 90s to the ritzier parts of Midtown Manhattan. Most theaters radiate out from around **Times Square**, the best possible after-dusk advertisement for the Broadway experience: the lit-up billboards, the digital readout for the number of people who have watched *'Les Miserables'* worldwide clocks up every minute (it currently approaches 30 million), and people saunter by either dressed to the nines or outfitted in punky gear and sporting outrageous hairdos. In the immediate vicinity of Times Square are the theaters where the big shows play and in the tiny triangle of pavement in the middle of the square will be found **TKTS**, the ticket booth which sells off the unsold evening's tickets at discounts of up to 50 percent. It makes a lot of sense to draw up a list of shows you would like to see, have some idea of the theaters' locations, and then check the availability and prices of tickets at the booth. The length of the queues varies according to the time of year and it sometimes makes sense to turn up the night before and check out the scene before enquiring at one of the booths when the crowds have departed. To help you choose a show there are a few helpful publications. The Friday edition of the *New York Times* has a hefty weekend section full of reviews and news on ticket availability. The *New York* magazine features its own reviews and a free *Broadway Theater Guide* is available from the Visitors Center at most hotels.

less than 100 seats with an average ticket price of US$10 (sometimes with a two-drink surcharge).

Classical Music & Dance

The **Lincoln Center for the Performing Arts** lies at the heart of the classical arts in the city. The six concert halls and theaters provide a home for the Metropolitan Opera Company, the New York Philharmonic Orchestra, the American Ballet Theater and the New York City Opera and Ballet, not to mention the numerous visiting ballet companies and orchestras who regard performances here as the highlight of their tours. In 1968, Pavarotti made his Metropolitan Opera debut in *La Boheme* and New York

The grand interior of the Metropolitan Opera.

art columnists were prescient enough to spot a major new talent. "Any tenor who can toss off high C's with such abandon and successfully negotiate delicate diminuendo effects," proclaimed the critics, "has the goods." It is true to say that anyone performing at the Lincoln Center can deliver the goods and the variety of programs available during any one week is astonishing.

The New York Philharmonic's reputation as a group of virtuoso players has not only been confirmed but enhanced. If they are not performing at the Avery

Competing for your ear is **Carnegie Hall** (tel: 247 7800) which does not boast a resident orchestra but can instead claim to attract the very best orchestras from all parts of the Inited States and the world. The Vienna Philharmonic regularly performs here as do popular singers and bands of all persuasions.

The New York City Ballet experienced an artistic crisis with the death of George Balanchine in 1983 but the troupe has maintained an impressive schedule. In 1991, it broke its contemporary focus with Peter Martins's staging of *The Sleeping Beauty* and has never looked back. In fact, in this respect it is exceptional. Over the last few years all the ballet companies associated with the city – with the notable exception of the New York City Ballet – have experienced fiscal problems resulting in fewer dancers and less exciting choreography. One reason for the New York City Ballet's financial stability is that it has never been as dependent on touring as other companies are. The New York State Theater is its regular home and it is reliably locked into a schedule of winter and spring seasons. The American Ballet Theater which for so long was under the artistic direction of Mikhail Baryshnikov, usually performs at the **Metropolitan Opera House**.

The equivalent of the TKTS for the Lincoln Center and Carnegie Hall is the **Music & Dance Booth** located in Bryant Park, just behind the New York Public Library on 42nd Street. Half-price tick-

Fisher Hall, another symphony orchestra will be in their stead. Every summer there is a Mostly Mozart Festival when all the seats are reduced to a special low price. At the **Alice Tully Hall**, a string quartet or a chamber orchestra can be enjoyed in conditions that are generally considered to be acoustically unsurpassed.

Talent Off The Street

Pavement art in Greenwich Village.

The ancient art of busking is alive and well in New York and nowhere more so than on the platforms and along the passageways of the subway system. Most of the performing artists have been licensed by the transport authorities. Not only are the standards of music invariably high but the range of styles is delightfully wide; on one day a singer with accompanying acoustic guitar, on another a banjo or mouth organ, or else it will be a couple playing Central American calypso or a Viennese waltz. Standing in the Union Square Station amidst the bleak architecture while listening to a finely-played piece of classical music can be an uplifting and slightly surreal experience. More so when an elderly lady, with a trace of an Eastern European accent in her Manhattan voice, requests Strauss' Blue Danube and the musicians are pleased to launch into the piece.

Street talent on the sidewalks of New York is anarchic; no tickets and no schedules. Throughout the summer there is usually someone performing an impromptu show or other around popular locations like Times Square, East 34th Street or Greenwich Village and any visitor to the city would be unlucky not to encounter some display of talent. Quite common are the mime artists who dress in black, their faces daubed with white powder. Their methodology is sometimes explained by a placard with the cryptic message: "No money, No move." They remain totally immobile until coins are dropped

ets, if available, are sold on the day of performance. Telephone 382 2323 to give you an idea of availability.

Ballet is by no means confined to the Lincoln Center. The Brooklyn Academy of Music (BAM), at 30 Lafayette

into their tin, whereupon they begin to mime some amazingly complicated action complete with sound effects. Or at least they begin the action, for if more coins do not materialise from the audience, the artist will once more freeze into immobility.

The short stretch of Fifth Avenue outside the Central Library is a favorite stomping ground for enterprising street artists and there is no better vantage point for viewing the show than the broad steps of the library itself. A familiar figure amongst the lunchtime crowd from nearby offices is a mime artist who specialises in stepping in line behind unsuspecting pedestrians. Within a second of taking up his position the performer is able to accurately imitate – and often exaggerate – the gait and mannerism of his walking model, and continues to do so for about a hundred meters, to the amused delight of his audience.

The improvised shows on the streets open another window on the creative soul of New Yorkers. The performers are rarely there just to milk tourists for there is never any obligation on the part of the audience to part with money. When money is the only motive, like the putative rap artists who offer a personal serenade to tourists resting on the steps of the Metropolitan Museum, the quality of the performance is invariably shoddy.

The really talented artists are performing for fellow citizens of the city as much as they are for visitors; sometimes, like the highly skilled skateboarders in Central Park, they perform out of self-esteem or, like the Native American bands that play their traditional instruments and distribute leaflets describing their plight, the show is a form of "agitprop" theater. Whatever their motives they are willing to be judged by the quality of their performance and monetary reward is completely at the discretion of the audience. How many artists are prepared to be paid on this basis? Only the best is part of the answer.

Avenue in downtown Brooklyn (tel: 718 636 4100), can be relied on for designing and hosting talented experimental

dance. Mark Morris is the current creative force at BAM and his programs always attract attention from mainstream critics who recognise the importance of an alternative venue for composers and choreographers. BAM also attracts performances by the **Dance Theater of Harlem**. The **City Center**, located at 131 West 55th Street (tel: 246 8989), usually holds rich and diverse programs from the **Joffrey Ballet** and troupes like the **Paul Taylor Dance Company**. Modern and experimental dance is the forte of the **Joyce Theater** at 175 Eighth Avenue (tel: 242 0800).

All the places mentioned so far are just the regular and better known venues and for each of these there are two or three more venues that quietly organise highly individual programs. Recently, the **Christ Church United Methodist** on Park Avenue was the scene of the *Four Saints in Three Acts* opera, composed by Virgil Thomson to texts penned by Gertrude Stein. These individual programs are frequently too bold and original for the more conservative, major companies.

Radio City Music Hall performances, a part of New York City culture.

Rock Music

There are many venues for major rock concerts in the city but the biggest is **Madison Square Garden** (tel: 465 6000). With seating capacity for 20,000 people, it can afford to host big bands on their world tours, and as New York is an almost obligatory stopover for these world tours, there will always be a big name scheduled.

Newspapers and magazines advertise the shows or, when you are passing along West 37th Street, pause to see the coming attractions lit up in digital splendor.

Radio City Music Hall (tel: 757 3100), when the Rockettes are not high-kicking their way through their winter season, still attracts big names in the rock industry who would rather not be tarnished with the tacky populism of Madison Square Garden.

Meadowlands Stadium (tel: (201) 935 8500) is as roomy as Madison Square Garden and concerts here are well advertised, unlike so many of the smaller clubs dotted around Manhattan where big names are scorned, and the atmosphere and the avant-garde are more highly regarded.

Only *Village Voice* will carry the current listings, but places where something interesting is usually happening include the **Lone Star Cafe Roadhouse** (tel: 245 2950) and the more punky **Rock 'N' Roll Church** (tel: 807 7850).

MOMA – Museum Of Modern Art

The MOMA contains some of the most effective galleries for modern art exhibitions.

After Monet the rooms continue with Picasso and lead up to the magical, fairy tale colours of **Marc Chagall**. The pictorial element in Chagall is recognisable even if it is not the most significant, but in the work of **Piet Mondrian** pure geometry becomes a mode of perception and there are two rooms of his work in the museum. New ways of representing reality – ways of *seeing* reality – continue with canvases executed by **Klee** and **Kandinsky** and post-cubist Picasso.

At any one time about a-third of MOMA's collection, that is, art from the Impressionist period onwards, is on view in its recently renovated home on West 53rd Street near Sixth Avenue. Be prepared to have your sensibilities heightened – the paintings are dramatically presented in airy and light-filled rooms – in a journey through modernity in the company of its most profound artists. These major works of the late 19th and 20th century art scene, quite apart from their individual worth, are exhibited together in a way that re-creates the wonder and turmoil of the Western world's most recent cultural revolution.

Begin with the Post-Impressionists exhibited on the second floor where **Cezanne's** *The Bather* opens a new visual door on pictorial representation. The rooms that follow are filled with canvases by **Gauguin**, **Toulouse-Lautrec** and **Van Gogh**; the latter's *The Starry Night* probably being the single most precious, and valuable, painting in the whole museum. After Van Gogh there is a sudden and unexpected transition to the work of the Cubists – but this is the way it happened – and the fractured world of **Georges Braque** and **Pablo Picasso** are worthy of a room to themselves. They could hardly share a space with **Monet's** triptych of lily ponds that demands a vast space of its own just to accommodate the whole broad sweep of the painting.

Be sure not to miss the subversive anarchism of the **Dadaists** who set out to destroy classical notions of art and who might be just a little miffed to discover that they have been enshrined in an art institution.

MOMA has the best collection of Dada art under one roof and their surrealist spirit is continued in the work of **Dali** and **Magritte** who are also well represented here.

The third floor is devoted to post-World War II art. The main attraction here is the abstract expressionism of American artists like **Jackson Pollock** and **Mark Rothko**. Art criticism remains divided over the aesthetic and social significance of this movement and padded benches allow the visitor to sit in comfort and ponder over this issue while viewing the paintings. On the same floor ebullient Pop Art jumps off the wall with the likes of **Liechienstein's** *Drowning Girl* ("I don't care! I'd rather sink...than call Brad for help," she cries).

Before leaving the museum, be sure to relax in the ground floor **Sculpture Garden**, a haven for tired feet and exhausted sensibilities, with **Rodin's** *Balzac* to cheer the spirits.

The Guggenheim presents major contemporary works of art.

Art

New York has an embarrassing richness of art galleries but the **Metropolitan Museum of Modern Art** will come first in most people's wish list of places to see. With 32 acres of floor space devoted to permanent and temporary exhibitions the place is irresistible.

Some of the highlights include the substantial remains of the Egyptian temple at Dendur; an exquisitely re-created 16th-century Chinese garden; a Frank Lloyd Wright living room; a recently opened "Costume Institute" and, most famous of all, a staggering collection of classic Western art that has to be seen to be believed. The Museum of Modern Art has the greatest collection of 20th-century art in the world. Equally compelling to anyone interested in modern art is the **Guggenheim Museum** with its famous spiral ramp, which is the only building in Manhattan designed by Frank Lloyd Wright. More 20th-century art is found at the **Whitney Museum of American Art**, founded by the wealthy socialite Gertrude Vanderbilt Whitney. It is famous for its biennial exhibitions of contemporary American art.

Free Shows

The **New York Shakespeare Festival** decamps to the Delacorte Theater (tel: 861 7277) in Central Park from June to

August and free tickets are handed out at the theatre nightly starting at 6:15 pm. Not surprisingly, the queues begin in the afternoon! The **Metropolitan Opera** (tel: 362 6000) also presents free shows in Central Park and again the queues for the 8:00 pm performances start at around 3:00 pm.

Not to appear mean by comparison, the **New York Philharmonic** (tel: 875 5709) presents free summer concerts in city parks and, on selected weekday mornings between September and June, their rehearsals are open to the public for only $5 (tel: 875 5656 for the schedule).

The **Cathedral of St John the Divine** (tel: 316 7540) frequently mounts concerts during the day and at night. While the acoustics are not perfect, the free entry and the evocative setting more than make up for this.

Literature

If you have been asked to name a famous writer born and bred in New York it can prove surprisingly difficult to answer. Yet writers from all parts of America and the rest of the world are drawn to the city for inspiration. One of the best ways to prepare yourself for a visit to the city, or for reflection after a visit, is by reading some of the literature that New York has spawned.

A writer who settled in New York and spent a large part of his life there was **Thomas Wolfe**. Wolfe was born in

North Carolina in 1900 but before his untimely death in 1938 he made his home in the city where he was employed as a university lecturer of English.

New York features in most of his novels and *The Web and the Rock* is particularly interesting because it tells the story of a young man coming to the city for the first time and his impressions of the place are recorded in unforgettable detail. His almost-namesake, **Tom Wolfe**, has written one of the best modern New York stories in *The Bonfire of the Vanities*. This modern parable about the 1980s tells the tale of a rich young yuppie who accidentally drives his Mercedes into the South Bronx and discovers another America. The main character is very similar to **Jay McInerney's** character in *Bright Lights, Big City* although the story stays focused on his decadent lifestyle in Manhattan. The biting social satire is even more finely developed in his second novel, *Story of My Life*.

Books that are more concerned with the dispossessed of the city include *Bird at My Window* and *Measure of Time* by Rosa Guy. Both books are set in Harlem and poignantly recreate the experience of being black and poor. Another highly emotional tale about New York is *The Catcher in the Rye* written by the reclusive **JD Salinger**, which tells the moving story of an adolescent struggling to come to terms with life in modern America.

While New York burgeons with talented writers, so thrives the literary

The Museum of Natural History never fails to fascinate the young and curious visitors.

agents and the publishing industry. Recession or no recession, New York remains a strong market for books and it is unquestionably one of the leading publishing centers of North America, indeed in the English speaking world. Many of the major imprints are New York based, thus the literary scene can only surely form a segment of this vast intellectual merchandising by the publishing industry.

The Cinema

American movies, foreign films, talkies and silent movies, animated film, documentaries, non-narrative experimental film, revivals of old classics – all have their dedicated followers and venues. Where else would a showing of John Ford's classic western *The Searchers* receive full page reviews in the *New York*

you'll ever see and thoughtfully provide special recesses in every seat to accommodate this gargantuan tubs.

The movie event of the year is the **New York Film Festival**, a surprisingly purist affair when compared to the Cannes Festival. Approximately 50 new films are screened at the Lincoln Center every afternoon and evening for three weeks. Fortunately there are no hyped up awards or publicity stunts. For the rest of the year, a number of well-established cinemas specialise in independent and foreign films, revivals, art films, and the less commercially-oriented American movies. The **Angelika Film Center** on West Houston Street boasts six screens and a policy of being as "Catholic" as possible in its range of screenings. The **Museum of Modern Art** recognises film as a major component in its brief and shows up to six films a day from its archive of over 10,000 movies. Friday's *New York Times* and *Village Voice* carry comprehensive listings and reading what is on is rather like consulting a film encyclopedia.

While New York has inspired many a movie plot or scene, its moneyed influence has long been the financial force behind many a Hollywood production. The influence of the bankers, financiers and deal makers is thought to match the talent available in the Californian movie industry. How exactly this has suffered from the recession fall-out is not quantified but it could still be a prevailing formula that the studios look to New York to finance the productions.

Times and the *Village Voice* because a rare 35mm print was made available for the first time?

Movies matter in New York and it shows in the New Yorkers dedication to film trivia. Even the mainstream chain of **Loews Cinemas** will while away the minutes before the program starts by flashing questions on the screen about classic films or vintage directors and then reveal the answer a few moments later. The Loews chain of cinemas also sell the most massive tubs of popcorn

Architecture

The Manhattan skyline is the defining characteristic of the popular image of New York. Towering skyscrapers jostling for space and struggling upwards like plants in a jungle desperately seeking sunlight. The tall buildings, whether seen in bright sunlight or sparkling in the night sky, have become synonymous with the energy and frenzy of the city. If these man-made mountains were ever taken away, what place would New York occupy in the world's imagination?

The World Trade Center.

The enduring fascination of the Manhattan skyline depends on both individual buildings and an aesthetic response to the whole architectural *presence* of New York.

Take the main buildings first. Two of the earliest structures that impressed people were the **Chrysler Building** and the **Empire State Building**, and they continue to dominate the skyline. For less than a year the Chrysler Building was the tallest in the world, but the Em-

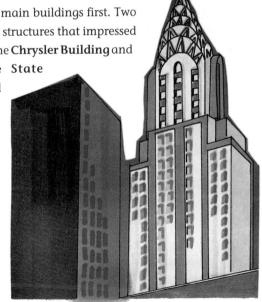

Brooklyn terraced houses.

pire State Building reached even higher in 1931 and retained the record for a long time afterwards. Although not the first skyscrapers in the technical sense of the word, that is, constructed from a supporting metal frame, these two build-ings have come to represent that burst of architectural mania that began in the mid-1920s.

The endeavor of this era was self-consciously futuristic as well as plainly pragmatic. The reaching up to the skies

Skyline of the latest among the older buildings.

was an imaginative feat as well as a literal one, partly inspired by the Paris *Exposition des Arts Decoratifs* of 1925 and the modernist urges of Europe that were giving shape and form to a new set of urban sensibilities.

The word skyscraper is now common currency and has lost much of its evocative power, but when the term was first being introduced, it really did convey the idea of touching the skies. This was before the advent of aeroplanes and the idea of conquering the skies was still an audacious and breathtaking ambition. In fact, the pinnacle of the Empire State was planned as a 150-foot-high spire that dirigibles could moor onto and dock on the roof. The more pragmatic motivation for building ver-

tically was, of course, the scarcity of ground space in Manhattan. No one can afford to build horizontally on an island 13 miles long and only two miles wide, but when some of the big buildings first started to go up, their squatness of design blocked out so much light that yet another problem was created! This was partly solved by the "Zoning Law of 1916" that insisted that buildings could not simply extend themselves upwards by continuing to use their original ground space. The law meant that, after a certain height was reached, the structure could only occupy 25 percent of the allocated plot. This piece of legislation heralded the emphasis on streamlined sleekness that is so much a part of the elegant architecture of New York.

New York Architects

Two of the earliest architects to leave a permanent mark on the cityscape were Joseph Mangin and John McComb. They were an unlikely pair, coming from different cultures and architectural traditions. Joseph Mangin was a French architectural engineer, who harked back to ancient Greece and Rome for inspiration. The hallmark of Mangin's style was a yearning for stately grandeur which, at its best, combined this with a lightness of tone and at its worst resulted in a monumental and graceless heaviness. John McComb hailed from Scotland and sought to imbue his buildings with a Georgian style that could express both confidence and flights of the imagination.

Mangin and McComb worked together on **City Hall** and it remains their best achievement. The exterior faces south and betrays the Renaissance influence of Mangin. In appearance it resembles a chateau and consciously evokes the classical past. More impressive is its interior, especially the flamboyant but controlled majesty of its marble staircase. This was the work of McComb and stands as eloquent testimony to his skill and flair as an architect.

From the end of the civil war in 1865 to the end of World War I in 1918, nearly every architect winning a commission in New York was influenced by one European tradition or another. The firm of McKim, Mead and White emerged as the most influential group of architects and a roll-call of their achievements includes the **Brooklyn Museum**, the **Bronx Hall of Fame for Great Americans** and **Columbia University**. Although they worked as a team, they (like Mangin and McComb) possessed quite different personalities. Charles Follen McKim was the professional architect *par excellence* who managed to completely upstage his partner Rutherford Mead. Stanford White, on the other hand, relished his role as the *avant garde* artist who was not afraid to interpret European forms with reckless abandon. He even managed to die with rare style, being shot dead by a jealous husband on the rooftop of one of his own buildings.

The Bauhaus school of art was founded by Walter Gropius in Germany in 1919 and soon developed a seminal and controversial style that was to have important reverberations in New York. Before World War II, the New York architect Philip Johnson was championing the modernist spirit behind Bauhaus that rejected ornamentation and historical references. The new style favored simplicity and geometric designs. Then, in the wake of Hitler's closure of the Bauhaus School, architects like Gropius and Mies van der Rohe fled to America where they took up residence. The **Seagram Building**, designed by Mies, is just one of the many buildings inspired by this school of art.

Another early admirer of Bauhaus was Philip Johnson, who later came full circle and renounced his own architectural pedigree by

Skyscraping Ingenuity

Manhattan's skyline could never have developed the way it did without two technological concepts that only seem obvious in retrospect. One of the earliest exponents of building vertically was the architect Jenney. The story goes ... one day he observed a large book falling accidentally onto a fragile birdcage. Wondering why the cage suffered no serious damage led to his momentous realisation that a core of metal frame was capable of spreading and sustaining a weight many times greater than itself. This was the powerful secret to skyscraper technology and remains so to this day. The other great development owes its existence to Elisha Graves Otis, an engineering mechanic and inventor who was posted to New York in

discovering the pleasure of art for art's sake. In his design at the flamboyant **AT&T Building**, functionalism is left far behind and the doors are opened for another new school of New York architects.

Gropius and his Modernist ideals was have a major influence in yet another admirer, I M Pei. For Pei, who studied under him in Harvard, there was instilled this principle that the architectural plan "was to flow from the purpose of the building and the human activities it was to contain, rather than from a preconception of how it might look as a piece of sculpture."

One of his earliest projects was the Kip Bay apartment complex on Manhattan's East Side. it demonstrated his skill at form and functionality. Pei went on to design more ambitious projects: the NCAR in the foothills of the Colorado Rocky Mountains – here the complex of buildings merges aesthetically with the majestic wildness of its surroundings; the East Building of the National Gallery in Washington D C – a powerful expression of American Modernist architechture.

Pei, who runs on of the largest architectural firms in New York, **Pei Cobb Freed & Partners**, is a visionary who was able to communicate the 'essence' of architecture. Instead of faceless, sterile towers, his designs are idealistic: they are meant to touch and inspire the millions that walk through them.

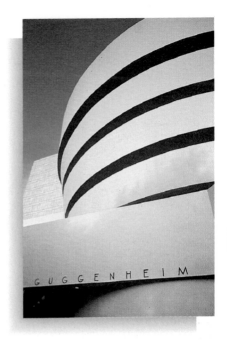

The Guggenheim, distinctive and bold.

when the first skyscraper was finished in 1889 an elevator was built to take people to the top of its 12 storeys. The architect, incidentally, lived on the 11th storey as living proof that such a tall building was safe!

1852. Here, he worked on his idea of replacing the rope-based hoist in lifts by an elevator cabin that would be steam-driven and capable of carrying people. A mechanical clamping device ensured that the cabin would not plunge its passengers to death even if the lifting rope frayed and broke, a common enough failure in the old freight hoists. In 1857, the first public elevator was introduced in a department store and

Architectural Antics

The architects that created so much of what is valued as the quintessential New York skyline are sometimes portrayed as being like children playing with building blocks who try to upstage each other by simply constructing something taller. The architect William Van Alen was quite openly engaged in a competition with one of his own part-

The classic Gothic facade of St Patrick's Cathedral.

out and extended from the highest point!

Such antics should not detract from the seriousness and sense of vision that inspired so many of the classical creations in the 1920s and 1930s. The **Rockefeller Center**, which was finally completed in 1940, occupied a ground space that could easily have fostered a giant of a building that would have literally overlooked all the existing structures. The architects bypassed this opportunity to immortalise themselves into the record books and busied themselves with a more comprehensive vision. There is no one construction that defines the Center and to experience the thrill of the place, it is essential to get inside and move about. Unlike so many of the buildings in Manhattan, the architectural grandeur is not just a visual, exterior spectacle. In the words of Le Corbusier, it is "rational, logically conceived, biologically normal, harmonious in its four functional elements: halls for the entrance and division of crowds, grouped shafts for vertical circulation (elevators), corridors (internal streets), regular offices." The futuristic overtone of this is fully borne out by the experience of walking inside the Center.

ners to see who could reach highest. Alen was working on the Chrysler Building while his associate was drawing plans for a building in Wall Street and when the Wall Street building was complete, it turned out to be higher than the Chrysler. But Alen had a secret design feature, a spire positioned on top of the Chrysler that had been kept inside the top section of the building. Just as his partner thought he had won the competition, Alen gleefully had the spire brought

The New York Public Library in classical style architecture.

Post-war Architecture

The end of World War II ushered in a new architectural phase that was the result of many new influences. Important architects fleeing Nazi Europe settled in the city and, on the technological front, there were developments in the use of reinforced concrete and air-conditioning. The most characteristic feature of the new architecture, called "the International Style," is the glass curtain wall. Countless arrays of windows on all sides create the illusion of a sheer mirror of glass. These are the buildings that have become part of Hollywood's iconography; the business magnate in his huge but sleekly elegant office, seated at a desk that almost touches a vast window that looks out over Manhattan.

All styles reach their apotheosis and the glass curtain wall reached its ultimate expression in the twin towers of the World Trade Center. Looking up at them from the outside it is difficult to imagine that 50,000 people work behind the glass and it is even more difficult to contemplate doing what Philippe Petit did: walking on a tightrope between the two towers. More awesome it is to contemplate the greater disaster had the 1993 bombs blast been on a more massive scale.

The **World Trade Center's** towers are undeniably impressive. They reach a quarter of a mile into the sky and, in winter, the plaza below has to be

Brownstone, Glass and Concrete

When most people think of viewing New York's architecture, the natural tendency is to gaze upwards at the Himalayan peaks of concrete and glass. But the city also possesses some architectural delights that can be appreciated without an accompanying ache in the neck. Texture, not size, is what distinguishes a number of 19th-century houses that can still be found scattered around Manhattan. The houses are identified by the name of the dark-coloured cladding material that was applied over the bare bricks and mortar – brownstone. The sandstone was quarried from the banks of rivers in New Jersey and Connecticut and transported to the metropolis in great quantities. It was in great demand as a speedy and relatively inexpensive way of surfacing the bare brick exterior of townhouses and proud home-owners embellished the brownstone with cast-iron railings and banisters.

A subsequent generation of New Yorkers dismissed the brownstone as a mark of vulgar, bourgeois taste and, sadly in the 1930s, thousands of the houses were demolished. However, the style is highly valued today for its successful evocation of the past and its European flavor. It is well worth seeking out and houses on Lexington Avenue and Third Avenue contain some extremely well-preserved brownstone houses, complete with steep flight of steps leading to the front doors.

There is some leeway in any discussion about which building was the first skyscraper. The **Tower Building** was certainly the first structure with a steel skeleton but at 12 storeys high it plainly lacks charisma. The **Flatiron Building**, at 175 Fifth Avenue, is often credited with being the first true skyscraper and there is certainly some poetic truth to this claim. It is a building of distinction, not least because of its odd angle and it fairly bristles with pride since its recent steam cleaning. When it was first erected, in the first decade of the 20th century, there were no other buildings in the vicinity that came anywhere near its 286 feet and its sharply angled sides caused unexpected wind currents to blow down its sides and along the ground. Female pedestrians were constantly being embarrassed at having their undergarments exposed and there were even times when the police arrived to disrupt the crowds of male spectators who gathered to observe this spectacle!

Which of Manhattan's skyscrapers will pass the test of time and still be applauded in 50 years time? A good case can be made for the **Seagram Building** which has retained the respect it has earned amongst architects the world over. Situated on Park Avenue between 52nd and 53rd Streets and dating back to 1958, it is easy to stroll past the building and see it as just another curtain-wall skyscraper. In one sense this is just what it is; but it is the purest and epitome of this particular style of architecture. It is rendered outstanding by its perfect proportions, use of the best-quality materials and its liberating use of the plaza space.

closed off because icicles falling from above would gather such momentum that they can kill. However, some say that the towers are monumentally boring and the aesthetic pleasure they create is one of awe but little else.

Post-modernism

Not surprisingly, a reaction set in against this style of architecture and in the 1980s a different style started to emerge. Called Post-Modernism, there is more than a hint of nostalgia in the return to the reckless bravado of the 1920s and nowhere is this more apparent than in the **AT&T Building**. This building is everything the World Trade Center is not – eclectic. The base of the building is a Renaissance-style atrium while the roofline wittily imitates a Chippendale

The upper reaches of the Chrysler Building has become one of Manhattan's most distinctive landmark.

chest-of-drawers. The whole concept is slightly outrageous and yet perfectly in keeping with the spirit of the city. It deliberately harks back to the past. Ironically, the Sony Corporation bought the place in 1991 and within the interior is a shrine to this new electronic age.

Trying to predict the architectural future of New York is impossible. The most recent buildings added to the canon have little in common and point in wildly different directions. On the one hand there is the **Holiday Inn Crowne Plaza** in Times Square, multi-coloured, brash and cocking a hoop at pretension, while the new skyscraper for **Citicorp** in Queens raises the possibility of a new era of tall buildings located outside Manhattan.

The enigma that lies at the heart of the city's architecture is that there never has been any master plan, or even a consensus, amongst the many talented architects and builders. New buildings continually ascend, old ones are regularly destroyed and this anarchist spirit of revolt and renewal continues to produce an astonishing and arresting array of sights.

Yet a tour of architectural fare and flair hardly misses the undeniable sight of the derelict and disrepair among the aging buildings, something that even the most elegant soaring spirits fail to hide. These sites are crying out for the healing hands of urban renewal, which hopefully may rise again when property developers rise above the recession.

The east side of Upper Manhattan is in a class of its own. Many of the city's most prestigious museums are found here as are many of New York's most prestigious people. The social and mental landscape of Woody Allen is mapped out in this area, home to the cultured upper middle-class urbanites that personify his films mostly set in New York. Exclusive apartment blocks with high profile security systems are found along the upper reaches of Fifth Avenue and the surrounding streets; the criteria for success is owning an apartment in Upper Manhattan which commands a view of Central Park. In the post-World War I period in 1918, this part of town was appropriated by the extremely wealthy and the *New York Times* described this end of Madison Avenue as being like a string of pearls, each pearl being "a double block of millionaires." However, it was not always so. Before the turn of this century the city's patricians lived out their elite existences to the south of the

East Room, Pierpoint Morgan Library.

Upper East Side

113

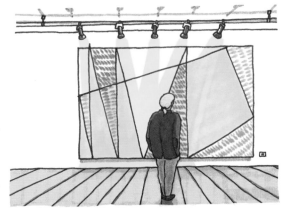

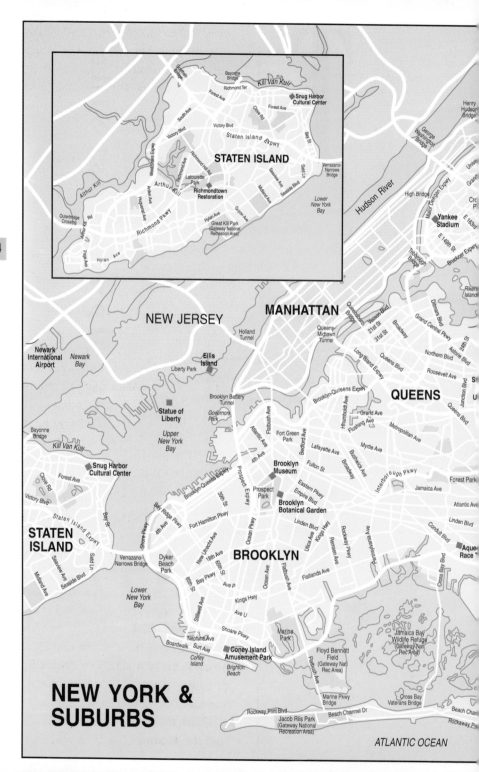

NEW YORK & SUBURBS

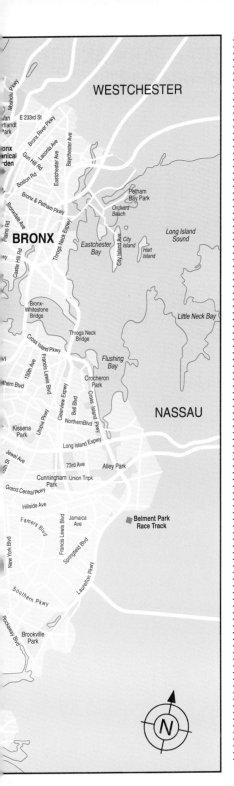

newly opened Central Park and the east side of upper Manhattan was sought out by the *nouveau riche* who were never fully accepted by the old aristocratic families.

The Central Set

The **Metropolitan Club** at 61st Street stands as a permanent reminder of the in-fighting that went on between the monied classes during the closing decade of the 19th century. J P Morgan, of Pierpoint Morgan Library fame, was a highly successful financier who was viewed with barely concealed contempt by the established upper class. Tired of being snubbed by their exclusive social clubs, Morgan and his friends commissioned Stanford White to design and build a new club that would be more exclusive than anything the old establishment had to offer. Morgan's obsession with 17th-century Italy must have been made clear to the architect because the Metropolitan Club evokes more of a Renaissance flavor than anything the Renaissance actually produced!

Not far away, at 10 East 60th Street, is a very modern kind of club. The **Copacabana Club** is really just another disco and at the moment not one of the best, but its claim to fame is assured by its immortal role in what is probably Barry Manilow's best song – *Lola*.

From the profane to the sacred, the **Temple Emanu-El** is a magnificent

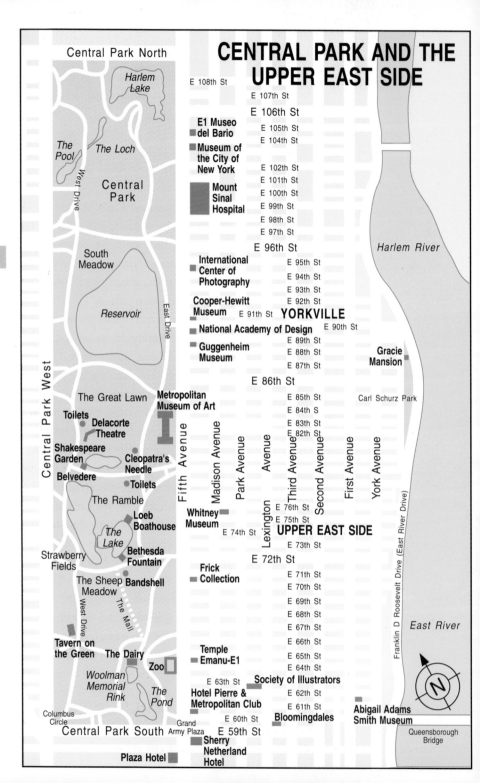

CENTRAL PARK AND THE UPPER EAST SIDE

Central Park North

Harlem Lake

E 108th St

E 107th St

E 106th St

E1 Museo del Bario

E 105th St
E 104th St

Museum of the City of New York

E 102th St
E 101th St

The Pool

The Loch

Mount Sinal Hospital

E 100th St
E 99th St
E 98th St
E 97th St

West Drive

Central Park

E 96th St

South Meadow

International Center of Photography

E 95th St
E 94th St
E 93th St

Cooper-Hewitt Museum

E 92th St

Harlem River

E 91th St   YORKVILLE

Reservoir

East Drive

National Academy of Design

E 90th St

Guggenheim Museum

E 89th St
E 88th St
E 87th St

Gracie Mansion

E 86th St

The Great Lawn

Metropolitan Museum of Art

E 85th St
E 84th S
E 83th St
E 82th St

Carl Schurz Park

Central Park West

Toilets

Delacorte Theatre

Shakespeare Garden

Cleopatra's Needle

Belvedere

Toilets

The Ramble

Loeb Boathouse

Fifth Avenue

Madison Avenue

Park Avenue

Avenue

Third Avenue

Second Avenue

First Avenue

York Avenue

Whitney Museum

E 76th St
E 75th St
E 74th St

Lexington

UPPER EAST SIDE

The Lake

Bethesda Fountain

E 73th St

Strawberry Fields

Frick Collection

E 72th St
E 71th St
E 70th St

The Sheep Meadow

Bandshell

E 69th St
E 68th St
E 67th St

West Drive

The Mall

E 66th St
E 65th St
E 64th St

Tavern on the Green

The Dairy

Temple Emanu-E1

Society of Illustrators

Franklin D Roosevelt Drive (East River Drive)

East River

Zoo

Woolman Memorial Rink

The Pond

E 63th St

Hotel Pierre & Metropolitan Club

E 62th St
E 61th St

Abigail Adams Smith Museum

Columbus Circle

Grand Army Plaza

E 60th St

Bloomingdales

Central Park South

E 59th St

Sherry Netherland Hotel

Queensborough Bridge

Plaza Hotel

Waldorf Astoria, one of the ranking hotels of the world.

synagogue situated at East 65th Street and Fifth Avenue. It is America's largest Reform synagogue, with room for well over 2,000 worshippers and should be seen from within to be really appreciated. It was built in 1929 in an eclectic style that manages to combine the Romanesque-Byzantine with touches of Moorish art and even hints of art deco. The cavernous interior, which comes as a color shock especially after viewing the limestone exterior, contains some lovely mosaics. If possible try to be there on a Friday evening after 5:00 pm when an organ recital takes place.

Two blocks to the east of the temple, at 643 Park Avenue between 66th and 67th Streets, is the **Seventh Regiment Armory**, an unlikely looking structure to find in this supremely elegant part of town. Appropriately enough, it has a militaristic exterior, yet within, everything is subdued by Victorian wood-panelling and some fine stained glass. The glass is the work of Louis Comfort Tiffany whose use of opalescent glass caused a sensation when it first appeared; this in turn led to many commissions including one to decorate the White House. Each January a big antiques fair is held in the Armory and a variety of other summer events tend to pop up here every now and again.

Shops Aplenty

There are many good reasons to spend

Bloomingdale's on Lexington, where choice will never be a problem.

time in Upper Manhattan's East Side and one of the best is the opportunities it presents for people-watching. Visitors are not usually allowed in the exclusive social clubs and luxury apartment blocks, unless the doormen can be persuaded otherwise, but the regular stores are open to the public and they are often fascinating places.

The really top-notch designer shops actually installed their own security systems that bar doors to none but recognised customers. However, a place like **Bloomingdale's**, on 1000 Third Avenue at 59th Street, is well worth strolling around even if shopping is the last item on your agenda as the fashion department is not to be missed.

Nearby at 655 Madison Avenue, at

60th Street, is **Boyds**, another one of those places which sells ludicrously expensive items, cosmetics and vanity pieces, and whose customers look like they have just walked off the set of a long-running soap *Dynasty*.

The Suburbs

The not-so-rich in this part of town live in **Yorkville**, the area that lies between Franklin Roosevelt Drive and Lexington Avenue and bordered northwards by 96th Street and southwards by 77th Street. By tradition this is the German part of New York, dating back to the mid 19th century when German-speaking Europeans fled to America after the

The East River, between Manhattan and Roosevelt Island.

failed 1848 revolutions. Nowadays, it is more the haunt of city yuppies and the only reminder of an ethnic past is to be found in the few remaining bakeries and coffee houses which sport names like **Schaller and Weber**, at 1654 Second Avenue between Second and Third Avenues.

The nucleus of the extant German community is 86th Street, where newsagents can still be found selling German newspapers and delicatessens serve *wienerschnitzel* and *plockwurst*. For a tempting choice of typically ornate German pastries, try the **Cafe Geiger**, at 206 East 86th Street between Second and Third Avenues, which has retained a reputation that goes way back.

A coffee and cake at the Cafe Geiger is perfect just before or after taking a walk towards the river and the Carl Schurz Park at the end of 86th Street.

Just before crossing East End Avenue to the park is a row of two dozen small cottages that make up the **Henderson Place Historic District**. The cottages, now priced at millions of dollars and aimed at the very upwardly mobile, were originally built as servants' quarters for long-demolished mansions.

On the other side of the road is the **Carl Schurz Park** which looks across the East River to the borough of Queens. This part of the river is known as **Hell's Gate** due to the meeting of dangerous currents meandering from the Harlem River, Long Island Sound and New York

Gracie Mansion, handsome residence of the Mayor of New York.

Harbor. The park itself is named after an immigrant from Germany who led an eventful life in his new country, reaching the rank of major-general in the Union Army. He later served as a senator representing Missouri, before being appointed Secretary to the Interior dur-ing the government of President John Quincy Adams (1797-1801) and he also achieved fame as the editor of *Harper's Weekly.*

The park is home to **Gracie Mansion**, built in the 18th century as a home for the wealthy shipowner Archibald

exterior ones: shutters over the windows, a handsome verandah and two sets of pretty lattice railings.

Art and Old Money

One stretch of Fifth Avenue is known as **Museum Mile**, and with good reason. Enthusiasts with stamina could easily spend an entire vacation cloistered within the walls of the many and varied institutions.

In practice, it makes more sense to see some of the smaller museums on separate days and visit the big ones on more than one occasion. The **Metropolitan Museum of Art**, the really big one, could hardly be visited too often (see the Arts & Culture chapter), while the **Guggenheim Museum** (see the Architecture chapter) demands to be stared at and entered into. It is difficult to forget a visit to either of these two places and return visits can become compulsive.

The **Frick Collection**, although tiny in comparison to the Metropolitan, is very unique in its own way. It is wonderfully uninstitutionalised and an utterly relaxing place for the weary pedestrian. And because the emphasis is on quality and not quantity this is one museum where the visitor is not burdened by dutifully trying to take in too much in a single excursion.

Henry Clay Frick himself was such a ruthless, thoroughly unpleasant man that it is puzzling to try and reconcile his

Gracie. It is now the official residence of the Mayor of New York and the high security surrounding the place helps to make the park a particularly safe piece of greenery.

Unfortunately, the security also means it is difficult to see the place at close quarters, though the characteristic features of the architecture are mainly

The Metropolitan Museum of Art

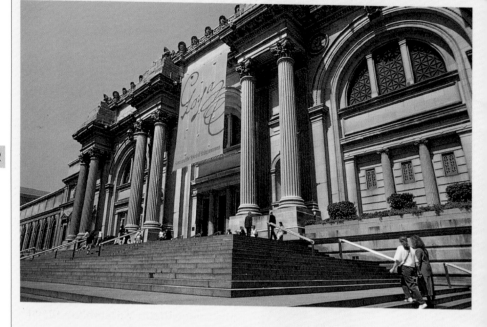

Metropolitan mecca of art.

Warning! Do not attempt to see the entire Met in one visit. It occupies 1.4 million square feet and stretches from 80th to 84th Streets. Even without the full collection of two million works of art on show, any one visit can only take in a fraction of the treasures displayed. So, collect the floor plan from the information desk and make some decisions about what to see and what to leave for the next visit.

If you intend to spend the better part of the day, or the week, in the Museum, these details should help to orientate you; the Museum is closed on Monday but opens from 9.30 am to 5.15 pm every other day, except Fridays and Saturdays when it closes at 8.45 pm. Admission is US$6 and $3 for senior citizens and children over 12. The Foreign Visitors Desk in the Great Hall has brochures and assistance is available in Japanese, French, Spanish, German, Italian and Chinese. For refreshments, there is a cafeteria, a restaurant and three bars. You might also wish

to have a look at the gift shops in the Museum which sells books, postcards, prints, posters and reproductions of sculpture, jewelry and other works from the Museum's collection. The Museum also conduct tours, in English and other languages.

The Metropolitan Museum of Art is the largest depository of art and antiquities in the Western Hemisphere. The five major collections are European Painting, American Painting, Primitive Art, Medieval Painting and Egyptian Antiquities. There are also collections of prints, photographs, costumes, musical instruments, sculpture and decorative arts and a recently opened Arms and Armor Galleries that not only displays European armor but also the finest collection of Japanese arms and armor outside Japan. To top it all, unique exhibitions, (especially put together for the Met) are also regular features.

Of course, everyone has their own interests

but the collection of European art is unparalleled. Flemish art and the Netherlands is represented by the work of Jan van Eyck, Rogier van der Wyden and Bruegel while Spanish paintings by El Greco and Velazquez include the incomparable *View of Toledo* and *Portrait of Juan de Parej*. Painters from the Italian Renaissance range from Botticelli and Raphael to Bronzino and Mantegna.

Some would justify a visit to the Met just for the five Dutch works created by Vermeer whose calm and haunting interiors seem a million miles away from the bustling street life that unfolds on the pavements outside the hallowed rooms of this museum. The Impressionist and Post-Impressionist art where Manet and Monet rub shoulders with Cezanne, Renoir, Gauaguin and Toulouse-Lautrec, not to mention Van Gogh, and Seurat and gems like Rousseau's *Reclining Lady in the Tropical Jungle* can be found in their own art gallery.

The Egyptian Art galleries are stupendous. Everything seems to be on a massive scale, not just the giant sarcophagi that commands your attention but even door jambs taken from a set of temple doors (at a time when non-Egyptian archaeologists could retain almost half of whatever they excavated) are absolutely huge. To cap it all virtually the entire Temple of Dendur that was presented to the United States in recognition of UNESCO's help in saving monuments in Nubia from flooding caused by the building of the Aswan Dam in 1960 stands in the Met.

The American Wing has three storeys of nearly 20 different period rooms from the early 17th to 19th centuries and includes some of the very best Tiffany glass to be found anywhere. The Primitive Art collection span three millennia and exhibits range from artefacts from Gabon's Fang tribe to the fascinating Asmat Mbis poles of Pacific Islands.

And if you have the time for return visits, seek out the treasures of Islamic, Asian, Chinese, Greek and Roman art. The Lila Acheson Wallis Wing has some extraordinary 20th-century art and on the roof above this wing, is a contemporary Sculpture Garden that opens in the summer and offers panoramic views of Central Park.

insensitive nature with his ability to put together such an amazingly fine collection of art. His fortunes were made from coke and steel and any attempts by workers to form unions were ruthlessly crushed. On more than one occasion striking workers were killed by his private army of strike-breakers.

In return, more than one attempt was made on his own life; the most famous would-be assassin being Alexander Berkman whose unsuccessful attempt in 1892 led to a life spent behind bars. Incidentally, his *Prison Memoirs of an Anarchist* is an unrecognised gem of prison literature.

The **Whitney Museum of American Art** is housed in such a forbidding-looking building, it could almost put one off entering inside. Yet inside, the huge collection of 20th-century American art is presented in a most aesthetically pleasing and intelligent manner. Over the recent years the gallery has been at the center of numerous controversies, partly due to an adventurous and imaginative director who refuses to allow the place to become a stuffy museum. The originator of the gallery, Gertrude Vanderbilt Whitney, was an equally energetic champion of the arts. She was a sculptor in her own right whose inherited wealth allowed her to build up an unrivalled collection of American art.

She founded the museum in 1931 and had been dead for 24 years before the Whitney Building became home to her inspired collection. A biennial high-

Art at its finest at the Metropolitan.

Museum Mile

Gently spiralling displays of art at the Guggenheim.

Ten museums occupy the stretch along Fifth Avenue from 104th Street in the north down to the Metropolitan Museum of Art that ends at 80th Street. If you start at 80th Street you will probably never leave the Met which is the best argument for traveling up on the train to 103rd Street and walking three blocks west. If you do not like the idea of walking the three blocks across Puerto Rican El Barrio, then take the M1, M2, M3 or M4 bus up on Madison or Fifth Avenue and hop off at 104th Street.

The first museum is **El Museo del Bario**, which has undergone a renovation, and was reopened in January 1994. The name translates as "the museum of the neighborhood" and while it started out as just – this a cultural centre for the surrounding Puerto Rican community – it has become a showcase for Hispanic culture. The collection of Puerto Rican *santos* (small wooden saints worshipped at home) shares a home with some stunning examples of Pre-Columbian art and the newly enlarged exhibition areas allow for bigger special displays.

Almost next door, at 103rd Street, the **Museum of the City of New York** charts the development of the city from a small Dutch trading post to today's vibrant metropolis. The 20-minute multimedia presentation is an excellent introduction to the historical evolution of the city.

The **International Center of Photography** at 94th Street is situated in a relatively small building (for Fifth Avenue). It is an attractive half-Georgian and half-Federal townhouse with entire rooms devoted to single photographers like Adams, Cartier-Bresson and Capa. The special exhibitions warrant a visit.

Two blocks down is the **Jewish Museum** which exhibits a wide-ranging collection of Judaica in the tenderly personal memorabilia of

light (between March and June on odd-numbered years) is a major exhibition that turns the spotlight on current movements in contemporary art. Everyone turns up hoping to spot the new Edward Hopper or Andy Warhol and, because time has not allowed any consensus to emerge, the critics are at their most vociferous and vicious.

Henry Clay Frick, unlike Whitney, collected art for his own edification and the Frick Collection is basically a collection he bought to furnish and decorate his home. Andrew Carnegie was a busi-

poor Lower East Side settlements as well as tackling the major crisis of the Holocaust.

At 91st Street is the **Cooper-Hewitt Museum**, the 64-room former home of the magnate Andrew Carnegie which now displays an extremely eclectic collection of design items. Exhibits range from furniture and glassware to candlesticks and contemporary objects of interesting design. The house itself is a living museum of 19th-century high culture and the ground floor conservatory is enviously attractive.

The **National Academy of Design**, at 89th Street, is not as dull as it might seem. There is no permanent collection but the frequently changing exhibitions are often some of the best in town and it pays to make a telephone call (tel: 369-4880) to see if the subject on show is of special interest to you. The National Academy of Design is often passed over by tourists simply because the world-famous **Guggenheim Museum** which no one wants to miss is located just next door. Before entering, step across to the Central Park side of the road and take in Frank Lloyd Wright's "organic architecture." Saunter inside up the gently curving ramp to feast on Kandinsky, Chagall, the Cubists, the *Dancers* by Degas, Van Gogh's *Mountains at Saint Remy* and a whole host of other masters of the modern form.

And within walking distance the grand **Metropolitan Museum of Art** further south beckons....(see Box). If the vast American Museum of National History at Central Park West is the mother of all museums, then the Metropolitan Museum of Art has to be the father of them all.

ness associate of Frick's who later fell out with the former.

Both of them have one thing in common, their homes have been transformed into public museums. In Carnegie's case, his 64-room mansion is now home to a vast collection of decorative arts which surfaces in the form of constantly changing and invariably fascinating exhibitions. Regardless of the exhibition that happens to be on, visitors have the opportunity of viewing the home of a man rich enough to sell his steel company for US$250 million – in 1901!

The remaining museums on Museum Mile tend to be dwarfed by the fame of those already mentioned but they are still well worth visiting.

At 94th Street is the **International Center of Photography**, the new kid on the block, having opened in 1974. Permanent collections of all-time great photographers are complemented by imaginative thematic exhibitions.

The **Museum of the City of New York**, at 103rd Street, is housed in a modern neo-Georgian building where upper Manhattan meets Spanish Harlem. The museum has devoted itself to the history of the city, not in a particularly exciting way but interesting nevertheless, and the audio-visual show does a good job of encapsulating the 400 busy years of the city's evolution.

The **National Academy of Design**, although it does not possess an exciting name, is one of the least visited museums but it is still well worth checking out to see what temporary exhibition is being mounted. The Academy was founded in 1825 by Samuel Morse, the inventor of the telegraph and its binary code. Recently, some of these exhibitions have surprised everyone by their cleverness in both content and presentation.

Fifth Avenue has justifiably become a synonym for elegance and high class consumerism but it is only one section of this very long avenue that contains glitzy boutiques and department stores with private dressing rooms. Fifth Avenue itself begins near Union Square, not far from Greenwich Village and goes all the way north to the fringes of Harlem. It is too long a street to even walk in one trip, let alone visit the sights along the way. The consumer strip, and the most walk-worthy part, stretches between the Empire State Building and the Plaza Hotel. Between these two buildings is an incredible array of shops, and the sheer variety of consumer goods on sale is staggering.

Where Fifth Avenue meets 38th Street, the august **Lord and Taylor** is a champion of top American designer styles but in close proximity are gaudy souvenir emporiums that keep their own supplies of fake brand-name watches. One moment you see a pavement entrepreneur trying to unload his suitcase of T-shirts in front of a window

An uptown view of Fifth Avenue.

Hailing a cab, a common sight on the avenues.

display featuring tacky miniatures of the Empire State Building and then a block later – lo and behold ! – **Saks Fifth Avenue** at 49th Street caters to the wealthiest citizens and visitors to the city. **Gucci** is at 689 Fifth Avenue, at 54th Street, and one block up – between 55th and 56th Streets – **Henri Bendel** is another top-of-the-league sophisticated department store. At 56th Street the world-famous Italian fashion house, **Fendi,** has three floors of merchandise set amidst a classical Roman setting. Other top-notch shops include the 12-floor women's salon at 54th Street, **Elizabeth Arden**, and **Steuben Glass**, on 715 Fifth Avenue at 56th Street, where an extraordinary range of functional and artistic crystal is available.

Madison Square Park

At the bottom eastern end of Fifth Avenue where it meets Broadway, is **Madison Square Park**. The park's main claim to fame is that it was here where the new game of baseball was first developed in 1840. A few years later the baseball pitch was laid out as a public garden as this part of town became highly fashionable and elitist. The original Madison Square Sports Center stood nearby and it was on the roof of this building, designed by Stanford White, that the playboy architect was shot dead by an irate husband. Legend has it that the outraged husband was driven to his crime of passion after realising that

Elite interiors of the Waldorf Astoria, which until 1929 stood where the Empire State now is.

White's design of a revolving statue of Diana, centered conspicuously above the center of the sports complex, bore more than a passing resemblance to his own wife! The original Madison Square Sports Center is long gone and since those torrid times, a second Madison Square Garden has also come and gone. The third Madison Square Garden, the only one that now stands, confuses people by being situated many blocks away from Madison Square Park, to the north-west.

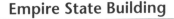

Empire State Building

The north-west corner of Madison Square Park is at East 26th Street and Fifth Avenue. If you stroll further up Fifth Avenue to its corner with 34th Street, the unmissable **Empire State Building** can be found. The site where the Empire State Building now stands is another one of those corners in the city where the ghost of a newly demolished building continues to inhabit the present. Up until 1929, the legendary **Waldorf Astoria Hotel** stood at the junction of Fifth Avenue and 34th Street, and an invitation to one of the hotel's balls was the only sure way of knowing that New

York society endorsed your *beau monde* aspirations. Four hundred invitations would be sent out for one of the dances and the cream of the city's socialites were dubbed "The Four Hundred." By the end of the 1920s the nucleus of the upper class had moved uptown and the hotel followed suit, shifting to its present position on Park Avenue.

Plans were immediately made for the construction of the Empire State Building but as the lorries shifted away the last vestiges of the Waldorf Astoria the almighty economy of Wall Street came crashing down. The first bricks of the Empire State building were laid in the immediate aftermath of the Crash and among the building's many claims to immortality is the fact that the final construction bill turned out to cost millions less than the original estimates.

The Empire State retains its preeminent status as the *icon* of New York. The observatory is open from 9:30 am to midnight and a ticket costs US$3.50. Although the building is no longer the tallest in New York, you will feel an indefinable pleasure from just being at ᶠthe building. In fact, some 2.5 ᵉople make the trip to the top , ᵤᵣ. A constant ever-changing stream of exhibitions is seen daily at the lobby by the Fifth Avenue entrance, and there is always an animated King Kong display and up at the observatory there is often a costumed King Kong posing for photographs. Down at the concourse level is a Guinness World of Records exhibition with separate admission charges.

Central Library Hall

Just a short walk from the Empire State is the **Pierpont Morgan Library** at 29 36th Street, between Park and Madison Avenues. The ubiquitous firm of McKim, Mead and White built it to house the financier's private library of books and artefacts and, with various additions to both the buildings and the contents, the Library is now one of the best in the city. Many many priceless books are on display, including a 15th-century bible printed on a Guttenberg press, and the only extant originals of Aphra Behn's plays. Aphra Behn was a contemporary of Shakespeare and her plays were just as popular before they sank into oblivion and until they were rediscovered by feminists a decade ago. Pierpoint Morgan did not just collect Renaissance books and manuscripts, he commissioned the architects to design a 17th-century Italian building to house them. A glass-covered court connects the origi-

nal building with a brownstone house that is now a well-stocked museum shop, specialising in art books.

Back on Fifth Avenue, just before 42nd Street, is another library, the **New York Public Library**. Non-bibliophiles should consider climbing the Vermont marble steps and stepping inside, just to admire the *beaux arts* decor and the sheer style of the whole place. The Central Hall comes alive with four large murals that date back to 1940 and the Reading Room possesses a state of the art computer system that can retrieve a single item from among the staggering collection of six million books and twice as many periodicals in minutes. The books are all stored in eight vast levels located directly beneath the Reading Room. This was where Leon Trotsky chose to study before he sailed off to ignite the 1917 revolution in Russia. The library offers informative, free tours and there is a useful shop worth browsing through.

Rockefeller Center

Five blocks further up Fifth Avenue is the beginning of **Rockefeller Center**, between 47th and 52nd Streets. It was conceived as a "city within the city" and lives up to its ambition by connecting nearly 20 buildings through a complex system of underground walkways, replete with shops, theaters and restaurants. On an average workday a quarter of a million people come and go, mill-

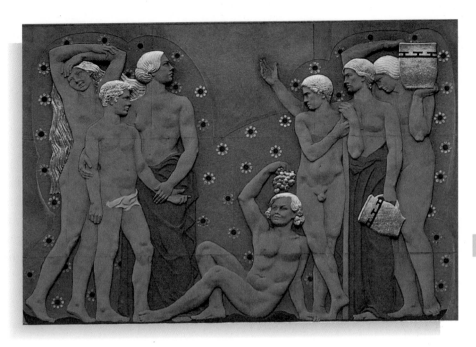

Wall decorations in the Rockefeller Center.

ing about inside, or working in the dense layers of office space. It was originally the property of John D Rockefeller Jr, the oil tycoon, after his plan for a joint investment with the Metropolitan Opera was scuppered by the 1929 Wall Street Crash.

The center was subsequently owned by Colombia University but now belongs to a Japanese consortium who took control in 1989. Forming part of the complex is the **Time and Life Building**, where the magazines of the same name are published as well as other illustrious titles like *Fortune* and *People*. It is easy to spend the best part of a day wandering about inside the Rockefeller Center as apart from the numerous shops and amenities there are countless dis-

plays of art in the form of murals and sculptures. The most famous artwork commissioned by Rockefeller was a huge mural in the lobby of the GE Building that so incensed the patron that he had it wrapped up and taken away on the day of the grand opening. The communist artist, Diego Rivera, had refused to remove the portrait of Lenin from the mural. The mural was recommissioned and what now stands in its place is an idealistic mural executed by Jose Maria Sert.

To organise shopping in the Rockefeller Center, it is best to visit the information desk at 30 Rockefeller Plaza on the concourse level, where you can obtain a free copy of the Center's directory of shops and services. Everyone will

Trump Tower, the ritziest shopping complex in Manhattan.

have their own favorites, but the **Metro-politan Museum of Art** is good for souvenirs and presents, and **Larium** is a quality leather store, with its entrance on 50th Street between Fifth and Sixth Avenues.

Saint Patrick's Cathedral

An unlikely neighbor to the modernist Rockefeller Center, on the other side of the road, is the Gothic **Saint Patrick's Cathedral**. The church is so utterly European and medieval-looking that it might seem that the whole structure was transported here from somewhere in France.

In one sense it was, for the British architect James Renwick went on a professional tour of France to collect design details from all the cathedrals there. He then returned to New York and produced this amalgam of classic Gothic; everything but flying buttresses have been incorporated into the faultless design, and they would have been added if not for the constraints of space! The artificiality of the design accounts for the cosmetic feel of Saint Patrick's, although the blue window glass inside is very impressive. Strangely enough, the church, which is the ecclesiastical seat of the Archbishop of New York, gains from being surrounded by the concrete of the Rockefeller Center, across the road, and the glass of the Olympic Tower to the rear.

Trumping Ahead

Further up Fifth Avenue the infamous **Trump Tower** can be found and wondered at on 56th Street. Built in 1983, the Trump Tower attracts modern voyeurs fuelled by the media hype surrounding the multimillionaire Donald Trump.

Donald Trump was not one who lived in restraint or reclusiveness, and his showmanship revealed itself in this glitzy building. The atrium is spectacular, capable of provoking diametrically opposed reactions in different people, and the 80-foot high waterfall is a sight to behold.

Above the atrium are 200 lavishly luxurious apartments, each one of which commands a three-fold view over its surroundings. Residents include the likes of Stephen Spielberg as well as Donald Trump the man himself! Architecturally, the building has been both acclaimed and condemned although it is probably difficult to dissociate feelings about the building from feelings about "the Donald."

The pretentiously new constantly rubs shoulders with the classically old in New York so it quite fitting that the Trump Tower should be located only a short walk away from the supremely elegant **Plaza Hotel**, at Fifth Avenue and 59th Street. It is equally appropriate that they should both be linked to the same person. Although it has undergone extensive renovations, both the

Children's paradise in FAO Schwarz.

exterior and interior continue to exude charm. Built in 1907, it gained notoriety during the inter-war years when it was the favorite watering hole of notable celebrities. It was here that Solomon Guggenheim, the millionaire art collector, stacked up his favorite paintings after each shopping spree in Europe. But, even the hotel's largest suite became too small for his burgeoning collection and so he had to consider building his own museum to house them. His chosen architect Frank Lloyd Wright, who constantly shuddered at what he saw as the monstrosity of most of the city's architecture, was content to live at the Plaza.

Inside the Plaza, the **Palm Court** makes no bones about evoking

A Walk Up Fifth Avenue

Shoppers pound the pavements
of Fifth Avenue.

of shop exteriors, an estimated US$40 million is traded *every hour*. Business is mainly conducted by Hasidic Jews, who can easily be recognised by their traditional dress.

Back to Fifth Avenue and on the right at #611 is the prestigious **Saks Fifth Avenue**. This exclusive store is now over 70 years old. In fact, their carrier bags have come to be a New York City memento. Back on the other side of the street, between 49th and 50th Streets, the sloping **Channel Gardens** lead down to the **GE Building** (also still known by its earlier name, the RCA Building). The Channel Gardens were named after the Channel that divides Britain and France, which are both represented here by the **British Empire Building** and the **Maison Francaise**. In the lobby of the GE building, tickets can be purchased for a tour of the television studios upstairs. Free tickets are also available for seats to the live recordings. Channel Gardens is the most picturesque way of entering the Rockefeller Center. If you feel like resting, head for the beautifully restored **Rainbow Room**, located high up on the 65th storey and commanding magnificent views. The decor and the views alone make the price of a drink seem quite reasonable, the only drawback being that men need to be dressed in jacket and tie, whatever the time of day.

The really glamorous part of Fifth Avenue is north of 52nd Street. This is where the beautiful people draw up outside the designer stores in their chauffeur-driven limousines, leaving their equally well-groomed poodles perched on the back seat. The number of famous stores is legion but one in particular deserves special mention. **Bergdorf Goodman** located at 754 Fifth Avenue, is one of the classiest department stores to be found anywhere in the world. Even the escalators seem posher than those found in other stores!

Fifth Avenue is fun, not just because of the thrill of people-watching but also because of the number of fascinating sights tucked away down its sidestreets. For instance, starting where 42nd Street meets Fifth Avenue and walking two blocks north on the left hand side of the road to 44th Street is the infamous **Algonquin Hotel** because of its literary associations, which started in the 1920s when a group of city intellectuals regularly met at their favorite table and made witty remarks published in the *New York World*. Other figures who frequent its portals Noel Coward, Bernard Shaw and Brendan Behan at who stayed the Algonquin in the 1960s. Today, despite renovation, the faded elegance is scrupulously maintained and the "Rose Room Bar" is eminently suitable for soaking up the atmosphere.

Back on Fifth Avenue, and continuing northwards for another three blocks until comes 47th Street, **Diamond Row** on the left into view. Diamond Row is at the heart of New York's diamond-dealing and behind the small number

The Empire State Building

Looking up the Empire State Building.

Now over 60 years old, there is nothing quite like it. Every day of the week visitors descend like pilgrims to a secular shrine, just happy to be there and relive their film memory of the sensitive ape waving away the planes as he climbed to the top clutching the "very reluctant" female mortal. In 1945, a B-52 bomber, that was not hunting King Kong actually did crash into the side of the building causing damage that came to millions of dollars. Fortunately, the building's structural integrity was not affected. Apart from the thrill of just being at the top, you can enjoy panoramic views of the city. Definitely a satisfying orientation exercise at the beginning, or very end, of your visit to the city.

Over the years, nearly 20 people have jumped to death from the Empire State, although the netting that is visible around the first floor was not constructed to try to save them. Surprisingly, it is to collect coins that might be dropped from the top of the building and which, if unlucky enough to hit someone walking below, would prove fatal.

The lift climbs up to the 86th floor and the observatory but if you prefer to walk, there are 1,575 steps to climb. The initial impression, on stepping out onto the observatory, can be disappointing because of the security wire that has been errected but if you stick your nose up against it and look through, the effect can be dramatic. The obvious landmarks are the Statue of Liberty to the south and the expanse of Central Park to the north, while on a clear day you can see parts of four states. A windy day proves an unsettling experience, as the building sways more than an inch and visitors who are unprepared for this can receive quite a shock.

On the 86th level there is another claustrophobically small lift that will take you up the final 16 floors to the 102nd level. There is yet another observatory here which is completely closed in by glass. This is the beginning of the mooring station that was supposed to act as a dock for passing airships and balloons. This idea was actually added to the design at a fairly late stage and had just as much to do with increasing the height of the building. The original summit at the 86th floor made it only marginally higher than the Chrysler Building but the designers of the Empire State wanted no room for equivocation; they were consciously striving for a world record. For 40 years, from its completion in 1931 and until it was overtaken by the World Trade Center in 1971, it remained New York's tallest building.

By including its television antennae in the measurement of its height it still rates, at 1472 ft, as one of the tallest buildings in the world. Only the Sears Building in Chicago and the World Trade Center are taller. In recent years there has been talk of Donald Trump masterminding the ultimate skyscraper for New York, taller than anything else in the world, but even if it does materialise it will not detract from the enduring appeal of the Empire State.

Greenery in a concrete jungle – rooftop garden overlooking Fifth Avenue.

Fitzgerald's "Gatsby" era and English high tea is served to the accompaniment either of live piano music or even a small orchestra. The **Oak Bar** is equally popular and the 1920s decor has been wonderfully preserved.

Just beyond the Plaza Hotel, the junction of the **Grand Army Plaza**, at Central Park South and Fifth Avenue, marks the beginning of the residential section of Fifth Avenue. At various points along the avenue, especially around the Grand Army Plaza at Fifth Avenue between West 58th Street and 60th Street,

near 47th Street. The even bigger rail-road and shipping magnate, "Commo-dore" Cornelius Vanderbilt, imitated the idea and by the turn of the century, real estate prices rose sky high in this part of town. The fancy department stores set up shop to be close to their wealthy patrons and the living legend of Fifth Avenue was created.

One block south of the Plaza Hotel, at 765 Fifth Avenue on 58th Street, **F A O Schwarz** can be found on the ground floor of the General Motor Building. This is the most engaging toy shop to be found anywhere in the city. With or without children, this is an Aladdin's cave of toys, games and books – three floors of them!

Finally, mention must be made of some of the notable bookstores to be found along Fifth Avenue.**Barnes & Noble** is at 105 Fifth Avenue, at both corners of 18th Street, and it's the "most capacious individual bookstore in the world measured by square footage," ac-cording to the Guinness Book of Records. Most of the books on the 20.71 km of shelving are discounted from 10 to 50 percent.

At 666 Fifth Avenue on 52nd Street, **B Dalton Bookseller** is one of the larg-est outlets of this huge bookstore chain that has 800 shops across the United States. **New York Bound Bookshop** at 50 Rockefeller Plaza, is one of the city's many specialist bookstores, specialising in old and new titles on New York itself and including old maps and prints of the city.

young performers gyrate, breakdance and roller skate to the sounds of a mot-ley collection of musicians, all of whom are grateful for any tourist dollars that come their way.

The palatial residences of Fifth Av-enue date back to 1837 when a railway magnate decided to get away from the crowds by building a mansion

By the middle of 1993 only three of New York's 75 precincts recorded no killings. One of the three precincts covered Central Park. It is a startling statistic, not least because of several highly publicized violent crimes in its past, and it ably reflects the generally very low level of criminal activity in the park.

A location that was once considered a mugger's paradise now has the police announcing that their biggest problem is bicycle robberies that occur here during the summer.

One possible explanation for this most comforting of transformations is that the park has been completely taken over by law-abiding Manhattanites intent on enjoying their leisure time so much so that muggers and other miscreants feel outnumbered and intimidated! Bordered by Central Park South to the south, Central Park west to the west, Fifth Avenue to the east and Central Park North to the north, the park's 843

Restful respite from the budgeoning buildings.

Central Park

141

The common sight of a jogger.

acres certainly does buzz with the hum of concerted activity: hordes of children on school trips, tourists, out-of-towners and New Yorkers everywhere – ensconced on park benches while chatting amiably to cyclists enjoying a rest, belting past on a punishing jog or more jogging calmly along, whilst conversing with their running mates or gliding past in lurid sports gear on futuristic-looking skates.

At times it seems to be only the police in their cars or on their horses that are not sporting Walkmans®, but, then you spot a young couple engrossed in each other's company and utterly oblivious of the cyclists who seem equally unaware of the 15-mile-an-hour speed limit.

Activities in the Park

The range of possible activities in the park encompasses both the purely personal – a solitary walk or with a friend or loved one – and the theatrically public. A concert in Central Park provides the ultimate recognition a band needs; no one can question a group's popularity when 750,000 spectators turn up, as they did for Paul Simon's most recent concert there. (In 1944 nearly one and a half million turned up for the "I am an American Day" celebrations). The **New York Shakespeare Festival** is such a popular event (the tickets are free) that it may seem that just as many people turn up for the events then. Tickets for the **New York Philharmonic** and **Metropolitan Opera** at the Great Lawn are in equally great demand. To find out what live entertainment is on or being planned in the near future, there is a daily update available by telephoning 794 6564.

The personal and the public activity can be combined by taking a ride in a horse-drawn carriage, the minimum cost for a half-hour ride being US$40 and US$60 for an hour. The carriage can be picked up on many of the streets bordering the park but the main starting point and terminus for rides is on Central Park South. The romantic image of a buggy ride through sylvan glades goes right to the heart of some New Yorkers and more than one proposal of marriage has been delivered within earshot of the driver.

On Central Park South and throughout the park, you can generally observe an activity that keeps the park, and most of the city for that matter, free of empty tin cans. The down-and-outs who rummage through the bins, an on-going activity when warm weather increases the consumption of soft drinks, diligently search for empties for which they will earn a nickel a piece. Each individual collector hands his quota to a larger collector who in turn passes them on until eventually they reach the entrepreneur responsible for recycling the soft tin alloy.

The chances are you would rather wish to engage on some other activity, but do not worry for there is a lot to

Mounted police on patrol.

choose from. **Walking Tours** are available during the summer, conducted by the Urban Park Rangers (tel: 427 4040) and at weekends a general walk is available through the **Conservatory Garden**. Ask to be shown the treehouse where Bob Redman was finally "captured" in 1985. The young Redman had a passion for treehouses and lived in his own constructions in the park for eight years. One had five rooms spread across five levels and when his congo drum-playing brother came to practice his music in the trees, speculation was rife as to the source of the tree music. After his capture Redman was offered a job as a tree pruner in the park and he now owns his own tree maintenance business. It is also possible to purchase a

Central Park in late spring.

US$0.50 brochure from **The Dairy** that outlines informative self-guided walks through the most interesting regions in the park. If walking is too slow for you, the prime jogging arena is the 1.58-mile track surrounding the Reservoir.

If you need rejuvenation after that jog, there are two places to eat in the Park. The **Boathouse Cafe** at Loeb Boathouse serves lunch and dinner. Ring 517 3623 to check what's available – the menu changes regularly. The **Tavern on the Green**, located at Central Park West and 67th Street, is an establishment that has been in the Park since the 1930s. New Yorkers like to use the Crystal Room for private celebratory dinners while the Terrace is open for casual cocktails, and lunch and dinner can be enjoyed for around $25. Call 873 3200 to reserve a table.

If the weather or your disposition dissuades you from too much walking then consider **The Park & City Trolley Tour** (tel: 360 2766) that takes you up-and-down and from side to side on a 90-minute excursion. The tickets can be purchased from the information kiosk at 60th Street and Fifth Avenue. For general information about the park, including free maps and calendars of special events, check out the **Visitors Center** at The Diary, located in the middle of the park on line with 64th Street. Incidentally, the way to check your location in the park is by way of the numbers marked on the lampposts. The first two sets of numbers indicate the cross streets and the second set indicates

Horse and carriage, an old-fashioned way of seeing Central Park.

whether it is the East or West Side. Biking is the best way to see the park and the only place to hire bicycles within the park is the **Loeb Boathouse** (tel: 517 3623). The safest time for cycling is at weekends when the roads are closed to cars and two-wheel traffic moves in a strictly one-way anti-clockwise direction. The Loeb Boathouse is also the location for boating in the nearby lake. All the boats are rowboats and can be rented by the hour.

Skating, on rollers in the summer and on ice in the winter, is one of the supreme pleasures to be enjoyed in the park due to the stupendous backdrop formed by the skyscrapers on Central Park South at the **Woolman Rink** (tel: 5174800). In winter ice skating is also possible at the **Lasker Rink** (tel: 9961184) which becomes a swimming pool in the summer. Horseback riding is possible along nearly five miles of bridle trails and the horses can be rented from the **Claremount Riding Academy** (tel: 724 5100) at 175 West Street. Children will enjoy the **carousel rides** (tel: 879 0244) on the Coney Island-made carousel, featuring nearly 60 hand-carved horses, that have been a feature of park life for over forty years. On the other hand, bird watching is most productive in the dense woods that occupy the Ramble, situated in the center of the park. The **Audubon Society** (tel: 691 7483) organises regular early morning ornithological trips during the spring and summer.

Clowning around with Alice in Wonderland, the March Hare and toadstools.

The **Zoo** has recently emerged from a four-year renovation exercise and remains a firm favorite for families. Although some of the animals can be seen from the surrounding walkways it is necessary to enter the zoo to enjoy the landscaped garden with the attractive sea lion pool situated at its center. There is a separate **Children's Zoo**, where toddlers can explore Noah's Ark and meet various farm animals. Unfortunately, it is badly in need of renovation.

Sights To See

Watching people at play is part of the fun of Central Park, whether it is children exhibiting their skills at the frisbee, skaters at the Woolman Rink baseball and softball players on the **Great Lawn**, or just the whole kaleidoscope of people moving through the park "doing their own thing." Street life in Manhattan is conducted at such a frenetic pace that it is totally therapeutic to just observe New Yorkers as they relax and unwind.

The Metropolitan Museum of Art is actually located in the Park and a visit to the museum can be followed by a park stroll that takes in some of the more notable sights. The Museum is located at 82nd Street and Fifth Avenue and just at the South at 79th Street, there is a road leading into the Park. After entering the Park, follow the path to the right under the stone bridge. To the right of the bridge is **Cleopatra's**

Man-made Oasis in the Concrete Jungle

The story of the park goes back to the mid 19th century when the poet William Cullen Bryant was the first to suggest that he and his fellow city dwellers might benefit from some greenery in their habitat. Luckily, Bryant owned a newspaper and he was able to vociferously campaign for his plan in the face of property dealers who argued fiercely against the inanity of the idea – potentially valuable real estate left for trees and grass and no rent to be collected? It took a number of years before they were overruled. Ironically, what helped to get the project off the ground was the perception among many property dealers that Manhattan's northern waste of swamp and rock could never really realise much profit. To be on the safe side the owners demanded the exorbitant rate of US$7,500 an acre.

A competition was organised to find the best plan and design submissions started to flood in. The winners were Frederick Law Olmsted and Calvert Vaux, a formidable couple who between them possessed the talents of landscape designing and architecture. They also had prodigious ambitions for the park and the realisation of this dream vision involved more than 3,000 workers who were employed at the same time. Swampland was cleared and drained, the land that wasn't swamp was cleared

of the shanty dwellings erected by the poor, many tens of thousands of trees were planted and endless tons of earth and rubble were shifted elsewhere. Work began in 1858 and the lake, the first attraction, was opened on 25 December of the following year. Work was finally completed in 1873 and even then the majority of New Yorkers still lived way below Central Park South, the park's southern most border, and a horse and carriage was employed to reach the park's formal Mall.

It took over 15 years for Olmstead and Vaux's plans to be completed and since then a number of features have been added while their basic vision has been preserved: a place to stroll and relax in and escape, as Olmsted put it, "the bustle and jar of the streets." To help appreciate the scale of the human and engineering achievement that the park represents, it is worth reminding oneself that almost everything seen by the contemporary visitor was created out of wasteland without the benefit of earthmovers, power drivers and power drills and that the idea of constructing roads that ran below the pedestrian level 150 years ago represents an engineering wonder.

Today no one reads the poetry of William Cullen Bryant but his immortality has been preserved in the park he helped to create.

Needle, an Egyptian obelisk presented to the city in 1881. There are only three other obelisks in the world outside Egypt. The hieroglyphics inscribed on this particular obelisk in the Park date to the reign of Thutmose III, around 1600 BC.

One of the sights worth seek-

ing out is **Belvedere Castle**, located just south of the Great Lawn and near 79th Street, now well over a 100 years old but still looking whimsically younger. It is a miniature mock castle perched on a hill which allows for excellent views over the Great Lawn and the diverse human activities unfolding there.

Nearby is the **Swedish Cottage**, a thoroughly uncosmopolitan-looking wooden chalet that serves as a venue for occasional puppet shows and other inexpensive events. Between the castle and the cottage is the **Shakespeare Garden** which is just south of the **Delacorte Theatre** where you can enjoy the bard's plays being performed. The cuttings in the garden are said to be from the same mulberry and hawthorn trees that Shakespeare himself nurtured after he retired to Stratford.

The specialised art of model-boat sailing is the main activity in the shallows of the **Conservatory Water** and a weekend morning is the best time to watch the young and the not-so-young engage in this hobby. The statue of **Hans Christian Andersen** stands at the west side of the pond and is the site for story-telling sessions on summer Saturday mornings.

At the north end of the pond are sculptures of characters from *Alice in Wonderland*, another of the many literary commemorations in the park. Near the zoo, along the tree-lined **Mall** is a series of statues of Shakespeare, Scott, Burns and Christopher Columbus and a statue dedicated to the sled dogs that carried anti-toxins across the Antarctic in 1925!

If you walk past the statue of Columbus, cross the road and follow the marked path to the right for about 20

Cleopatra's Needle.

yards, you will reach **The Dairy** building, where cows were once milked. It has been tastefully renovated to preserve its Victorian origin and now serves as the main information center.

Night Falls

At night Central Park takes on another existence, providing a place of shelter for as many as 500 people during the warmer months. If you turn up early enough in the morning you will see park attendants removing discarded cardboard "beds," implicit recognition of the simple fact that homeless people must sleep somewhere. During the Depression the United States Post Office recognised a squat in Central Park as a legitimate address and as recently as 1984 a federal court ruled that a park bench is a recognised address for voter registration! But a time when prospective mayors conduct election rallies from within the park to address its constituency is as unlikely an event as a return to the days before air-conditioning when residents left their nearby apartments to sleep out in the open during hot summer nights.

In the last couple of years there has been a noticeable lengthening in the number of hours of purposeful activity pursued within the park's perimeters. The park's northern territory is not recommended for a night time stroll but you will find joggers and walkers almost up to midnight south of the reservoir, an unheard of phenomenon five years ago.

Real Estate

What will endure is Central Park's enormous popularity. It was a gigantic success from the day it opened and in 1860 – only its second year – two and a-half million people passed through it. Other cities like Detroit, Boston and Philadelphia were sufficiently impressed to copy the concept and quickly set about creating their own imitations of New York's pastoral oasis.

But, Central Park has never been content to just complacently exist and heated arguments continue up to the present about its proper line of develop-

ment. In 1890, a racetrack was proposed and rejected and in 1919 the idea of building an airport through the park was mooted.

When the construction of a subway line in the 1980s entailed excavation works to be carried out in the park, the force of public opinion was such that the authorities had to demonstrate how

The young and old come together at the boat pond in the Conservatory's waters.

every piece of rock was being numbered so as to be accurately replaced.

In 1993, one of the city's top brokerage firms pledged US$17 million to help in the renovation of the western side of the park if the city and Central Park Conservancy matched their gift, which they did within days. The injection of capital like this, funding the renovation of the park's infrastructure, will almost certainly help keep Central Park a fun place to be – an oasis in the concrete jungle – and New York's single greatest recreational facility.

Tthe Upper West Side stretches from Central Park across to the Hudson River and from Columbus Circle in the south to Columbia University in the north. The area is not so homogenous as its counterpart on the east side of Central Park. The refined and the rich live here but, unlike the Upper East Side, they *do not* define the area's character and, the area benefits in terms of the variety – in the people, streets, and places to visit.

Cathedral of St John the Divine.

Circling Columbus

Columbus Circle, named after the statue of the celebrated Christopher Columbus, founding father of the new world, to be found here, is also the home of the **New York Conventions and Visitors Bureau** where visitors can pick up free maps and leaflets and make enquiries. The Bureau is housed in what was originally an art gallery which

THE UPPER WEST SIDE AND MORNINGSIDE HEIGHTS

Riverside Church

Claremont

Morningside Park

W 123rd St
W 122nd St
W 121st St
W 120th St

Eight Ave

Powell Boulevard

Columbia University

W 119th St
W 118th St
W 117th St
W 116th St
W 115th St

Lenox Avenue

Barnard College

Broadway

Henry Hudson Parkway

Riverside Park

MORNINGSIDE HEIGHTS

Cathedral of St John the Divine

Nordglas Avenue

W 114th St
W 113rd St
W 112nd St
W 111st St

Fifth Ave

Cathedral Parkway

Central Park North

W 109rd St
W 108rd St
W 107rd St
W 106rd St
W 105rd St
W 104rd St

Manhattan Avenue

W 103rd St
W 102nd St
W 101st St
W 100th St

West End Avenue

Columbus Avenue

Hudson River

W 99th St
W 98th St
W 97th St

W 96th St
W 95th St
W 94th St
W 93rd St
W 92nd St
W 91st St
W 90th St
W 89th St
W 88th St
W 87th St

Broadway

Central Park West

Soldiers and Sailors Monument

W 86th St
W 85th St
W 84th St
W 83rd St
W 82nd St
W 81st St
W 80th St

UPPER WEST SIDE

American Museum of Natural History & Hayden Planetarium

Fifth Ave

Zebar's

79th Street Boat Basin

W 79th St
W 78th St
W 77th St

New York Historical Society

Central Park

W 76th St
W 75th St
W 74th St
W 73rd St

Dakota Apartment

W 72nd St
W 71st St
W 70th St

Freedom Place

West End Avenue

Amsterdam Avenue

Broadway

W 69th St
W 68th St
W 67th St
W 66th St
W 65th St
W 64th St
W 63rd St
W 62nd St
W 61st St

Lincoln Center

W 60th St
W 59th St
W 58th St
W 57th St

New York Coliseum

Columbus Circle

Henry Hudson Parkway

N

The Metropolitan Opera at Lincoln Center.

was not only a commercial failure but the building's architect was pilloried for what was considered an aesthetic flop.

Lincoln Center

From Columbus Circle, a walk up Broadway brings the **Lincoln Center** into view. Any place that provides a home to the Metropolitan Opera Company, New York Philharmonic Orchestra, American Ballet Theater – not to mention the New York City Opera and Ballet and a host of other important artistic events – has got to be a major landmark even though the exterior looks unprepossessing! Eight blocks of slum dwellings were demolished in the 1960s to make room for a set of six concert halls and theaters that can accommodate 18,000 people. Before the demolition work even began, the slums had achieved fame as the location for the filming of *West Side Story*. It was visionary to set about transforming such a run-down neighborhood into a cultural nucleus at that time but the grand conception has proved a memorable success. It stimulated, if not created, a process of gentrification which cynics say has turned a ghetto for the poor into one intended for the rich.

Of Halls, Theaters, Museums and Centers

Guided tours of the Center are available daily from 10:00 am to 5:00 pm. The tour includes the three main halls which are quite different in character. The **Avery Fisher Hall** underwent a costly technical renovation in 1976 to try and improve the acoustics and the architect Philip Johnson masterminded the work. Even if you are not on a tour, it is worth reaching the foyer to gaze at the hanging sculpture created by Richard Lippold, entitled *Orpheus and Apollo*. The foyer of the **New York State Theater** is equally memorable, not just for the art work created by Lee Bontecou and Jasper Johns but also because of the pleasing colors and design of the whole place. The **Metropolitan Opera House** is the grandest of all and, again, there is no need to follow a tour to appreciate the splendor

of the chandeliered staircase and the Chagall murals at the top. Tour guides invariably tell the story of how Chagall planned to work with stained glass but the administrators feared that it would would be vulnerable to passing neighborhood hooligans. The artist produced murals instead which were placed behind glass, partly to create a glassy effect as well as a protection. For a part of the day they are covered with cloth to minimise the damaging effects of constant sunlight.

Opposite the Lincoln Center is the **Museum of American Folk Art**, a refreshing reminder of the lives of ordinary Americans from colonial times onwards. The emphasis is on objects of domestic use – kitchen gadgets, signboards, furniture and the decorative arts – and the useful little shop has an array of modern folk-designed items for sale.

Central Park West is the part of Eighth Avenue that runs alongside Central Park from Columbus Circle up to Douglas Circle near Columbia University. Even when street gangs were fighting it out where the Lincoln Center now stands, Central Park West was an exclusive residential area which has become more so now than ever before. Unlike Fifth Avenue, its counterpart located on the other side of the park, the glamour of Central Park West is understated and not given to such ostentatious displays.

Dakota Dreams

Dakota Apartments, at the corner of West 72nd Street, is a good example of how the area developed. As the 19th century was drawing to a close, the burgeoning middle class found it in-

Upper West Side apartment buildings.

creasingly difficult to find space in the city for the large brownstone houses where they traditionally resided in. The first apartment blocks built for the bourgeois had to be sufficiently classy to distinguish them from the blocks of tenement buildings that the *hoipolloi* lived in. Places like the Dakota Apartments convinced the rich that they could indeed live in apartments, and so far uptown that jokes were made to the effect that the name referred to the State of Dakota where the wild Red Indians lived.

The individual apartments have as much space as a small house and the Germanic exterior was designed to give the place a dandy European atmosphere. Over time it has acquired a rather sinister appearance. It was the location of Roman Polanski's film *Rosemary's Baby*. Famous inhabitants of the past include Lauren Bacall, Boris Karloff and Leonard Bernstein. John Lennon, who also lived here, met his untimely end at the 72nd Street entrance on 8th December, 1980.

Almost directly across the road from the Dakota is **Strawberry Fields**, a small garden space dedicated to the memory of John Lennon in Central Park. The site was instituted by Yoko Ono, Lennon's widow, who still lives in the Dakota.

A few blocks further up Central Park West, the vast **American Museum of Natural History** comes into view on the left. This, the mother of all museums, demands to be seen but anyone trying to see it all in one visit is likely to come out shell-shocked and in need of a holiday.

Being selective about what to see is not just good advice, it is essential. It is best to collect a floor plan and make some choices. The first story has the "Ocean Life and Biology of Fishes," which is far more exciting than the title might suggest. Here is the largest museum exhibit in the world - a monstrous model of a blue whale. The second floor is devoted to human societies and although the content is scholarly, the range of techniques used to enliven the displays will fascinate visitors of all ages. The "Hall of Asian Peoples" is a trip through time and cultures but to view all this and the "African Peoples" section will leave no time or energy for the

Exhibits in the Museum of Natural History.

"Hall of South American Peoples" which is the newest of the three, having only opened in 1988! The museum also houses an incredible collection of minerals and gems, stuffed mammals and a dinosaur area which is presently being renovated but with some skeletons on exhibit. Children will find exhibits to wonder at in every room while the "Discovery Room," which is only open at weekends, is superb for anyone under the age of 11.

The museum is joined to the **Hayden Planetarium** on 81st Street which can also be separately visited. It is not spectacularly different from most other planetariums, just bigger; however the laser concerts are dazzlingly good (tel: 769 5921 for details of times).

A Churchy Tale

The northern parts of the Upper West Side are decidedly unglossy and there is little worth seeking out until 112th Street. Here, at the junction of 112th Street and Amsterdam Avenue, stands the yet unfinished **Cathedral Church of Saint John the Divine**. Although work on the church began in 1892, it will probably only be completed in the second half of the 21st century. Being American, it should come as no surprise to learn that when it is finally complete it will be the largest cathedral in the state. It is situated close to Harlem and the stonework has been painstakingly carried out by workers from the local community, who are being trained by English stonemasons. When finished, the authenticity of the work should prove a more enduring legacy than simply knowing that the nave will be twice the size of an American football pitch.

How could a building take perhaps 200 years to complete? From the very beginning the pace of construction was slow, for reasons no longer fully understood. When a new architect took over in 1911 there was a complete change of style from the romanesque to the gothic. This, coupled with financial problems, helped to slow things down even more and when the United States went to war in 1942 everything completely halted. After the war, the financial problems continued and for much of the 1970s no construction occurred at all. Matters now seem to be moving on a more even keel and by the year 2000 the two towers are expected to be finished. Despite, or because of, such a sorry history, a visit to the cathedral is fascinating and the experience of seeing such a construction in progress is quite historic. A work of its kind will probably never be attempted again.

Ivy League

From the unfinished medievalism of Saint John the Divine, it is a short walk north to the thoroughly cosmopolitan **Columbia University**. This is one of the most prestigious universities in the whole country, up there with Harvard, Yale

and Princeton as one of the illustrious Ivy League seats of learning. The architectural firm of McKim, Mead and White were responsible for the design. Their best creation is the **Low Library** which boasts a broad set of white marble steps leading up to the columned portico constructed in the grand neo-classical style.

From the university campus it is easy to walk across Broadway to **Barnard College**, which opened in 1889 for women at a time when Columbia University had a policy of male enrolment. The college can be seen on the way to **Riverside Church** in Riverside Drive, at 122nd Street. This church holds the distinction of being situated in a skyscraper. Its French gothic style is a conscious imitation of Chartres Cathedral and the altar alone is worth viewing for the carving that forms its backdrop. From the 20th floor, a flight of steps lead to an observation deck which offers panoramic views of the Hudson River and New Jersey.

From the observation deck it is easy to make out **Grant's Tomb** and while it is only a quick walk away back down on the street it is debatable whether the final resting place of the Civil War hero, Ulysses S Grant, is worth seeing. In both senses of the word it is a monumental failure, unattractive to look at and surrounded by a set of mosaic benches that seem ludicrously out of context. This area north of Central Park and bordering Harlem is called **Morningside Heights**. Despite the rich nuggets of culture, that is, the university and the

Columbia University, one of America's bastions of academic excellence.

Harlem

A friendly smile in Harlem.

An impoverished landscape of mean streets, riot-ravaged buildings, illegible graffiti, hostile adults and "crack babies" born with an addiction to crack cocaine ... the media images of Harlem go back to the riots of the 1960s when the streets became a battleground and stores were engulfed in flames but, the subsequent years of municipal neglect have done little to improve the neighborhood's infrastructure or its attractiveness. White New Yorkers will tell you they never go there – their nightmare scenario is being stuck on a subway train that breaks down in Harlem – and while it is not really that bad, it is difficult not to feel apprehensive if you travel there by yourself as there are some dangerous quarters.

An equally good reason for seeing Harlem on a bus tour is that the places worth seeing are

spaced out across a large area and the tours offer good value for their comprehensive coverage. Choose between **Gray Line Tours** (tel: 397 2620) and **Harlem Spirituals** (tel: 302 2594), both reputable and experienced companies whose tours usually include a visit to a Black gospel church service.

Harlem was founded by the Dutch. In the aftermath of the Civil War the area was settled by rich white families who later moved further away to Connecticut and elsewhere. Their grand homes were rented to professional blacks, and it comes as a surprise to discover that Harlem possesses some very desirable residences in its middle-class areas, like **Sugar Hill**. In the 1920s, the neighborhood's black identity started to take shape and whites from outside the area were attracted to the nightclubs and cabarets that featured the likes of Duke Ellington, Ella Fitzgerald, Billie Holiday and Aretha Franklin who performed at the famous **Apollo Theater**, which was only open to white customers, and which was recently reopened after its restoration in 1986. The houses where Duke Ellington and Ella Fitzgerald lived are passed on the tour,

two churches, it is not a very salubrious area.

Harlem Nights

Harlem – of course, is notoriously insalubrious and tense; for many white New Yorkers it is regarded as strictly a no-go

area. There are good reasons to treat parts of Harlem with extreme caution, especially at night, but this vibrant non-white community is as much part of New York as Fifth Avenue and the Empire State Building. There are a number of interesting places to visit and it would be a pity to leave New York without ever having ventured into a neighborhood as is Sugar Hill which was christened with its name by Duke Ellington as the "only sweet place to live in Harlem."

After 1945 the area suffered from massive influxes of poor black people from the southern states and later waves of Hispanics travelling from Puerto Rico and neighboring Caribbean islands. The politicians paid no attention to the increasing social problems and emerging political players like Malcolm X became increasingly militant as they raised the consciousness of fellow backs.

The mostly demolished **Audobon Ballroom**, the scene of his assassination, has preserved the facade which will front a museum dedicated to the black leader. Alex Haley, the famed author of *Roots*, also lived in Harlem and his interviews with Malcolm X provided much of the source material for Spike Lee's recent film of the man who rejected his own surname – a legacy of the plantation owner whose slaves were named after him – and adopted an X as a surname.

Harlem's main shopping precinct, **West 125th Street**, is of interest to the visitor mainly for the pavement stalls selling the most colorful tee-shirts to be found in the city. Nearby on Lennox Avenue at 126th Street is a colorful street market where Harlem's most recent immigrants – from Senegal and the Ivory Coast – still don their West African dress. On Sundays their stalls can be found along Martin Luther King Boulevard, selling a variety of trinkets and souvenir items.

which, with sound advice and common sense, is quite feasible and safe to explore (see box).

The western side of Harlem, **Hamilton Heights**, is named after Alexander Hamilton, a leading figure in the American Revolution and one whose face is stamped on every US$10 bill. He fought on the battlefield, became George Wash-

ington's aide and later Secretary to the Treasury before dying in a duel at the hands of his bitter enemy Aaron Burr. The story goes that, after drawing their duelling pistols, Hamilton the gentleman fired his harmlessly into the air only to provide Burr with the opportunity of shooting him down in cold blood.

Beyond Hamilton Heights, in the northwest corner of Manhattan, is **Washington Heights**.. This area boasts two attractions. On Broadway at 155th Street, **Audubon Terrace** is a complex of museums belonging to the **Hispanic Society of America**, the **American Numismatic Society** and the **American Academy and Institute of Arts and Letters** (the Museum of the American Indians has moved downtown). The museums are fascinating for anyone with an interest in Spanish culture, coins and medals, or literary documents.

The other, more principal, attraction in Washington Heights is the **Morris-Jumel Mansion** at 161th Street between Amsterdam and Edgecombe Avenues. It was built in 1765 to a basic Georgian design but with a Federal overlay that is now in need of renovation. During the Civil War, George Washington was headquartered here and later it was purchased by a French couple, Stephen and Eliza Jumel. Most of the furniture in the house belongs to their residency, including a bed that reputedly belonged to Napoleon. It is an engaging place to visit and the history of Eliza Jumel adds an element of spice. Before marrying her rich merchant hus-

Washington Heights.

band, Eliza was a prostitute and later while Stephen Jumel was bleeding to death in the house, she was said to have sat in another room and waited for his passing. She had an affair with Aaron Burr, the man who shot Hamilton, and although she married the latter within a year, they later separated and Burr is said to have died on the day their divorce came through. With a story like that, it is not surprising that the house is supposed to be haunted.

Both the Morris-Jumel Mansion and the Audubon Terrace Museums can be reached by the number 1 or A trains.

Cultural Cloisters

The best reason of all for straying into the northern limits of Manhattan is to visit the **Cloisters Museum** located in **Fort Tryon Park**.

The Cloisters is actually a branch of the Metropolitan Museum of Art, spectacularly sited on a wooded hill and guaranteed to induce a sense of having travelled through time and space to medieval Europe. The founder of this eccentric enclave was George Grey Barnard who was dedicated to the idea of recreating a monastery from the Middle Ages and filling it with authentic *objects d'art*. His vision was magnificently achieved and when the whole place went up for sale in the 1920s, John D Rockefeller bought it for the Metropolitan and added some treasures of his own. An enjoyable and perfectly safe way to reach this northern extremity is

Treasures of the Cloisters

Bas relief at the Cloisters.

The Cloisters shares with the Gugggenheim the very special status of uniting its form with its content. The Cloisters is a 20th-century museum, devoted to the art of the Middle Ages. It manages to incorporate parts of five medieval cloisters into its design and structure. Just as a cloister is defined by its covered walkway surrounding a courtyard with paths leading off to other monastic buildings, so too does this museum's cloisters provide passageways to the various galleries. And just as medieval monks would engage in contemplative repose within the confines of their cloisters, the modern visitor is just as likely to want to rest and relax in the shaded walkways that make up this wonderful museum. However, unlike the views available to 15th-century monks, glimpses of the George Washington Bridge are discernible in the distance.

Everything here is a treasure but **The Campin Room** has one of the most engaging paintings ever produced in the Middle Ages. It consists of a three-paneled altarpiece painted by Robert Campin, depicting the arrival of the Archangel Gabriel's arrival to the home of the Virgin Mother. The angel is about to announce to Mary that she will give birth to Christ and every detail of the scene including the furniture, utensils and Joseph's carpentry work, is rich with religious symbolism. Some of the symbolism is obvious to the viewer but there is enough left unexplained to leave the visitor musing over the details while lost in wonder at the astounding beauty of the colors.

The **Unicorn Tapestries** are extraordinary, woven in Brussels in the early 16th century, and like Campin's painting so rich with symbolism that they leave the viewer astounded at the combination of intellectual rigor and the sheer excellence of the craftwork.

The **Treasury,** entered through a heavy glass door, is a sanctuary devoted to priceless works of medieval art. The walrus **ivory cross** is so full of iconographic significance that it takes longer to "read" than the *Daily Post* (and is far more interesting). The wooden **rosary bead box** is so intricately crafted that a magnifying glass is needed to see fine details like Saint Peter cutting off the guard's ear. It is just one part of one of the cameos that forms the Crucifixion scene making up the lower half of a box that measures only a few inches across.

In the **Langon** chapel the profound faith of the Middle Ages is manifested in the **Autun Virgin and Child**, a wooden sculpture carved from a single block of birch. It was originally painted but even in its existing state the sculpture conveys a remarkable sense of the profound holiness with which artists imbued their work.

by way of the M4 bus which will take you through Harlem and stops outside the museum.

If you travel by subway to 190th Street, be prepared for a 12-minute walk through the adjoining woods or you can catch the shuttle from the Metropolitan Museum.

M

urray Hill is a well known area of midtown Manhattan but some of its boundaries are indistinct. Fifth Avenue marks its western limit and it stretches eastwards to Third Avenue taking in, roughly, the area between 32nd Street and 42nd Street. Tourists mostly throng the area because of the number of hotels and reasonably priced restaurants, or because they are making their way across to the United Nations Headquarters by the East River. During the day Murray Hill is packed with office workers and at night it can seem tranquil but deserted, and the residents of this respectable and comfortable niche can have the place to themselves.

United Nations Building.

Midtown East Manhattan

167

Illustrious Avenue

Cutting through Murray Hill are some of New York's most illustrious avenue names: Madison, Park and Lexington. Between them, they evoke the fast world of power

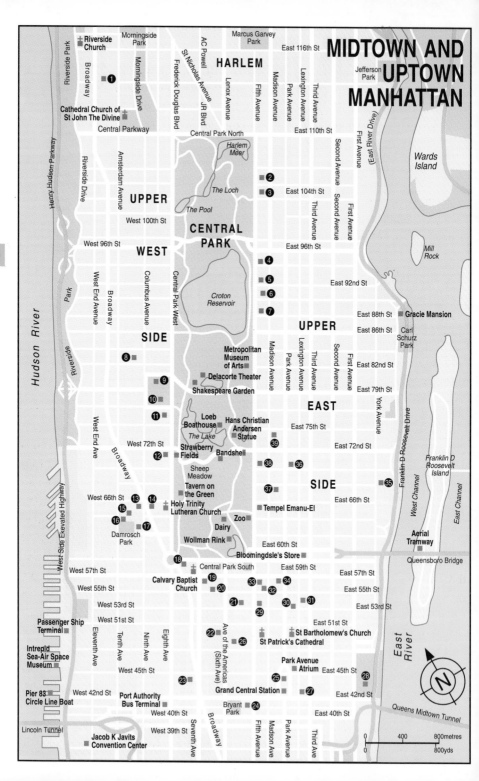

MIDTOWN AND
UPTOWN
MANHATTAN

LEGEND

dressing, executives dashing between yellow cabs and the vast, anonymous buildings that house their corporate offices. Any of the three avenues makes for an impressive company address and major companies invest a fortune in order to create a landmark building that will bear their name and broadcast their prestige. A good example of this is the **AT&T Building** at Madison Avenue and 56th Street, which is famous for its non-functional design and which now belongs to the Sony Corporation. The new owners are planning to make changes to the open ground space surrounding the AT&T and in time, the building's name may well change to that of the Japanese company. Visitors are beamed up to the fourth story in a sleek and purring elevator and given an electronic card that accesses an exhibition of the latest wonders of the microchip revolution. Very close by, the **IBM Building** boasts its own modest style and achieves high marks as one of the more pedestrian-friendly buildings in Manhattan. The glassed plaza is a pleasant place for a drink and a snack, often enjoyed to the accompaniment of live classical music. The basement of the building sometimes hosts some excellent art exhibitions.

East of the AT&T Building, where Lexington Avenue meets 55th Street is

Midtown towers along Madison.

the **Central Synagogue** which has been a meeting place for Sephardic Jews since 1872. It was designed by Henry Fernback, one of the first Jewish architects in the city and incorporates typical features of Mediterranean-style synagogues like the inverted U-shaped windows and swollen cupolas.

Still on Lexington Avenue, just two blocks down at 53rd Street, is the 900 foot-high **Citicorp Center** which makes a distinctive mark on the cityscape. The roof which slopes at an angle of 45 degrees was originally designed to garner solar energy but sadly, economics proved more compelling than environmentalism. The building is one of New York's most impressive; spectacular at night and gleamy white during the day.

Tucked away between the four massive columns that support the Citicorp Center is the minuscule **Saint Peter's Church**. The church replaces an older one that was demolished for Citicorp. Its thoroughly modern look blends in well with its context.

Behind Citicorp and its adopted church, another interesting building which is known to all New Yorkers as the **Lipstick Building** can be found, so named partly because of its shape and also because the designation collectively expresses their disdain for the inappropriateness of the design. It was unveiled in 1986 and has been labelled as the unacceptable face of post-modernism.

A short walk further down "Lex" (as Lexington Avenue is often referred to)

The rush hour as people empty the buildings.

look out for the pavement grate on the righthand side of the street between 52nd and 51st Streets. Marilyn Monroe fans still pay homage to the spot where she stood over the grating and let the breeze from the subway blow out her dress in movie *The Seven Year Itch*, a moment of cinematic history and a much-reproduced still that seems to capture the whimsical side of the actress's personality.

Park Avenue Power

Between Madison and "Lex" is Park Avenue, a powerhouse of material wealth, as represented by the array of banks, and internationally renown advertising agencies and top-notch plastic surgeons. Some of the city's most interesting architecture is be found along Park Avenue. One example is **Lever House** situated at the junction with 53rd Street, it definitely is a building well worth a closer look. The designers broke new ground in the early 1950s by making the two steel and glass sides of the building come together in a right angle, thus creating a dramatic space that is filled with light and which breaks up the monotony of the surrounding tower blocks.

Wonderful Waldorf

Between 49th and 50th Street stands the

Nightfall in Midtown.

St. Bartholomew's on Park Avenue.

Waldorf Astoria Hotel, one of the city's most illustrious and expensive hotels, which was sited here in 1931 after moving from where the Empire State building now stands. The decision to demolish and rebuild was dictated by the desire to be at the center of fashionable New York which in the 1930s meant Park Avenue.

The new hotel was determined to capture both the attention and the wallets of the super-rich and it still continues to do just this. The original hotel boasted of 2,200 rooms, now it numbers 1,692 and the best of all are in the renovated Waldorf Towers section. The Towers has its own entrance on 50th Street reserved for pop stars, presidents and ex-presidents who like to stay here.

Like many of the buildings on Park Avenue, the Waldorf Astoria is built above the railway tracks of the nearby Grand Central and the hotel stores its wine on the 5th storey so as to escape the train vibrations. The main lobby is a wonderful place to sit down, whilst people-watching and feasting your eyes on the splendid art deco style that has been lavishly revamped.

The Waldorf Astoria takes up an entire block but just behind it, between 50th and 51st Street is **Saint Bartholomew's Church**, tucked away on a far smaller space. The salmon-pink splendor of the exterior lures the visitor within, to a Byzantine world of mosaics that turns into a home for the destitute poor of the city at night. The church stands on prime real estate and various attempts to buy

Grand Central station.

all or part of the church have been made over the years. All the attempts were finally scuppered by a Supreme Court decision that ensures the church's future. Walking south from the Waldorf Astoria, still on Park Avenue, it is difficult to miss the **Helmsley Building**, formerly known as the New York Central Building.

Cars drive through its arches and pedestrians should check out the baroque lobby and ponder the rise and fall of Leona Helmsley, wife of the billionaire Harry Helmsley. The building that bears their name was constructed as office space for the managers of New York Central's Railway and for years it dominated Park Avenue's vista, until Pan Am, an airline company, built their own office building and stole Park Avenue's limelight.

Towering Towers

Among the many towering blocks of Manhattan, the one that has been consistently singled out for criticism for the 30 years of its existence is the **Met Life Building** (formerly the Pan Am Building) at Park Avenue and 45th Street looking south down to lower Manhattan.

The reason is resoundingly clear the building does not just steal space, it robs Fifth Avenue of any view. Bauhaus guru Walter Gropius contributed to its design which goes to show that great architects can make mistakes.

In 1977, the building was also the scene of a horrific accident when a helicopter landed on its rooftop heliport and lost its undercarriage, causing one of the rotor blades to sheer off. Parts of the helicopter were blown as far as Madison Avenue and five people were killed.

Grand Central

From the lobby of the Met Life Building it is possible to take an escalator to **Grand Central Terminal** but walking from Park Avenue allows for a more dra-

matic entrance. Heading south, take a right turn onto 46th Street and then turn left onto Vanderbilt Avenue. Just opposite 43rd Street is an entrance to a bar that makes the ideal viewing platform for the unfolding human drama which occurs down below on the main concourse of the station.

The concourse is a magnificent sight to behold, an absolutely huge cavern that reaches up to a painted vaulted ceiling that displays thousands of stars in a night sky. Train passengers are now mostly city commuters but the station has an intoxicating atmosphere that

evokes the drama of travel. It is not difficult to imagine the awed excitement that Americans must have experienced when they first travelled to New York and stepped off a train that had looped its way here.

Grand Central is a terrific place to explore via the ramps, escalators and glass catwalks that honeycomb their way up, down and across the station. Do not forget to travel down to the levels below the main concourse where shops and restaurants abound. Here is found the infamous **Oyster Bar**, renowned for the quality of its seafood and its alarming acoustics that make it the nosiest eating place in town.

Ford Philanthropy

From Grand Central a walk eastward along 42nd Street brings the **Ford Foundation** building into view. Atriums have now become a standard feature of New York architecture and are often just a token concession to the needs of pedestrians, but the Ford Foundation deserves full credit for this genuinely relaxing oasis. Considering that this was the first atrium to appear, there seems no good reason to excuse the rush of inferior and

The Ford Foundation atrium at Midtown.

unfriendly imitations.

The Ford atrium is a jungle greenhouse with a startling variety of real plants and trees. Above it all is housed the headquarters of the largest international philanthropic organisation in the world, founded by Henry and Edsel Ford.

United Nations

A block to the east is home to another international organisation, the **United Nations Headquarters**, built on land donated by John D Rockefeller Jr. The 175 member countries display their flags along United Nations Plaza. After one crosses the plaza and steps into the building, one officially leave United

42nd Street

A single visit to 42nd Street rarely reveals its many-faceted appeal; schizophrenically divided between its western and eastern halves, both of which change their character during the course of any 24-hour period.

During the day, West 42nd Street presents a depressing vista of closed club fronts, dirty pavements and the occasional grimy souvenir or soft pornography shop that seem designed to deter anyone from entering. In the early evening some of the clubs begin to open and the number of pedestrians increases but there is still little of interest. It is only when night falls and envelops the street in darkness that the street comes alive with people. The neon signs come into their own and every second shop is transformed into a glittering setting of pornographic cinema, striptease joints and peepshow galleries. Nowadays there is a noticeable police presence and it is quite safe to wander up and down before midnight; indeed, many of the people you will see are fellow tourists drawn to the street for the same reasons as you are: a curious mix of sightseeing, awe and voyeurism.

Leaving the sleaze behind and walking eastwards along 42nd Street brings one to a number of interesting intersections. At the corner with Madison Avenue the time of day and temperature can be checked by looking up Madison to the digital readout located at the top of the thin column of the Newsweek Building. Further along, at the corner with Sixth Avenue, is another digital readout recording the country's

States territory. Just to prove it, there is a UN Post Office inside which provides its own stamps for mail posted from within. The Headquarters are made up of three buildings: the 39-storey Secretariat Building which houses the permanent bureaucratic staff, the low-lying Conference Building and the grand General Assembly structure where those much-televised meetings take place. Perhaps

42nd and 9th Avenue, plastered with billboards.

national debt, with the numerals constantly changing. A terrific view can be enjoyed by standing on the corner outside the pizza joint and looking back at the cluster of old buildings over Bryant Park. The elderly, dark buildings are both evocative and photogenic, reminiscent of movie images of New York in the 1940s.

At the junction with Park Avenue, between 5:00-6:00 pm, 42nd Street bears witness to a phenomenal vanishing trick as thousands of office workers advance upon the imposing Grand Central Station and disappear from sight into the maze of underground pathways. Outside the station, shoeshine merchants are busy on the pavement cleaning, polishing or calmly waiting for the next customer. If it is spring or summer and unexpectedly rains, men appear from nowhere brandishing foldup umbrellas for US$4.

East 42nd Street would be a uninspiring testimony to corporate America – governed as it is by monolithic office blocks – were it not for the aerial beauty of the Chrysler Building situated at the corner with Lexington Avenue. Gaze up at it from the other side of 42nd Street and it is so easy to believe that the whole structure might just take off and fly away!

After the sun has gone down this section of East 42nd Street – taking in the imposing edifice of Grand Central Station, the Chrysler Building, and the nearby Grand Hyatt hotel – achieves a rich grandeur and magnificence. It is astonishing to walk half a mile to the west and encounter the gaudy vulgarity of West 42nd Street. Then again, this is New York in a nutshell; the beautiful rubs shoulders with the profane.

Le Corbusier should have been awarded the whole commission as, although he was initially consulted, the final design of the whole complex was created by an international group of architects and the overall effect is not as impressive as most visitors expect it to be.

The only way to look around the buildings is by taking one of the hourlong tours that depart every 20 minutes from the General Assembly Building. The highlight of the tour, after seeing the assembly halls, is the display of art donated by member nations. Exhibits include a Barbara Hepworth sculpture, an imposing ivory landscape from China and a host of pieces from around the world. The tour ends in the basement where a shop which sells ethnic items and UN postcards can be found.

Fifth Avenue divides midtown Manhattan in more than one way. The eastern half is the upmarket New York of the 1990s, all ready and willing to embrace the 21st century, a place which creates the feeling of sensation and awe because of the people, the individual and corporate wealth and the mesmerising architecture. The scenery west of Fifth Avenue is different, presenting more of a throwback to past decades rather than open embrace of the ones to come. Famous locations like Times Square and Broadway, which despite the new hotels and the crowds that still pour in and out of the theaters, are taking on a more nostalgic tone. In time to come there may be nothing left except nostalgia but, at the moment there is still plenty of glamour and Broadway still packs a punch.

The theatre district has a life of its own in the evenings.

Midtown West

179

Lights of Broadway

Broadway is both a geographical marker and a cultural signifier. The two overlap where Broadway, the city's longest avenue that stretches diagonally across the whole of Manhattan, meets Seventh Avenue.

Here in **Times Square**, and in the immediate surrounding streets, some 50 theaters once stood in close proximity. Nowadays, Broadway the theater district can be found between Sixth and Eighth Avenues, bounded on the south by 42nd and 55th Streets to the north. Times Square has earned the nickname of "The Great White Way," because of the sense of awe that first greeted the dazzling white neon lighting that lit up the square.

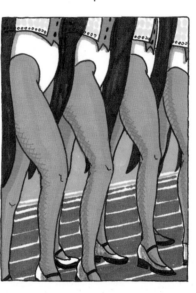

Broadway's first electric advertisement appeared in 1891, with a slogan that read "Buy Homes on Long Island Swept By Ocean Breezes," but it was in the 1920s that the neon craze really took off and made this part of the city buzz with brightness.

The statue in Times Square is that of **George M Cohan**, the Irish impresario who sang, danced and acted his way through Broadway with a legendary panache. "The Broadway Man," he boasted, "has a better idea of life and things in general than any other class of man in the world. He sees more, meets more and absorbs more in a day than the average individual will in a month."

Early this century, when Broadway was rapidly acquiring its theatrical reputation, the staple fare was dancing girls clad in knee-length bathing suits. In the years before World War I, Dublin's Abbey Theatre and the Parisian Vieux-Columbier both made seminal visits to US shores. In the years to come, serious American playwrights turned to New York for a more critical audience. At the same time, the Broadway musical was making its unique contribution to world drama and theaters could not get built quick enough to meet the demand. In the year before the Wall Street Crash of 1929, some 280 Broadway productions were mounted, an incredible phenomenon! Nowadays, while Broadway is still leading the world in terms of the sheer quantity of its productions, about 70 new shows appear each year.

Most of the old theaters that created Broadway's unrivalled reputation have now been pulled down. One of the few remaining and one of the best, is the

Radio City Music Hall, home of the Rockettes.

Paramount Theater Building at 1501 Broadway, between 43rd and 44th Streets. The building is unmistakable with its clock and globed top and when it opened in 1927 it was hailed as the ultimate in glossy sophistication. Many of America's most popular singers, Frank Sinatra for instance, only became big stars after successfully performing at the Paramount.

Another classic theater is the **Lyceum** at 45th Street, which successfully preserved its original and very ornate facade. An apartment on the second storey had a window surreptitiously built into the wall so that the theater-addicted tenant could view the stage show whenever he wished. The **Schubert Theater** at 225 West 44th Street has also retained its original facade, behind which Barbara Streisand first appeared and where *A Chorus Line* kept running for 15 years!

Radio City Music Hall

The Avenue of the Americas is where 50th Street meets Sixth Avenue. This is where **Radio City Music Hall** stands as another shrine built to the world of entertainment. It is big in a number of ways, it boasts: the world's largest chandelier (weighing two tons), the world's biggest contour curtain (weighing three tons) and the biggest indoor theater for rock music in the world. The really enduring appeal of Radio City rests with its classic art deco interior, a key factor which helped to save the building from its proposed demolition in 1970. It is now a protected building and will not suffer the same fate as Penn Station. Unless you have a ticket to a show, the best way to explore and appreciate the place is to take one of the hour-long guided tours that run on most days. A real highlight which is not to be missed is the stage in the shape of an enormous scallop shell!

Radio City was built in 1932 and went spectacularly over the top in luxury and extravagance. No expense was spared in the decoration of the theater which also featured 1930s state-of-the-art technology whilst incorporating the flair and imagination of its designers. The audience on opening night was so unused to the scale of Radio City that spectators in the rear actually thought that the horses on-stage were trained mice! The opening show also displayed the talents of a 36-member team of female dancers known as the Rockettes, a dance-troupe of the same name is still touring the country. They have earned an enormous following all over America and Radio City is their home base. Their synchronised dance routines are based on long hours of practice and you might be fortunate enough to see them rehearsing on-stage on your tour of the building. A character in J D Salinger's novel, *The Catcher in the Rye*, is always praising them: "You know what that is? That's precision".

The area worth seeing to the west of Radio City are the West 50 streets which run between Sixth and Eighth Avenues. Ninth Avenue has many restaurants and delis but the area further west is not recommended for sightseeing. The few gentrified spots do little to alleviate the general shabbiness and the streets are mean places during the day and particularly menacing at night.

However, back in the West 50s, you are safely in tourist territory and one of the places worth seeing is the **Equitable Center** located on Seventh Avenue between 51st and 52nd Streets. The building itself is nothing to rave about, but

The renown Carnegie Hall, founded by Andrew Carnegie, where operas and concerts are always a sell-out.

Whizzing trolley traffic in the Garment district.

step into the lobby and a giant mural by Roy Lichtenstein is impossible to miss. The title of the piece four storeys high, is *Mural with Blue Brush Stroke.* The Center is also home to two excellent restaurants: Le Bernardin, one of the very best places for fish dishes and the far less expensive Sam's which serves superb American dishes. Either place is ideal for dining before or after a visit to a Broadway show.

Carousing at Carnegie

Also in the vicinity, at 154 West 57th Street, is the world famous **Carnegie Hall**. Operas and concerts are always a sell-out here, not just because of the renowned acoustics. The music of the all-time greats have been heard here, starting with Tchaikovsky on the opening night and followed by the likes of Mahler, Rachmaninov, Toscanini and Leonard Bernstein.

And, with the addition of icons of popular music like Frank Sinatra, Judy Garland and the Beatles having performed here, it is not surprising that performers are as anxious as the public to get in! Perhaps that is why there is no resident orchestra; the Vienna Philharmonic and all the top American orchestras are queuing up to appear. Even if a ticket for a show is not available it is still possible to view the renovated interior by joining one of the twice-weekly tours.

"Slightly to the left of Carnegie Hall"

The General Post Office. Note the poetic resolve on its columns.

is how **The Russian Tea Room**, at 150 West 57th Street, advertises its location. It also shares the distinction of being one of those places worth viewing even if you are not a fully paid-up customer. Prices are impossibly high which probably explains why some of the biggest names in entertainment are attracted to the place and celebrity spotting is the name of the game here. If you are strolling by at lunchtime or in the evening, a glimpse of Woody Allen or Lisa Minnelli is not unknown.

The area south of 42nd Street as far as Madison Square Garden and bounded by Sixth and Eighth Avenues, is justifiably known as the **Garment District**. The manufacturing of clothes is New York's largest single industry, supplying America with 80 percent of its women's and children's clothing. Most of the manufacturing goes on within these blocks.

There are no flashy retail outlets but in shops around West 38th Street, clothes can be purchased at wholesale prices. Apart from the garbage skips heaped with remnants cloth, and the racks of garments trundling along the pavements, you would hardly be aware of the work going on inside the buildings.

A building worth seeking out in the Garment District is the **General Post Office**, a good example of the architectural insight of the firm McKim, Mead and White. The apocryphal story is that the size of the building was adjusted to

Times Square

When the *New York Times* decided to set up office here in 1904 they could never have guessed that they were bequeathing a name to one of the city's most famous squares, a perennial name that would still be around as the century draws to its close although this newspaper office has shifted to a new address. **Times Building**, the slim volume of concrete in the southern side of the square, was the place where the newspaper built up its enduring reputation as one of the country's more sane and independent broadsheets. The newspaper's boast was "All the news that's fit to print" and the building's association with news is preserved in the digitized display of world events that encircles Times Building. On 31st December every year the building becomes the focus of the city's New Year celebrations when a giant illuminated apple makes its way down from the top, watched by a crowd of 100,000 revellers.

Times Square is one of those New York landmarks that has to be seen and experienced. It is the best to pay a visit at night, as during the day it is just a particularly busy and noisy interchange. At night it is even busier and noisier but there is also a terrific atmosphere that makes you feel that you really are in the city of New York. Stay on the pavements because it is mayhem on the half dozen streets that come together in a frenzy of cars, coaches, motorcycles and horse-drawn sedans. On the central island of the square, the very talented buskers often perform for the crowds flooding out of the theaters nearby. And all around you the billboards are alight with neon and electricity, advertising brand names that can be seen all over the world but which somehow look sharper and more original here. Some of those classic neon pictorials such as the giant face of the smoker out of whose mouth poured steam in the form of oversized smoke rings and the woman blowing her nose on a certain brand of paper hankies – are now relegated to a nostalgic past.

Traditionally, Times Square was the ultimate den of iniquity, a place where tourists were supposed to feel lucky if only their wallet was pickpocketed. The reality is a lot more reassuring. The area has been the focus of police action and civic improvement programs for some time and the sleazy image is well out of date. It still is not advisable to wander the sidestreets in the early hours of the morning but, that's also true for many other parts of the city as well as for many non-American cities. Reliable evidence of the new-look Times Square can be gleaned from the fact that more than one prestigious hotel chain has chosen a site here. Hotel chains like the Ramada Renaissance and the Holiday Inn Crowne Plaza are happy to be associated with the "Great White Way."

accommodate the poetic resolve inscribed along the top of the columns: "Neither snow nor rain nor heat nor gloom of night stays these couriers from the swift completion of their appointed rounds."

Sports and Shopping

Next to the post office and slightly underground is **Pennsylvania Station**. Unfortunately, there is nothing special about the new station, the original Penn Station has been posthumously hailed as the architectural masterpiece of McKim, Mead and White, but it was pulled down in 1968 to make way for **Madison Square Garden**.

The name is a misnomer in two ways, firstly because Madison Square is over to the east where Madison Square Park can be found and secondly because there is precious little greenery

Store window at Macy's, the world's largest department store.

Both claims are probably true. Macy's is gigantic, filling an entire city block and seeming to sell everything and its image has been going steadily upmarket over the years. When the store was founded, in the mid-19th century, Macy's slogan was "It's smart to be thrifty." Nowadays it is worth leaving your plastic cards at home because this is the sort of place where your budget can be swamped by a surge of impulse buying.

The food emporium located down in the basement is not to be missed and if you want to eat on the premises, there are more than half a dozen places which serve light as well as full meals.

around this sports and entertainment complex.

In fact, the present building is the fourth Madison Square Garden and is home to the famous *Knicks* basketball team and the *Rangers* ice hockey team. Some 20,000 seats in "the Coliseum," as New Yorkers call it, fill with sport fans when a convention, a wrestling extravaganza or a world title fight is being staged.

Madison Square Garden proudly considers itself the world's most famous sports complex; nearby at 131 West 34th Street West, **Macy's** is equally proud of its claim to be the world's largest department store.

Ice hockey in progress at Madison Square Garden.

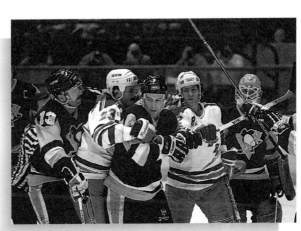

Union Square, where the subway trains can be clearly heard rattling below the streets, has enjoyed a chequered past but holds a more promising future. Originally a smart part of town known for its theaters and shops, it rose to prominence in the 1920s and 1930s as the focus for political unrest in the city. In 1927, the execution of two labor anarchists in 1927 brought together a tremendous crowd of protesters in the square and up until America's entry into World War II, a variety of socialist and syndicate organisations housed their headquarters in the vicinity of Union Square. After the war, the square degenerated and travel guides of a decade ago advised visitors to give the area a wide berth. Since then, there has been a successful effort to clean out the drug pushers and pimps and nowadays there is no need to worry about walking around the large square or sitting on a bench and watching the squirrels in

Inside a Union Square cafe.

Downtown

189

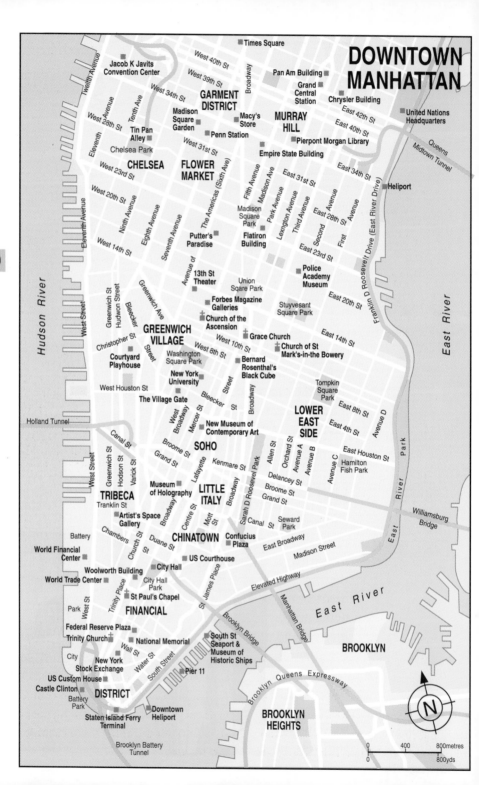

DOWNTOWN MANHATTAN

Times Square

Jacob K Javits Convention Center

West 40th St

West 39th St

GARMENT DISTRICT

Pan Am Building

Grand Central Station

Chrysler Building

West 34th St

West 28th St

Tin Pan Alley

Madison Square Garden

Macy's Store

MURRAY HILL

United Nations Headquarters

East 42nd St

East 40th St

Penn Station

Chelsea Park

West 31st St

Pierpont Morgan Library

CHELSEA

FLOWER MARKET

Empire State Building

East 34th St

West 23rd St

Heliport

West 20th St

East 31st St

Madison Square Park

East 28th St

West 14th St

Putter's Paradise

Flatiron Building

East 23rd St

Avenue of

13th St Theater

Union Sqare Park

Police Academy Museum

East 20th St

Forbes Magazine Galleries

Stuyvesant Square Park

Church of the Ascension

GREENWICH VILLAGE

Grace Church

East 14th St

West 10th St

Church of St Mark's-in-the-Bowery

Courtyard Playhouse

Washington Square Park

Bernard Rosenthal's Black Cube

New York University

Tompkin Square Park

The Village Gate

East 8th St

New Museum of Contemporary Art

LOWER EAST SIDE

East 4th St

SOHO

East Houston St

Museum of Holography

LITTLE ITALY

Hamilton Fish Park

TRIBECA

Franklin St

Artist's Space Gallery

CHINATOWN

Confucius Plaza

Seward Park

World Financial Center

US Courthouse

East Broadway

Woolworth Building

City Hall

Madison Street

World Trade Center

City Hall Park

Elevated Highway

St Paul's Chapel

FINANCIAL

East River

Federal Reserve Plaza

BROOKLYN

Trinity Church

National Memorial

South St Seaport & Museum of Historic Ships

New York Stock Exchange

US Custom House

Pier 11

Castle Clinton

DISTRICT

Brooklyn Queens Expressway

Staten Island Ferry Terminal

Downtown Heliport

BROOKLYN HEIGHTS

Brooklyn Battery Tunnel

Hudson River

Holland Tunnel

West Street

Twelfth Avenue

Tenth Ave

Eleventh Avenue

Ninth Avenue

Eighth Avenue

Seventh Avenue

The Americas (Sixth Ave)

Fifth Avenue

Madison Ave

Park Avenue

Lexington Avenue

Third Avenue

Second Avenue

First Avenue

Franklin D Roosevelt Drive (East River Drive)

Queens Midtown Tunnel

East River

Avenue A

Avenue B

Avenue C

Avenue D

River Park

Williamsburg Bridge

Greenwich St

Hudson Street

Christopher St

Bleecker

Greenwich Ave

West 8th St

Mercer St

Street

Bleecker St

Broadway

West Broadway

Broome St

Grand St

Lafayette

Kenmare St

Allen St

Orchard St

Delancey St

Broome St

Grand St

Canal St

Greenwich St

Hodson St

Varick St

Centre St

Mott St

Sarah D Roosevel Park

Canal St

East Broadway

Chambers

Church St

Duane St

James Place

Brooklyn Bridge

Manhattan Bridge

Battery

Park St

West St

Trinity Place

Wall St

Water St

South Street

City

New York

Battery Park

0   400   800metres

0   800yds

N

Farmer's Market at Halloween.

the cherry blossom trees.

At weekends it is especially attractive due to the **Farmers Market** that floods the square with fresh food and flowers. At the corner of East 16th Street there is a pleasant pavement coffee shop where meals and drinks can be downed whilst watching the scenery unfold around you. Just down East 16th Street the **Union Square Café** serves excellent food at reasonable prices and a couple of doors along is a large left-wing bookshop, a reminder of the square's proletarian past.

Warholian Art

It was on the 6th floor of Union Square West that **Andy Warhol's Factory** operated during the late 1960s and early 1970s. Warhol's paintings of multiple sets of objects like soup tins and celebrities like Marilyn Monroe catapulted him into the higher ranks of the Pop Art movement. He spearheaded a movement that championed the art of the ordinary. He later went on to create films.

Union Square was an exciting place to be when Warhol's manifesto proclaimed that everyone could be "world famous for fifteen minutes." It was here that Lou Reed came as an impressionable young musician and met the characters that make up the litany of his song "Take a Walk on the Wild Side.

Chic Chelsea

One of Warhol's better known films is *Chelsea Girls* which was filmed in the area to the west of Union Square known as **Chelsea**. Back in 1830, a writer named Clement Clark Moore inherited the land and laid it out in blocks for sale. Some of the original brownstone houses remain but over the years there have been successive waves of rebuilding, mostly for residential purposes, and today the neighborhood tends to lack a distinctive sense of identity. However, very recently, there has been an injection of energy in

Hotel Chelsea.

the form of art houses, off-off Broadway shows and a smattering of pubs and restaurants which have livened up the area.

One notable place to visit is the **Chelsea Hotel** at 222 West 23rd Street, between Seventh and Eighth Avenues, which dates back to the late 19th century when it was constructed for luxury apartments. Chelsea could never attract the middle classes and in 1905, when the neighborhood was respectably working class, the building became a hotel and began attracting artists.

Famous guests include Mark Twain, Sarah Bernhardt, Thomas Wolfe, Jack Kerouac, Bob Dylan and, more recently, Sid Vicious of *The Sex Pistols* who stabbed his lover Nancy Spungen to death whilst

Inside Roosevelt's home.

staying there. The hotel seems to live off its image, as the lobby, stuffed with 1960s memorabilia, makes obvious.

East Of Union Square

The east side of Union Square offers more of interest and just up Broadway and along to the right on East 20th Street is **Theodore Roosevelt's Birthplace**, a reconstruction of the house in which the President, whose term of office lasted from 1901-1909, was born in 1858. This was no mud cabin as the plush Victorian interior makes clear. The numerous big-game trophies on show attest to the macho image that Theodore, a sickly child, was brought up

on by his parents. When the more sensitive side of his nature revealed itself (when he declined to kill a helpless bear), the "teddy bear" was born, the very first of which is on show in his house.

Historical Haven

Carry on along East 20th Street and after crossing Third Avenue, **Gramercy Park** comes into view on the left. Gramercy Park is also the name of the few surviving blocks of elegant houses that have successfully held out against corporate blandishments.

The area has now been designated a **Historic District** so it is unlikely that skyscrapers will ever replace them. Rail-

Bohemia and the Beat Generation

Sociologists trace the roots of New York's Bohemia back to the puritan days of pre-1960s America when young people yearned to escape the strictures of the older generation. They came to Downtown Manhattan, found apartments in the streets around Union and Washington Squares – highly unfashionable in the mid-1950s – and found a voice to speak for them. The voice was Lenny Bruce, a very offbeat comedian who would come on stage and stand still for five minutes cringing with fear and crying, "Don't shoot." It was the Age of Paranoia, the McCarthy era when artists who did not proclaim their love of the American way of life would be branded communists and could wave goodbye to promising careers. Lenny Bruce himself found it increasingly difficult to find a club owner willing to risk his license by hiring a known dissident. Fortunately, club owners could sense a new mood among the young – Elvis Presley was on his way to stardom — and parts of New York were acquiring a reputation as hangouts for the Beat Generation.

By the 1960s Bohemia was no longer just a state of mind; it was acquiring a geographical fix that centered around Greenwich Village. Before the beatniks and the bohemians moved in, the area was an all-Italian one, insulated from the middle-class world of Uptown Manhattan which began at 14th Street. One of the first literary-underground cafés was the **Remo**, at the corner of Bleecker and MacDougal Streets, and like all the bars in the area it was originally very Italian and very macho. In its ironic transformation from a very macho area to one renowned for its "gay" ambience, the streets witnessed more than one conflict between hotblooded Italian hoods and young gays.

Bohemia's ability to attract artistic talent is well recorded. It was where a young writer by the name of Norman Mailer came to listen to Lenny Bruce; it was where Jack Kerouac's *On the Road* found its first audiences and some years later it was where an unknown band called the *Velvet Underground* started to appear.

The band's talent came from the music of John Cale, the lyrics and soul of Lou Reed and the beautiful voice of the young Nico (who at the age of 15 won a small part in Fellini's *La Dolce Vita*). They were about to be thrown out from a club where they were performing when they were noticed by the platinum-haired Andy Warhol who hired them immediately and nurtured them into the greatest rock musicians that New York has ever produced.

Village Voice

Bohemia and the *Village Voice* were once spoken of in the same breath. Writers like Mailer and Kenneth Tynan were associated with its early days when it was printed in Washington Square and where crowds queued to buy the first copies. It was not the polemical and highly political articles that caused the queues to form; simply the desire to read the advertisements for vacant apartments and reach a telephone before anyone else did. This still happens, although now the paper is printed at the New Jersey plant. The paper remains invaluable for anyone searching for accommodation and continues to be read more for its listings and advertisements than what are now mildly radical articles. Without the *Voice*, it has been noted, only the projectionist would turn up for a screening of avant garde films in a renovated fire station somewhere at the back of Union Square.

ings surround the square and only the private residents possess keys to the gates. So the nearest you can get to seeing the statue of Edwin Booth in the square is by peering through the railings.

Edwin Booth was a 19th-century actor, whose brother John Wilkes assassinated Abraham Lincoln. Edwin Booth did, however, establish the **Player's Club** in his house at #15, on the south side of the park. Next door (which is now the **National Arts Club**) is where Samuel

Police Academy Museum.

Tilden lived and had a steel block fitted over his front door.

Tilden went on to become Governor of the city after smashing the corrupt regime that was running New York. He never took his security for granted and he had a tunnel dug from under his house to 19th Street so that he could make his getaway in the event of an assassination attempt or a rioting mob attacking his home.

Police Story

Still on East 20th Street, across Third Avenue and near the Second Avenue corner, is the city's police academy where the **Police Academy Museum** can be found on the second storey. The emphasis is on the lawlessness of New York's past and exhibits include one of Al Capone's machine guns, a set of lethal knives hidden in a book, a fruit machine of the type that gangsters distributed and controlled, counterfeit notes and various types of handcuffs.

There is little that evokes contemporary crime in the museum itself but this is a real police academy and a police-station-like atmosphere pervades the place. Uniformed officers chat with plain clothes detectives and children will enjoy the scene.

There is no entry charge and, although they prefer visitors to ring beforehand (tel: 477 9753), it is unlikely that you will be turned away. Be sure to

Literary pursuits abound Downtown.

collect your identity sticker from the officer seated at the high desk.

down Third Avenue to the junction with 14th Street.

14th Street Vicinity

There is little point in walking further east to **Peter Cooper Village** and **Stuyvesant Town** because they are just private housing estates. It should prove more interesting excursion if you take a walk

Do not go left for it is sleazy-looking and uninviting, instead turn to the right and pass the **Palladium** theater, easily identified by the large mural overhead.

This was once one of New York's prime movie houses which

Browsing in a bookstore.

was converted into a modern club about a decade ago.

At the junction of East 14th Street and Fifth Avenue it is worth pausing to take in the views, the twin towers of the World Trade Center at one end and the Statue of Liberty at the other.

West 14th Street is exuberant in its dedication to bargain shopping and it is difficult not to be tempted into buying something. Street stalls sell cheap tee-shirts, souvenirs, bags and a hundred other consumables.

There are also many shops selling cameras and electronic items but avoid the man on the pavement with playing cards especially when he makes his apparently easy challenge to spot one card out of three.

Most, if not all, of the eager customers are working with him and no one can walk away the winner. West 14th Street is a good place to have your fortune told, from a crystal or tarot cards, or you can have a nail manicure for a reasonable price.

Within walking distance are two of the city's biggest discounted bookshops. **Barnes & Noble** is on both corners of Fifth Avenue and 18th Street and has a well organised collection on all subjects. They also have a wide selection of street maps and guides. Serious browsers collect a supermarket basket as they enter.

Even larger is the **Strand Bookstore** located at 8282 Broadway and 12th Street, definitely one of the biggest secondhand bookshops in the world.

U ntil the 1820s most New Yorkers paid scant attention to the swampy wasteland that lay to the northwest. In fact it was such a remote and rural backwater that the authorities chose what is now Washington Square as the site for executing criminals. However, in 1822 an epidemic of yellow fever broke out in the increasingly crowded community of Lower Manhattan after which the area started to improve. Those who could afford to, began to buy and build homes in Greenwich Village as a way of escaping the metropolis. For a while it was an upper class suburb, and real estate started to look elegant, hence many of the fine old houses here today create the charm and appeal of the "Village". By the end of the 19th century the suburb was another packed neighborhood and the rich moved further north to Fifth Avenue. The area now started to get interesting, as intellectuals and artists moved into the big houses that no longer

Stained glass in the Church of Ascension.

commanded high rents and the legend of Greenwich Village slowly began to take shape.

Celebrity Residents

Many famous names are associated with life in the Village. Henry James, Edgar Allan Poe and Edward Hopper all chose to live and work in the area. In the years before World War II, the Village attracted political and social radicals, like the anarchist Emma Goldman and the locale became the United State's equivalent of the Left Bank in Paris. The radicals gradually dispersed and the fashionable moved in, happy to be associated with the Village's *risqué* reputation. By the 1960s Greenwich Village had become run-down and plans were made to demolish and rebuild, but a hearty defense organised on its behalf by its residents turned the area into a national historic district.

Washington Square

Washington Square lies at the heart of the village and is *the* place to be. In an area where the streets abandon the usual topographical logic and seem to just head off in any old direction, the Square is the best place to begin and end your walk. And walking is the only way to see Greenwich Village. It is a safe area, even at night, but be sure to be armed with a street map or you will run the risk of

getting lost in the higgedly-piggedly twists and turns of the streets.

Of Arches & Churches

A good time to see Washington Square is during the weekends when tables and stalls are set up to sell bric-a-brac which

Washington Square Park, Greenwich Village.

brings together an attractive crowd of the young and old: New Yorkers, out-of-towners and foreign tourists. The square itself is not wonderful in any architectural sense and, like Greenwich Village when taken as a whole, it is the past history and the present atmosphere that makes it special. The most imposing physical feature is the **Triumphal Arch**, built in 1892 to commemorate the inauguration of George Washington as President a century earlier.

Inside the locked doors of the arch, designed by Stanford White, there

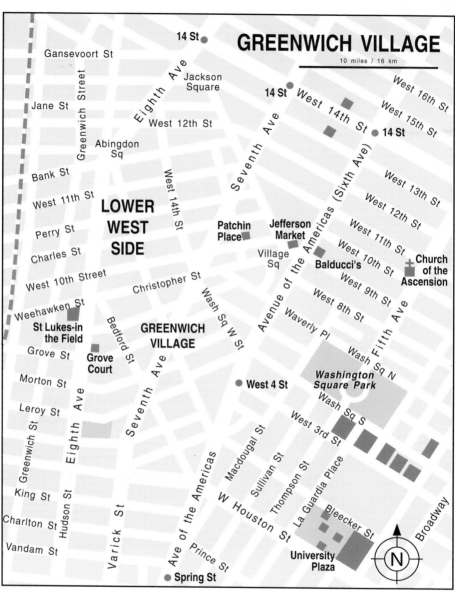

GREENWICH VILLAGE

10 miles / 16 km

14 St

Gansevoort St

Jackson Square

Jane St

West 12th St

14 St

14 St

West 16th St

West 15th St

14 St

Abingdon Sq

West 13th St

Bank St

West 12th St

LOWER WEST SIDE

West 11th St

West 14th St

Patchin Place

Jefferson Market

West 11th St

Perry St

Village Sq

Balducci's

West 10th St

Church of the Ascension

Charles St

West 9th St

West 10th Street

Christopher St

West 8th St

Weehawken St

Wash Sq W St

Waverly Pl

Wash Sq N

St Lukes-in the Field

GREENWICH VILLAGE

Grove St

Grove Court

Bedford St

West 4 St

Washington Square Park

Morton St

Eighth Ave

Seventh Ave

Wash Sq S

Leroy St

West 3rd St

Greenwich St

Macdougal St

Sullivan St

Thompson St

La Guardia Place

Bleecker St

Broadway

King St

Hudson St

Varick St

Ave of the Americas

W Houston St

Charlton St

Vandam St

Prince St

University Plaza

N

Spring St

are over a 100 steps leading to the top. Unfortunately, it is never opened to the public. Perhaps the authorities fear a repeat performance of the Dada antic in 1916, when Marcel Duchamp and fellow artists went to the top and announced to the world that the Village was an independent bohemian state

with no allegiance to the United States.

On the north side of the square are a few of the original brownstone houses built in the early 1830s for the wealthy citizens who decided to move here from the city. Henry James, who had a grandmother living in one of these houses, wrote his novel, suitably named *Wash-*

St Mark's in the Bowery was built in 1799.

ington Square which explored the sensibilities of the fine folk who lived here in the second half of the 19th century.

Little remains of the original south side of the square apart from the **Judson Memorial Baptist Church**, another creation of the McKim, Mead and White team of architects. A planned renovation of the building will do much to highlight the eclectic details of a basically Romanesque exterior. Funds are being collected for the cleaning and restoration of the stained-glass windows created by John La Farge. The congregation is very active and a stroll inside will reveal interesting current events.

Part of the church is used as dormitories for students of **New York University**, one of America's largest private universities with an enrolment of over 30,000 students. Nowadays, its departments are spread across the city but the main campus is sited around Washington Square and its proud ownership of many of the local buildings is shown by the flying of a purple and white banner.

To The South

From the southwest corner of the square is MacDougal Street, which is well worth strolling down, to its junction at Bleecker Street #130 and #132 once home to Louisa M Alcott, author of *Little Women* and #133 which is the **Provincetown Playhouse.** The theater still functions and is famous for having championed

Cafe Figaro, a popular meeting place.

Eugene O'Neill when he was an unknown playwright with modernist tendencies. Broadway had no interest in experimental theater and the Provincetown Players was the first American company to risk taking on something new and different.

Bleecker Street, and the nearby cafés are haunted with literary memories. This is the place to rest, have a cup of coffee and look through a copy of *Village Voice*. **Café Figaro** was where the Beat writers of the 1950s hung out, while **Café Borgia** was patronised by Kerouac and Ginsburg in the following decade. The **Minetta Tavern** is dedicated to the memory of Joe Gould, a bohemian artist who ended up in a mental institution and the documents on the wall recount the strange life he led in Greenwich Village.

Bleecker Street crosses the Avenue of the Americas (Sixth Avenue) and brings the **Church of Our Lady of Pompeii** into view. This is where Mother Cabrini, America's first saint, attended prayers. Italian by birth, she appreciated a church where the service was, and still is, conducted in Italian.

From the church it is a short walk down Leroy Street and across Seventh Avenue to **St Luke's Place** and its row of smart 19th-century brownstone houses. More literary associations at #16, where Theodore Dreiser wrote *An American Tragedy*, and the two lamps outside #6 commemorate the home of Jimmy Walker. Walker became mayor of the city in

Inside an Italian restaurant.

1926 and was a larger than life character who managed a shrewd political career until one too many revelations of his shady dealings resulted in his resignation. His popularity has never really plummeted and he remained a popular figure, well known for his song writing and legalisation of boxing.

The streets to the west all lead down to the **Hudson**, once a thriving buzz of activity where stevedores unloaded ships and lorries came and went throughout the day. Not the most salubrious part of town at night, it has an abandoned feel and many of the clubs and cafés are strictly for gays. **Bedford Street** is the most elegant street in the village, it connects Seventh Avenue with Christopher Street and contains two noteworthy houses, one claiming to be the narrowest and the other the oldest in the city. Edna St Vincent Millay, the first woman to win the Pulitzer Prize for poetry, lived here in the 1920s and the late actor Cary Grant also called it home for a while.

Bars

A place that is more difficult to find, but worth the trouble of seeking out, is a bar called **Chumleys**. The name does not appear outside, partly because it was once a speakeasy and partly because it is now so well known that there is no need to advertise its location. It is at #86 and the book covers plastered on the

East Village

Street fare in East Village.

A highly desirable area in the 19th century, East Village has been out of fashion for most of the 20th century but is now slowly reasserting itself in a steady process of increasing "yuppification." In the post-War years it was home to a Greenwich Village overspill of beatniks and bohemians

and at night **St Mark's Place** and the surrounding streets retain this atmosphere by way of lively clubs, restaurants and shops.

The sombre mass of the **Cooper Union Foundation Building**, located at East Seventh Street between Third and Fourth Avenues, is not easily missed. It is named after the man whose statue looks down on pedestrians from the small bit of grass located in front of the building. Peter Cooper became a millionaire without being able to read and write but he wanted to make it possible for other working class citizens not to feel the shame he experienced. He established a Foundation to finance a college that would offer free educational courses, a concept that was made even more revolutionary by his insistence that the college accept people regardless of their color. The college still functions in this way. Pop inside to see the public lectures currently being organised.

A short walk north along Fourth Avenue to St Mark's Place and off to the left is **Astor Place**, named after the city's first multimillionaire. The subway station is distinguished by a cast-iron sculpture located outside and the giant black cube sculpted by Bernard Rosenthal is called "Alamo" for an unfathomable reason. Check out the zany hairdresser the **Astor Place Hair Design**, for an astonishing array of styles.

From Astor Place the attractive **Stuyvesant Street** occupies land that was once part of the Dutch governor's farm and the house at #21 was built in 1804 as a wedding gift for Peter

walls advertise the fact that more than one illustrious writer found refuge here.

Grove Court is behind the locked iron gate where Bedford and Grove Street meet. This private mews, now the preserve of the wealthy, was built in the 19th century to house impoverished workers. There were apparently two nicknames for the row of houses: "Pig's Al-

ley," because of the disdain felt for the cheap houses and their residents and "Mixed Ale Alley" because the workers bought their beer in bulk and shared it amongst themselves.

Grove Street and Christopher Street, which the former runs into, are prominent gay areas and the **Crisis Cafe** at 59 Grove Street is a popular gay bar that

Stuyvesant's great-great granddaughter. The church at the end of the street, **St Mark's-in-the-Bowery**, is even older. Built in 1799, on the same ground as Stuyvesant himself was buried in 1672, the church boasts a Greek Revival steeple which was added to the structure in 1828. Church services are still conducted here but attendances are larger for the poetry, music and dance functions that take place within. In the 1950s, writers like Allen Ginsberg and Jack Kerouac gave readings here.

One reason why East Village is undergoing gentrification at such a slow pace is its proximity to the **Lower East Side**. Any further east than First Avenue brings one to **Alphabet City**, a very unattractive locality. By day it is safe to walk to **Tompkins Square**, between East Seventh and Tenth and Avenues A and B, where riots occurred in 1988 and 1989 when the police tried to remove the homeless by enforcing a night curfew. Much more interesting is **Lafayette Street** that runs parallel with Broadway from Astor Place down to Bleecker Street. At the end near East Fourth Street is **Colonnade Row** which sports a Corinthian facade and which boasts four houses dating from 1833. The magnate John Astor lived here. Across the road from his dwelling is the **Shakespeare Festival's Public Theater**. The theater opened in 1960 by staging an unknown (now infamous) musical called *Hair* and is currently presenting a Shakespeare Marathon with a production of every play ever written by the Bard staged over a five-year period.

was also the home of Thomas Paine (1737-1809), the English libertarian whose political writings had an enormous influence on American revolutionaries. Paine served in the Revolution before returning to England and upsetting the authorities there by writing in support of the French Revolution. He eventually fled to the United States after being charged with treason, only to find that the country he had helped establish no longer wanted him as a citizen. The gay bar makes its own statement by taking its name from one of Paine's titles, *The Crisis Papers*.

At night, Christopher Street attracts equal numbers of gays and tourists. It is a pleasant and safe thoroughfare although its history is associated with violence. In 1863 it was a focus of discontent for the Draft Riots and, more recently, in 1969 it witnessed an explosion of gay anger when a bar in the street, the **Stonewall Inn**, was raided by the police. The raid precipitated a siege of the bar and in the ensuing riot both police and protesters were injured. The fracas resulted in the official formation of New York's Gay Liberation movement and every June the city's Gay Liberation parade culminates in the west of Greenwich Village. The street also boasts the world's first gay bookshop, the **Oscar Wilde Memorial Bookshop**.

Christopher Street stretches westward down to the Hudson, becoming seedier and less welcoming along the way. It is more inviting to head eastwards to the busy junction where Christopher Street meets Sixth Avenue and Greenwich Avenue. The garden space between 10th Street and Sixth Avenue was where the notorious **Women's House of Detention** stood. The appalling conditions inside the prison led to its demolition in 1974. The adjacent building is the **Jefferson Market Courthouse Library** which dates back

One of the many quaint markets that dot Greenwich Village.

to 1876 and was reputedly modelled on a Bavarian castle. This is not too difficult to believe, given the splendid panache of its Gothic exterior. As the name makes clear, it has served various functions in its time and since 1967 has served as a branch of the New York Public Library.

The elegant style of Greenwich Village can again be enjoyed along West 10th Street which begins just opposite the library. The 19th-century houses have been carefully preserved. But before heading along the street to Fifth Avenue, look out for **Patchin Place**, which begins immediately on the right. This is another literary landmark in the city, a tiny mews which can boast of being home to socialist writers like John Reed and John Dos Passos as well as the poet E E Cummings. The most interesting resident was Djuna Barnes, the au-

An aerial view of downtown Manhattan.

thor of *Nightwood*, who hid here for over 40 years after leading a flamboyant and extrovert life as the archetypal bohemian. The story goes that E E Cummings would check up on his reclusive neighbor by occasionally shouting from his window, "Are ya still alive, Djuna?"

West 10th Street is also worth following through to Fifth Avenue if you want to see the **Church of the Ascension** at the corner. It was designed by Richard Upjohn, the architect of Trinity Church. In 1889,

McKim, Mead and White remodelled part of the interior. The most noteworthy element is the Tiffany stained glass and the altar mural created by John La Farge.

An alternative route to Fifth Avenue is by way of West Eighth Street if you want to unload some of those burdensome dollars on clothes. The street has a number of bargain clothes and shoe shops and **Andy's Chee-Pees**, at #16, is one of the best places to purchase cutprice gear.

Chinatown is utterly authentic and very touristic, making it ideal for the visitor who wants to soak up atmosphere, wander from shop to shop, eat ethnic food at a reasonable price and feel comfortable and safe.

Chinatown offers all this, and the restaurants which cater to visitors and the Chinese alike, offer some of the best value for money meals in the whole of New York.

Unmistakably Chinatown.

Motley Mott Street

The boundaries of Chinatown are no longer as rigid as they once were but **Mott Street** is still the main artery and cannot be missed. This is the place to buy stylish chopsticks, silk garments, jade ornaments, bamboo umbrellas, kimonos, woks, religious figurines, high-collared *Mandarin* dresses, or choose from the pavement stalls displaying 1,001 knick

FOOK KEE'S RESTAURANT

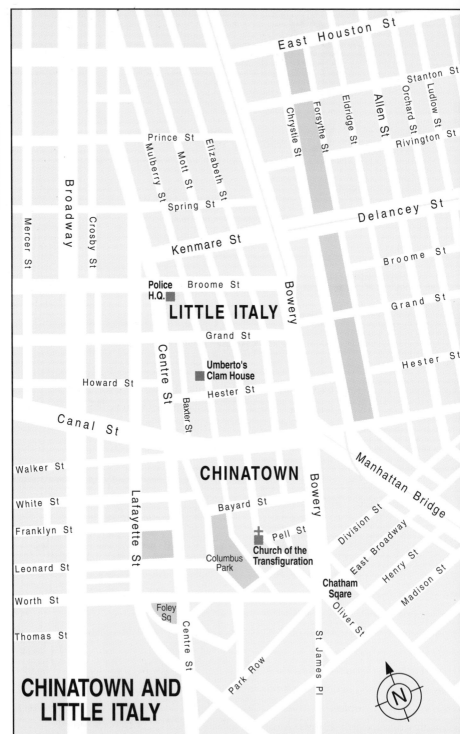

East Houston St

Stanton St

Chrystie St
Forsythe St
Eldridge St
Allen St
Orchard St
Ludlow St
Rivington St

Prince St

Mulberry St
Mott St
Elizabeth St

Spring St

Broadway

Crosby St

Mercer St

Delancey St

Kenmare St

Broome St

Police H.Q.

Broome St

LITTLE ITALY

Bowery

Grand St

Grand St

Hester St

Centre St

Umberto's Clam House

Howard St

Baxter St

Hester St

Canal St

CHINATOWN

Walker St

Bayard St

Bowery

Manhattan Bridge

White St

Lafayette St

Pell St

Division St

East Broadway

Franklyn St

Church of the Transfiguration

Henry St

Leonard St

Columbus Park

Chatham Sqare

Madison St

Worth St

Foley Sq

Oliver St

Thomas St

Centre St

Park Row

St James Pl

**CHINATOWN AND
LITTLE ITALY**

N

Chinese greengrocers.

knacks and souvenirs. The street is visually arresting, ablaze with color and character, with the color red standing predominate in banners and lanterns and the wine-soaked ducks hanging by their necks from poles.

Olfactory diversions come by way of the countless restaurants which prepare and serve the delicious varieties of Chinese cuisine, while the smell of incense emanates from the **Eastern States Buddhist Temple** at #64. It is a genuine temple but tourists are more than welcome (behind the golden statue there is a shop).

Nearby is **Quong Yuen Shing**, which opened as a general store in the 1890s. It is the oldest emporium in Chinatown and worth a browse around.

Further along you'll come to the **Church of the Transfiguration**, which offers services in Cantonese. Tourists are also welcome at the **Chinese Fair Amusement Arcade** at #8 where some fairly unique games can be observed.

Wander at will around the surrounding streets (Chinatown has one of the lowest crime rates in the city) and explore the exotica of food and consumer shops. Pell and Doyers Streets were once the haunt of the *tongs* (illegal Chinese societies that financed their welfare activities by controlling the neighborhood's gambling and drugs). The **Bloody Angle** is still remembered as the name given to the turn in Doyers Street where the bodies of men killed in the vicious "Tong Wars" were frequently

One of the many reasons to visit Chinatown – have your fortune told!

dumped.

Mott Street is just one of the 10 streets that come together at **Chatham Square**. Chatham Square was named after the Earl of Chatham – William Pitt, and is where Worth Street, East Broadway and the Bowery meet. While it is a nightmare of traffic when busy, benches are also located in the middle for rest and recuperation. Behind the seats is a memorial arch commemorating American-born Chinese war victims and nearby is a bank illustriously situated in a mock pagoda-style temple.

Boundary Between

The boundary between Chinatown and Little Italy used to be **Canal Street**, which meets Mott Street at the other end from Chatham Square. However since the post-1963 influx of Chinese this is no longer the case.

The street gets it name from what was once an open drainage conduit but nowadays is a busy road that links traffic from the Holland Tunnel with that coming across the Manhattan Bridge.

Between the Bowery and Greene Street the pavements are lined with an array of Chinese food, fruit and vegetable stores selling poisonous-looking but quite edible mushrooms, wet slabs of beancurd, even more poisonous-looking dried fungi and a host of exotic and strangely-colored fruits.

Eastwards to the Bridge

Heading eastwards for the bridge, Canal Street ends at the **Bowery**, a name derived from its early existence as a country road – the "Bouwerie" – when New York was a Dutch town.

Nowadays, it serves as a haunt for social misfits, the victims of alcohol abuse and drug addiction and queues of men will be seen lining up outside a soup kitchen giving away free meals. Individuals may politely request your loose change and it is worth crossing the road to admire the entrance to **Manhattan Bridge**.

The entrance was designed in the first decade of the century by the same team who designed the New York Central Public Library and it shows in the grand *beaux arts* treatment of the entrance. The frieze on top of the entrance shows some Indians (aided by winged horses) taking part in a buffalo hunt.

SoHo

Coined from South of HOuston, **SoHo** may sound like the red light entertainment area of London's West End but it has a very different character. In the early 1960s artists looking for adequate working spaces that did not cost the earth discovered the area they now call SoHo.

At the time it was a rundown ex-commercial area but the buildings had large unpartitioned rooms that stretched the length of a storey, were designed for storage or small industries but were also easily convertible into loft-type dwellings. Kitchens and bathrooms were installed, and word spread as more of the properties were taken over for conversion into art galleries, dance studios, offices for freelancers and so on.

Within a few years, the neighborhood was experiencing a renaissance as the trendiest place to live and work and enterprising proprietors opened up restaurants, shops and art galleries. Gallery hopping – there are about 140 – became a cultural marathon.

By the 1980s SoHo started experiencing the same cycle as Greenwich Village. Artists began to be outnumbered by Wall Street yuppies and rents began to soar as the lofts were converted into luxury apartments.

The Chinese In New York

New York has the largest Chinese community in the Western Hemisphere. The first great wave descended on its shores in the 19th century with another surge arriving in the second half of the 1960s. In 1965, Congress finally repealed laws that for more than 80 years had barred many Chinese while admitting Europeans. Since then, Asians have formed the single largest immigrant group arriving in the city and Chinatown has burst out of its original confines to occupy the area south of Canal Street, overtaken Little Italy, seeped into SoHo, given a fresh lease of life to the Lower East Side and created satellite communities in Brooklyn and Flushing, Queens.

Under the 1965 immigration laws, each country in the Eastern Hemisphere has a quota of 20,000 per year and in 1982, three years after the US established diplomatic relations with the People's Republic of China and broke off with Taiwan, the Republic also has a quota. Today there are at the very least 150,000 Chinese in Chinatown and as many again in the outer boroughs. They hail from the People's Republic, Hong Kong, Taiwan, Singapore, Malaysia, Laos, Indonesia, Thailand, Vietnam, Cambodia, South America and the Philippines.

The Chinese can be remarkably insular, an almost segregated thread in the multi-racial fabric of the city. Many Chinese live and work within the same square mile. There are over 600 factories in Chinatown, turning the area into the city's main clothing manufacturing center and a significant jewelry district has emerged which boasts an annual turnover in excess of US$100 million in gold and diamonds. Another source of employment is the 350 restaurants.

Chinatown is also one of the main centers of organised crime in the United States and the Justice Department regards Chinese- organised crime in the same way it does the Mafia. The Chinese Connection, shifting heroin from the Golden Triangle in Southeast Asia through Hong Kong to New York, has permanently replaced the French Connection that couriered the drug from Turkey through Marseilles to the United States.

Work ethics, abounds amongst the Chinese, and the typical Chinese man or woman in New York works up to 18 hours a day and leads a fairly spartan existence. Sharing a one-bedroom apartment with up a dozen fellow workers is not uncommon. Many have paid around US$30,000 to arrange their smuggled arrival in the city, thus they work like virtual slaves to repay the debt as quickly as possible. An average annual salary is between US$10,000 and US$12,000 for a unionised garment or shop worker. Garment workers are paid per piece, for example, the operator of a machine that sews seams will be paid between US$0.10 and US$0.20 a seam. Seamstresses add the collars, cuffs, zippers and pockets and the finished garment may end up in Bloomingdale's with a price tag higher than the worker's weekly wage. And for every unionised factory there is another sweatshop that violates all the laws regarding the minimum wage, compensation, the employment of minors and health and safety regulations. Such sweatshops are occasionally raided by the authorities who find the fire doors and windows firmly locked and metal gratings placed over the doors so that anyone passing by in the street assumes that the place is empty. A waiter can earn up to US$20,000.

Most Chinese in America dream of establishing a business of their own but a new shopkeeper would need to find US$100,000 "key money" to secure a 10-year lease and a rent of US$7,000 is not unusual for a 1,200 square foot store on Canal Street.

One of the few times of the year when the shops are really closed is during the New Year celebrations. The Wan Chi Ming Hung Gar Institute, founded in 1973 by kung fu master Sifu Wan Chi Ming, is one of the dozen or so kung fu associations that performs the lion dance through the streets of Chinatown.

Renaissance

Today, SoHo is chockablock with designer clothes shops, art galleries, *art nouveau* cafes, up-market restaurants and beautiful people all expensively

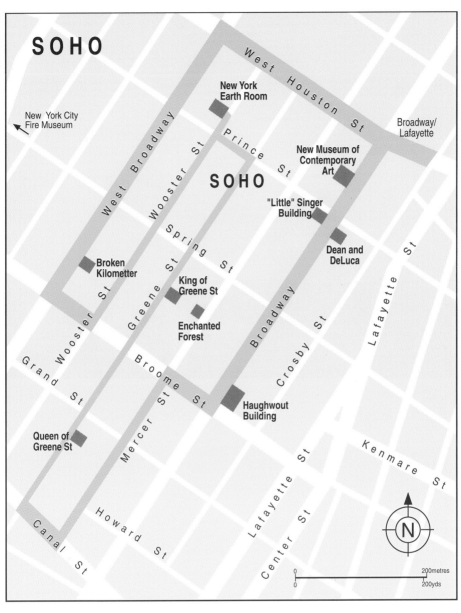

SOHO

New York City Fire Museum

West Houston St

Broadway/ Lafayette

West Broadway

Wooster St

Prince St

SOHO

New York Earth Room

New Museum of Contemporary Art

"Little" Singer Building

Spring St

Broken Kilometter

Greene St

King of Greene St

Enchanted Forest

Dean and DeLuca

Broadway

Lafayette St

Wooster St

Crosby St

Grand St

Broome St

Mercer St

Haughwout Building

Queen of Greene St

Kenmare St

Canal St

Howard St

Lafayette St

Center St

N

0   200metres
0   200yds

clad. Just like Greenwich Village, do not bother turning up too early as little will be open. Weekends are best when everything is open till 9:00 pm and the streets are abuzz with modish consumers.

SoHo is now so well established that the Guggenheim chose this location in which to open a new branch in 1992. The **Guggenheim Museum SoHo**, located at 575 Broadway near Prince Street, specialises in contemporary art and exhibitions from its permanent collections, all attractively presented in a wonderful cast-iron building with the cast-iron pil-

Art In SoHo

SoHo art gallery, one of the many in West Broadway.

It is a fitting coincidence that the area of Manhattan with the most important concentration of commercial art galleries should also be home to New York's most uniquely native form of art, the cast-iron building.

In the 19th century, when no one thought of living in SoHo, cast-iron structures were bolted together on-site allowing a small factory or warehouse to be errected in less than a month. Iron beams rather than heavy walls took on the weight, facilitating larger work areas, extra wide windows and allowing for decorative iron facades to be pinned onto the exterior.

The owner of the building would choose from a catalogue of designs that imitated the Italian Renaissance, ancient Greece, the French Second Empire or some imaginative architectural hybrid. Gargoyles and superfluous sculptural details would be added for fun. Most of the 200 surviving examples are now preserved for posterity as part of SoHo's National Historic District.

lars highlighted within. Continuing in the tradition of the main Guggenheim Museum, the building itself is the major work of art and the Broadway entrance is a sheer wonder of modern design.

Nearby, between Prince and Houston Street (pronounced How-ston), the **New Museum of Contemporary Art** offers a challenge to any art lover. Everything on show is so new as to escape being labelled and categorised by the establishment, with the result that visitors have little choice but to depend on their own judgement. There is no per-

Greene Street, between Canal and Grand Streets, has one of the best displays of cast-iron architecture which played a decisive role in saving the area from demolition in the 1960s. The building that occupies #72-#76 is magnificent, with a Corinthian-style porch that takes up the entire five storeys. Appropriately enough, the building now houses typical SoHo art galleries and a fancy antiques store.

When walking along nearby Wooster Street the aesthetic appeal is literally under your feet: the original stone block cobbles which were then known as Belgian Block. In other parts of SoHo, the asphalt pavements are being torn up and replaced with cobbles so as to make them resemble this original look. At #141 the **New York Earth Room**, run by the non-commercial Dia Art Foundation, boasts a 140-ton earth sculpture errected by Walter de Maria while the **Paula Cooper Gallery** at #155 is one of the more avant-garde and progressive galleries in the area.

Back on Broadway, if you can keep yourself out of the galleries, seek out #488 where the run-down **Haughwout Building** stands. It dates from the mid-19th century and consciously imitates Venetian architecture, but in cast-iron! The columned arch motif is repeated over and over again on the exterior and lends a remarkable fluency to the building. Inside, still in operation, is the first Otis elevator to be installed in a building in New York.

Also on Broadway, just past Prince Street, is another architectural gem, the **"Little" Singer Building**. This was one of the last cast-iron buildings to be erected – dating back to the first decade of the 20th century – with wide-framed windows.

manent exhibition and some of what you see will undoubtedly end up in the dustbin, but the next Picasso may also be on show...

Walking south on Broadway you will see a number of galleries exhibiting works for sale executed by both un-

Celebrating San Gennaro at Umberto's Clam House.

known and fairly well-established artists. Between #594 and #560, the **Broadway Gallery Buildings** is chock-full of galleries housing everything from the mildly modern to the outrageously avant garde that can only invite audience participation.

Turn right at Broome Street for Mercer Street on the left. At #85 there is a children's shop that stresses the entertaining and the innovative in a way that is becoming the norm for SoHo shops, and there are a number of craft and gift stores which are opening in the area that are great fun to look into even if nothing is purchased.

The western boundary of SoHo is marked by **West Broadway** where there are more art galleries and shops selling

SoHo is chock-a-block with designer boutiques, art galleries
and up-market restaurants.

artifacts culled from every obscure corner of the world.

Proprietors do not expect every visitor to purchase something and looking
around is more than half the fun. If you
visit on a Saturday, you will just be part
of the large crowd of window shoppers.

TriBeCa

When the artists of SoHo were forced out
by the purveyors of art who could afford
the escalating rents, they simply shifted
to the nearest affordable blocks. Their

heralded by the **TriBeCa Film Center** at 375 Greenwich Street, which was a former coffee warehouse which is now partly owned by the actor Robert De Niro, as is the attached restaurant. Fans of the *Ghostbuster* films may wish to take the short detour into North Moore Street, on the right at the northern end of the street where the fire station should be a familiar sight.

Little Italy

See it while it is still there. Little Italy is fast disappearing, subject to the unrelenting force of history and the encroachment of its territory by Chinatown. At the turn of the century Little Italy was a clearly defined area with around 150,000 immigrants who arrived on American shores to escape from the awful poverty of Naples and Sicily. Along with them came the Mafia who are likely to outlast the territory they first controlled as Little Italy has now shrunk to a couple of blocks on Mulberry and Grand Streets.

Along Mulberry Street, the sidewalks are lined with cafés and its atmosphere is almost mellow. Many Italian families have moved on to Bronx and Brooklyn but there is still a distinctly Latin flavor to the locality that invites one to slip into a coffee shop and laze away the time. Mulberry Street is best enjoyed during the ten days of the Feast of San Gennaro in September when music fills the air and *calzone* is served at every other food stall.

new domain, christened **TriBeCa** from the TRIangle BElow CAnal Street, is already well on its way to becoming indistinguishable from SoHo. However the recession is slowing down the transformation of an area that 15 to 20 years ago was a nondescript territory housing small garment factories and light industries. A sign of the area's future is

I will never forget the joy I felt when I saw the tall buildings of New York and the Statue of Liberty after so many dark days on board that crowded ship. There was the symbol of all my dreams – freedom to start out in a new life. Then came Ellis Island."

First impressions of anonymous immigrant.

For the millions of immigrants who arrived on America's eastern coast after a gruelling journey across the Atlantic, the **Statue of Liberty** was the first glimpse of the new land that beckoned. Before the new arrivals were officially allowed into America they were screened and processed on nearby **Ellis Island** and many visitors today unconsciously follow in their footsteps by beginning their stay in the United States by making a trip to the island and the statue. Tickets for the Circle Line Ferry include entry to both places and the boats regularly depart from Battery Park every half-hour from 9:30 am until 3:00 pm in summer.

The tallest lady in New York.

Lower Manhattan

Immigration Museum on Ellis Island.

During winter the schedule is subject to changes Call tel: 269 5755 for detail but there are never the long queues that make an early arrival so essential in the summer.

Ellis Island opened as an immigration station in 1892 and by the time it closed in 1924 an estimated 16 million individuals had disembarked here, passed the doctor's inspection and given acceptable answers to the examining officer's questions about employment and dependents. The unlucky ones were denied a landing card and mostly suffered the misery of a journey back to Europe, with some desperate rejects trying to swim from Ellis Island to Manhattan.

The **Immigration Museum** located on the island tells the somber and often depressing tale of the immigrant's ordeal. The majority of modern Americans who make the visit do so because this is where their ancestors once arrived. For them there is an added poignancy in listening to the taped recordings of the immigrants' experiences, the bleak photographs of their haggard faces as they awaited inspection and the memorabilia that ranges from children's shoes to train timetables.

Wall Street

Back on Manhattan the altogether different life of the financial district's fasttrack is on display. **Wall Street** is

The Stock Exchange Building.

the obvious place to head for but it is invariably an anti-climax if you are expecting an instant evocation of its fearsome image as the power house of world capitalism. The street's name comes from a wooden wall erected by Peter Stuyvesant in 1653 to keep out the Native Americans. The buildings that now stand here are not skyscrapers and the slow crawl of taxis between old buildings built in the style of ancient Rome and Greece does little to create the impression one might expect. Behind the classical facades, the big deals are being made and a visit to the **Stock Exchange** opens up the financial world which lies in the very heart of this part of town. Turn into Broad Street and collect a white ticket from the doorman to gain

entry to the **Visitors' Gallery** from where you can gaze down on the frenzied activities of the brokers. Their mystique diminishes when they pop out on the street for a quick cigarette; their crumpled jackets and worn faces betray the human side of their hectic work on the trading floor.

At the nearby corner of Wall Street and Nassau Street the **Federal Hall National Monument** (a Greek temple lookalike). The statue of Washington standing outside commemorates the fact that the first president was inaugurated on the steps of the monument in 1789. Inside is a small, free, museum devoted to Washington memorabilia.

To view the kind of building one expects to find on Wall Street, walk up to

The Statue Of Liberty

It is no longer just an American statue but a universal icon that befits New York, the world city that gave it a home. For the millions of immigrants who gave up everything they knew to risk a new life in a foreign land that they had only heard about or through letters sent home by their relatives, the giant figure of Liberty seemed to be bidding them a welcome as their ships sailed through the Verrazano Narrows to the New World. What the statue does enact is Liberty, holding in her left hand a law book inscribed 4 July, 1776, throwing off the shackles of oppression that lay at her feet and holding in her other hand a beacon to light a better world.

The spirit that the statue represents was captured in a poem penned by Emma Lazarus that was written to help raise money for its pedestal.

> Give me your tired, your poor,
> Your huddled masses yearning to breathe free,
> The wretched refuse of your teeming shore.
> Send these, the homeless, tempest-tossed to me,
> I lift my lamp beside the golden door.

Just over a hundred years later Lou Reed quotes the first two lines and offers his own comment in his 1989 New York album.

In fact the statue was never intended for America. The French sculptor Auguste Bartholdi was working on a lighthouse project for Egypt that would show a giant female figure representing progress. It was to stand at the head of the Suez Canal. While Bartholdi was working on this, a group of French republicans thought of commemorating the centenary of American independence by presenting the United States with a gift that would mark the fact that the American Revolution was partly inspired by the French philosophies of freedom. Edouard de Laboulaye, a French writer, came up with the idea of presenting a statue and Bartholdi was happy to rework his model. In the process he enlarged it by three times the original size and it took him a decade to complete.

It was made out of beaten copper panels, one-eighth of an inch thick and constructed with the engineering advice of Gustave Eiffel who made its interior steel pylon on which the panels laid. The gift shop in Castle Clinton, from where the ferries depart, sells an intriguing poster that shows the panels being relaid on the steel skeleton after the dismantled pieces had been shipped across from France in over 200 crates.

The cost of the statue was borne by public subscription in France but the American public was not so forthcoming when it came to raising the money needed to build the base upon which Liberty would stand. San Francisco, St Louis and Cleveland all offered to give Liberty a home but the problem was solved when a newspaper promised to print the name of every individual New York subscriber and eventually the statue was formally unveiled in 1886.

Bartholdi's wife posed for the modelling work but the face (even with eyes 2 feet 6 inches wide) was recognised to resemble his mother. Ironically, given the female dimension, women were not allowed to participate in the grand opening ceremony and it was left to a group of suffragettes to sail out in a rowing boat and futilely protest at the hypocrisy.

After you disembark on Liberty Island, there is a tiny elevator and step after step leading to the observation deck 10 storeys high. More stairs ascend a further 12 storeys – 168 steps – to the crown. There is a narrow staircase leading to the torch but this is no longer open to the public and by the time you reach the crown you hardly have the energy to climb higher.

the block between Nassau Street and Liberty Street where the **Chase Manhattan Bank** dominates the scene. It was designed by Skidmore, Owings and Merrill, the team of architects who inau-

gurated the flush of giant glass boxes and plazas that appeared across Manhattan in the 1960s. The 813-foot high building is undeniably impressive but the plaza fails to make use of its space

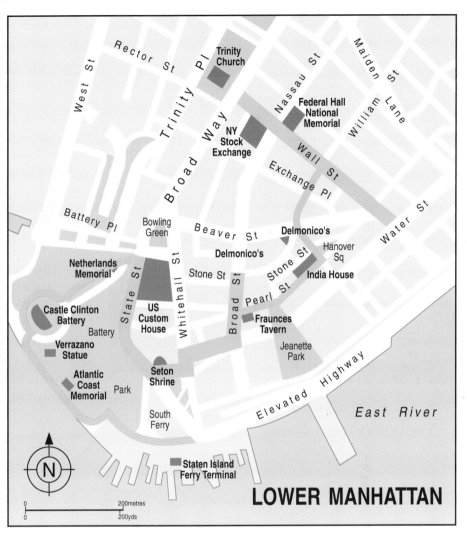

LOWER MANHATTAN

despite the sculpture and the huge photograph of the Manhattan skyline that stretches along one side. However it is a place to rest and orientate before decending the steps down to William Street.

The first left on William Street brings you on to Liberty Street where the massive **Federal Reserve Bank of New York** holds a commanding presence. It was Solomon P. Chase of Chase Manhattan

fame who established the Federal banking system. In the vaults of the grand headquarters 10,000 tons of international monetary gold are stored. Over ten million notes are processed daily and the gold bars are periodically moved to reflect international exchanges. The good news is that visitors can see all this on a guided tour; the bad news is that reservations must be made in advance. (Write to Public Information, Federal

Reserve Bank, 33 Liberty Street, NY 10045 or tel: 212 720 6130. A week's notice is usually required, more or less depending on the time of year.) It is worth arranging a tour if only to see the incredible security arrangement and the wheelbarrows of cash. It will be pointed out (presumably as a deterrent), that the entire building can be locked shut in 30 seconds and that three out of every five guards are trained marksmen.

every work day. Now, 20 years after its opening, the towers blend in comfortably with the surrounding buildings. When they are viewed from the Brooklyn Bridge or the Staten Island ferry one wonders what all the fuss was about.

But when you stand underneath and gaze upwards, or when you peer out across the 110th floor, they can become frighteningly tall.

It just does not seem credible that anyone would even think about walking on a tightrope between the two towers which is what Philippe Petit (dressed up as a construction worker) did!

The World Trade Center

The security at the nearby **World Trade Center** is also very tight especially since the terrorist attack in 1993 and while the famous *Windows on the World* restaurant has been indefinitely closed as a result, the observation decks on the 107th and 110th floors should reopen soon for visitors. When the two towers, aptly described as the twin Ronson lighters, were nearing completion in the early 1970s, they were heavily criticized. Aesthetically dismissed for the utter simplicity of design, urban ecologists also wondered how the area could cope with an added influx of 50,000 employees

Directly across from the World Trade Center on Broadway is the oldest church in Manhattan. **Saint Paul's Chapel** dates back to 1766. The bright blue and pink interior, lit by Waterford glass chandeliers, belies its authentic Georgian ancestry and English architecture, and it is worth venturing within to see the pew where George Washington always prayed during his first term of office.

Saint Paul's is 80 years older than the better known **Trinity Church**, also on Broadway but further south at the top of Wall Street. One reason for it being better known is simply its prime

Winter Garden, Battery Park City.

location though before the closing years of the 19th century it was noted as the tallest building in the city.

Nowadays, the church holds its own among the secular shrines that surrounds it and is usually full at the lunchtime concerts that attract office workers.

The adjoining cemetery has a Dickension feel about it and amongst the tombstones can be found those of Alexander Hamilton, US Secretary to the Treasury and Robert Fulton, the inventor and painter who was famous for his ferry service to Brooklyn.

A break for lunch in the Financial District.

The foundations for the World Trade Center go very deep indeed and the vast amount of earth that was cleared away was deposited in the nearby Hudson. In the process, the landfill added almost a hundred acres to Manhattan. It provides the basis for the construction of the relatively new **Battery Park City** which is still being enlarged and embellished. The area includes some of the city's most contemporary architecture, making up the adjoining **World Financial Center**. The concept of Battery Park City has been compared with the Rockefeller Center and time will tell if the section of West Street between Vesey and Liberty Street really does live up to its expectations.

The **Esplanade** provides a scenic walkway and there are constantly new shops and restaurants opening around the **Winter Garden**, a magnificent glass dome that encloses a small grove of tall palm trees. At weekends, Battery Park City comes into its own and makes the perfect place to enjoy a meal after wandering through the deserted financial district.

While in the city, do not miss a walk along Brooklyn Bridge.

Do not confuse Battery Park City with **Battery Park** located at the southern tip of Manhattan. This is where the ferries to the Statue of Liberty and Ellis Island depart and at the eastern end, near the subway stations, is where the Staten Island Ferry Terminal is located.

A walk across **Brooklyn Bridge** is not to be missed while in New York and access to the raised walkway usually entails walking along the opening stretch of Broadway as far as Park Row.

This part of Broadway has little to recommend it, though it does boast a

Life At the Stock Exchange

Gazing down at the floor of the New York Stock Exchange from the glassed-in visitors' gallery, it is difficult to credit the scene with any sense of purposeful activity. Even at 10:30am the floor is so littered with paper cuttings that your first impression may be that the whole place needs a thorough cleaning. Yet standing amidst the litter, leaning on tiny counters, talking on the telephone or just apparently idly chatting, are brokers who between them control trillions of dollars. Some of the brokers will be gazing at the small video screens angled on black rods and attached to a structure in a way that resembles some giant insect that are projected down onto the floor. Most of the floor space is taken up with a series of octagonally-shaped open-fronted "shops," the trading posts, where women key in the various orders to buy or sell.

What adds to the visitor's sense of disorientation is not just the complex machinery of pipes and video machines that seems to literally grip the entire floor, but the incongruous mixture of frenzied activity and seemingly indolent ease. One corner of the floor will be frantically busy with people shouting, telephoning and reacting to their electronic paging devices while adjacent to all this will be someone else calmly consulting his notebook or casually talking in a group.

The whole trading floor and all its facilities were completely overhauled in 1980 (without a minute's interruption to business) to bring everything electronically on-line. The building installation was completed on overhead platforms and then, once a week for 14 successive Fridays, an old trading post was dismantled and a new one lowered into its place. Back in the 1880s, over 5,000 telegrams were sent out and 2,000 messages delivered by boys on bicycles, everyday of the year. Everything is now logged-on computer and monitored by a team of investigators whose job it is to discover signs of uncharacteristic behavior that might point to some chicanery.

It helps a lot if you spend 10 minutes, viewing the film that tries to explain what is happening on the floor before you enter the **Vistor's Gallery**. The film is narrated by Leonard Nimoy of *Star Trek* fame and it will to help you make sense of the various personages milling about on the stock exchange floor. One can also consult an array of push-button computer screens that provide answers in five different languages to questions about bulls, bears, bonds, options and so on.

You might be tempted to invest some of your vacation funds in a few shares. One share in McDonald's stock cost US$32.75 when first floated on the market, 20 years later that same stock is worth US$2,800. But while the Stock Exchange is quick to advertise its success stories, there is little mention of the Crash of 1929 and only a photograph on the wall, showing the crowds gathering outside on the streets in October 1987, reminds one of a more recent glitch.

very posh McDonald's with a smiling doorman in coat and tails, live piano music at lunchtime and staff to help you find a seat.

Five and Dimes Fortune

Before turning down Park Row be sure to pause across the road from the **Woolworth Building** to admire its wonderful success in blending skyscaper technology with a sense of stylistic abandon. Built in 1913, it remains one of the city's loveliest creations.

And just as the Woolworth Five and Dime Store (everything was priced at either US$0.05 or US$0.10) were strictly cash only, so Frank Woolworth paid the whole US$13.5 million dollars when the building work was completed. The lobby inside is even more lovely than the exte-

The Woolworth Building, a successful blend of skyscraper
technology and stylistic abandon.

rior, a glittering mosaic of shining colors where even the mail box is an extravagant piece of gothic panache.

Enter via the Barclay Street entrance to observe the bas-reliefs in the corner that portray Frank Woolworth counting out nickels and dimes and the architect Cass Gilbert holding a model of the building like some medieval craftsman. In the other two corners, on the Park Place side, are another two caricatures, one of a builder and another of the renting agent.

The building, dubbed quite suitably the "Cathedral of Commerce" is still the headquarters of the Woolworth corporation.

Across the road from the Woolworth Building is the small City Hall Park where the mounted police rest their horses and where stone chess tables are set out for anyone who wants a game. The building that gives the park its name is on the other side, just past the municipal buildings that crowd in one another, **City Hall** is the most elegant and least offensive. On top of the cupola stands Lady Justice, facing south on what was the entire city of New York when the building was completed in 1812.

Lower Manhattan has its own share of museums and the most recent to open was the **National Museum of the American Indian**, at Battery Place between State and Whithall Streets. An extensive colllection of art and artefacts from Native American tribes all across America are housed in the US Custom House. The building itself is a superb example of the *beaux art* style, designed by Cass Gibert, and its front sports allegorical sculptures of the four continents.

Seaport Experience

South Sea Port, just south of the Brooklyn Bridge, is a major complex of shops, restaurants and museums. The museum block is between Fulton, Front, Beekman and Water Streets and a good introduction to the commercial history

of the seaport can be gleaned from the multiscreen **Seaport Experience** at the Trans-Lux Seaport Theater in Front Street.

The museum block is an innovative concept – an open museum without walls – that unfolds on the pedestrianised cobblestoned street that recreate the bygone era of sailing ships. Before

The South Seaport is a major complex housing many
shops, restaurants and museums.

the new steamships appeared on the
scene in the 1860s this part of the East
River was crowded with the tall masts of
cargo ships and commerce thrived in a
way that is now being recreated in the
business conducted by countless shops,
craft centers, restaurants and galleries.

Seven sailing ships can be visited at
Piers 15 and 16 and the century-old
schooner **Pioneer** regularly cruises
around the harbor. The **Visitors' Center**
at 14 Fulton Street has free literature on
everything that is available. Tickets can
be purchased here.

Outer Boroughs

Manhattan is where the action is. It is where nearly all visitors to New York stay, it is where most of the theaters, concert halls, galleries, landmarks, universities and department stores are concentrated. But New York City has four other boroughs – Brooklyn, Queens, The Bronx and Staten Island. Though only the Bronx is on the North American continent, all of them are linked with each other, and with Manhattan, by an extensive transportation system which includes 65 bridges and 19 tunnels. The outer boroughs are largely residential and industrial, but they have their own surprises.

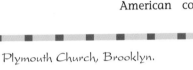

Plymouth Church, Brooklyn.

Brooklyn

If **Brooklyn** had not become part of New York in 1898 it would now be the third largest city in the United States and this guidebook would be entitled *New York & Brooklyn*. It is the most vibrant of the

The Promenade at Brooklyn Heights.

four outer boroughs, the most visited and the most visitable and has an ethnic mix that is every bit as diverse as Manhattan's. The best way to enter the borough is not by subway, where the sense of entering a new territory is minimised, but by the **Brooklyn Bridge**, whose name proudly proclaims its purpose. This magnificent 486-meter span took 14 years to complete. Upon reaching the Brooklyn side of the bridge take the left fork and turn right on the road to Cadman Plaza West and the elegant charm of Brooklyn Heights.

The first and most charming of all New York's suburbs, **Brooklyn Heights** conveys an atmosphere of peace and calm unique to the whole city. There are no major sites or places of interest that

have to be seen and the sense of enjoyment that is had by being here simply comes from walking the quiet tree-lined streets, taking in the elegant architecture and experiencing an uplift of the spirit that comes from momentarily leaving behind the clamor and claustrophobia that inevitably builds up after a stay in Manhattan.

Old Fulton Street is reached by turning back and following the course of the bridge on the street level. It leads to the old **Fulton Ferry Landing**, located directly opposite the South Street Seaport, where the commuters clambered aboard Robert Fulton's ferries to take them to their city offices before the bridge was opened. On the way to the water's edge you will pass the equally old **Eagle**

Warehouse where Walt Whitman once worked when the building housed a newspaper office. He was sacked after his abolitionist stance over the question of slavery became public. The anti-slavery connection crops up more than once in the Heights. If you continue along Fulton Street until #372, you will come face-to-face to an officially designated landmark, the **Gage and Tollner**. This engaging little restaurant opened in 1879 and the gas-lit 90's atmosphere still prevails.

Most of the fine old streets run between Henry Street and The Esplanade, the first street you encounter is **Middagh Street** where, at #24, the oldest home in the neighborhood, (an 1829 Federalist clapboard house) is to be found. The street was named in honor of the locally prestigious Middagh family but one member of this family objected so strongly to this that she succeeded in having the adjacent streets named after fruit and vegetables. One of these is Orange Street, where the **Plymouth Church of the Pilgrims** (where the abolitionist Henry Ward Beecher held mock slave auctions to collect money for their release) is found. Abraham Lincoln, drawn to Beecher's ardent anti-slavery sentiments, worshipped here, so did Charles Dickens and Mark Twain. His sister, Harriet Beecher Stowe, was the author of *Uncle Tom's Cabin*. Beecher himself lived at #22 in Willow Street and a number of the houses in this street made up part of the underground route for slaves escaping Canada.

Turn into Pierrepont Street and follow it to the end where you will see the Promenade. **The Promenade** is Brooklyn Height's showcase, a peaceful walkway backed by a park and overlooking the East River and the commercial monuments of Manhattan on the other side. It is a place to sit, reflect and gaze at after meandering through the 19th-century streets. This is where you can enjoy an unobstructed view from the Statue of Liberty northwards to Brooklyn Bridge all the way to the Empire State Building. This view of Manhattan is the best one possible enjoyed from the comfort of a stationary seat and it also makes the perfect spot for a picnic lunch.

Unlike Manhattan, though, the street corners have no mobile food stalls, but if you have not brought your own food it is no problem because Montague Street is nearby with a discriminating selection of cafés and restaurants. It is a

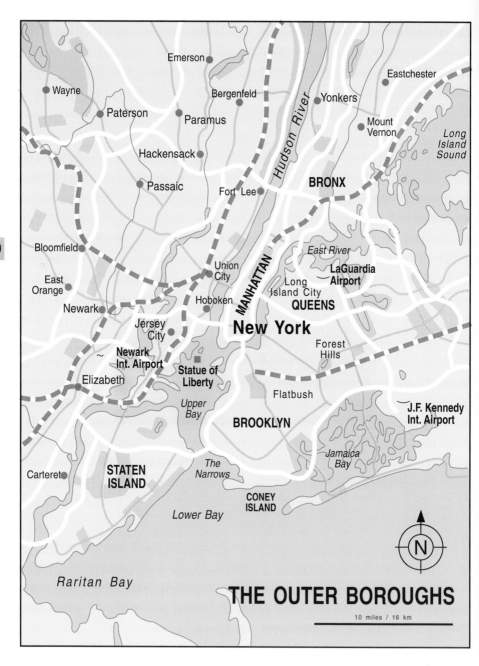

THE OUTER BOROUGHS

10 miles / 16 km

delightfully lively street with good record and bookshops but with none of the hassle sometimes encountered across the river.

Wander further south, through the quaint **Grace Court Alley** with its stable yards and classic brownstone town-houses, and you will reach Atlantic

Prospect Park in Brooklyn.

Avenue. After a few blocks you will find here ethnic restaurants, especially Middle Eastern ones on the border of South Brooklyn and the neighborhoods of Cobble Hill and Carroll Gardens. This is very sedate territory, relaxing and utterly safe for wandering through, but south of Carroll Street is the not-so-salubrious **Red Hook** neighborhood. Arthur Miller's *A View from the Bridge* is set in this part of Brooklyn and the ultra-rough world of *Last Exit to Brooklyn* was filmed here.

Central Brooklyn

Three locations – Park Slope, the Brooklyn Museum and Prospect Park –

are conveniently bunched together in Central Brooklyn. If you enjoyed the architectural grace of the Heights, then **Park Slope** offers more classic brownstone mansions built later in the century which boast the Georgian simplicity of the first half of the century combined with the Victorian fad – some would say neurosis – for ornate decoration and superfluous design details.

The main street, Seventh Avenue, is a busy shopping area where typical Brooklynites of varied races and budgets mingle in the stores and restaurants. Close by is **Prospect Park**, Brooklyn's answer to Central Park, which was created by the same architectural team of Olmstead and Vaux and considered by both of them to be superior in both design and execution. It managed to completely seal off the urban jungle outside and the pastoral idyll suffers from fewer organised activities than Central Park.

There is a small zoo, a 1912 carousel that bobs around at weekends, an 18th-century Dutch farmhouse, the **Lefferts Homestead**, that has conducted tours and off-beat gems like a Quaker cemetery where Montgomery Clift was buried! The broad expanse of the Long Meadow which offers a great view of the whole park is where people come to play and relax.

The **Brooklyn Museum** is well on its way to fulfilling the original intention – to become the largest museum in the world designed by McKim, Mead & White. Unfortunately, their original intention was arrested by financial problems which caused the construction work to come to a premature halt. The present expansion plans project well into the next century but the museum already houses enough exhibits to require repeated visits.

The Egyptian Galleries on the third storey are world-renowned and seriously rival similar exhibits in Cairo and London. The Assyrian reliefs in the Kevorkian Gallery is of particular interest. You will find wall sculptures depicting winged deities and griffin-headed genies, also ceremonial vessels and engraved silver bowls. There are also impressive displays of pre-colonial art from the Americas, Africa and the Pacific Islands as well as some of the best Ameri-

can paintings in the city.

A stroll through the neighboring **Brooklyn Botanic Garden** would do wonders to any nature lover. The Garden contain specialized gardens, including one with fragrances for the blind, three authentic Japanese settings with displays of bonsai, and a tribute to Shakespeare, incorporating 80 plant species mentioned in his plays.

Coney Island

In the days when the Dutch called it Konijn Island (Rabbit Island) it was a real island... but, over the successive years as the name became more and more anglicised, it evolved into **Coney Island**, with the sea silted up on one side. This made no difference to the millions of hard-working New Yorkers who, around the turn of the century, transformed a small elite resort into the most famous amusement location in the world. Its skyline, made up of roller coasters, a giant ferris wheel and the hugely successful *Parachute Jump*, became the paragon of beach resorts and every other amusement resort strived to emulate its appeal. The fact that the place started to decline only in the 1950s is proof of its enduring status. It was the Disneyland of its time, but there was no entrance fee, the food stalls did not hike up their prices and people of all ages found something to amuse them.

Today, it is still a functioning amusement resort and the crowds still hurl

Safety In The Suburbs

The outer boroughs contain some of the most dangerous neighbourhoods in the city. The 75th Precinct in Brooklyn, covering 5.6 square miles of streets, is currently the most dangerous area of the city with a murder occuring every 63 hours. With over 50 people killed in the first four months of 1993, the *New York Post* masochistically pointed out that this was higher than the number of fatalities in an entire year in Cincinnati. "This isn't a police precinct, it's a military base," remarked a precinct policeman, "There's gunfire here every night. There were nights in Vietnam when it was quieter."

However, from a visitor's point of view, such frightening statistics and lurid descriptions hold little significance. The area covered by the 75th precinct is a purely residential one and there is no reason why a tourist would be in or near this area. None of the places of interest in Brooklyn are close to this, the poorest area in the city where most of the killings are drug-related and involve members of street gangs. The dangerous parts of Brooklyn are clearly demarcated - Bedford Stuyvesant, East Flatbush, Buswick, Kensington, Crown Heights and East New York (where the 75th Precinct is) - and common sense dictates that one should stay away from these areas.

It is a similar story with the Bronx. There are dangerous parts of the borough in which it would be foolish to wander around in. But, no one does, certainly not New Yorkers who are not forced to live in this neighborhood, where even the police travel in pairs or threes for safety. Again, the neighborhoods with the high-est crime rates are clearly known - University Heights, Morris Heights, South Bronx, Bedford Park, Soundview - and the only one where outsiders are likely to find themselves is the South Bronx where the Yankee Stadium is located. But the stadium is only worth going to when a game is on and the subway is packed with supporters who provide one with safety because of their large numbers. A visitor just follows the crowd and returns home straight after the game. Travelling to a game on the subway, where the train comes up from the underground, provides despairing views of the devastating South Bronx ghettoes. In the 1970s, it became a common occurrence to burn down premises and collect on the insurance prior to leaving the area for good. The borough's infrastructure never recovered from this bout of self-destruction and subsequent underfunding by the authorities has meant that burnt-out shells of buildings still stand. Needless to say, there is little incentive for new businesses to move in and the vicious cycle of deprivation continues to trap hard-working poor families who still make up the majority of the neighborhood's population.

There is no good reason not to visit the places of interest in the outer boroughs. Sensible precautions are as valid here as in Midtown Manhattan. Do not walk down dark deserted streets at night, do not remove your wallet on the street or in a subway, do not ride in empty subway cars or wait at deserted sections of the platform. You are as safe in the suburbs as anywhere else.

themselves onto the three miles of sand every hot summer, but the thrill of being there depends on whether you can summon up a hefty dose of nostalgia. A sense of what it once was is helpfully created by the beguiling, run-down quality that Coney Island now exudes. Buy a cold beer and a hot dog and stroll along the boardwalk, take in the stalls and sights, and perhaps visit the Aquarium. Popular exhibits are sharks, whales, performing porpoises and electric eels. Go between May and October as some of these exhibits are flown to Florida for the winter. Then, wander down to Astroland Amusement Park where the dilapidated shell of a roller coaster evokes the past. Some of the old amusements are still working in the Park, for example the 1927 *"Cyclone,"* which

The Van Cortlandt Mansion stands in a preserved rural setting.

makes so much noise it seems that this roller-coaster has not been oiled in the last 50 years.

Further along is **Brighton Beach** (home to thousands of Russian emigrants) and stalls selling Russian dolls of Yeltsin and Gorbachev. The Russians arrived on US shores in the thousands during the 1970s when the beginnings of a thaw in US-Soviet relations was first discernible and sufficient numbers took up abode in Brighton Beach to cause the place to be rechristened "Little Odessa."

The Bronx

Contrary to popular Manhattanite belief, there are places in the Bronx worth visiting. The **Yankee Stadium** is hardly worth a visit if there is no game going on but if a match is on, especially if you are able to go with someone who knows the rules (See *Sports & Recreation*), then the stadium comes alive with exuberant supporters and cheerleaders.

The **Bronx Zoo** (see *Flora & Fauna*) is a major attraction at all times of the year. It is also ideal for children and big enough to contain most of your favorite animals. Across the road from the zoo is the **New York Botanical Gardens** with the Bronx River thrusting its way through the middle of what is left of the oak and hemlock forests that once carpeted most of the state.

The Gardens contain a horticultural museum, an immense rock gar-

The Bronx Zoo is home to 4,000 animals.

den, a rose garden, the unique **Lorillard Snuff Mill** and a large conservatory with equally large giant tropical plants. The conservatory, called the **Enid A Haupt Conservatory** is the centerpiece of the preserve, with its complex of ten connecting greenhouses. The conservatory is living proof of the influence exerted by the Garden's founders – **Dr Nathaniel Lord and Elizabeth Britton**, by their visit to Kew Gardens in England. At the right time of the year, the flower collection is magnificent.

Lovers of literature will be drawn to the melancholy **Poe Cottage** where Edgar Allan Poe lived out the remaining three years of his life. He moved into the cottage in 1846 in the hope that the fresher air would help his wife Virginia cope with the onslaught of tuberculosis. Her death bed and Poe's rocking chair look untouched in the cottage. Poe suddenly left his cottage only to be found dying in the street some time later. What exactly happened remains an unsolved mystery.

You would not find any mystery in the **Van Cortlandt Mansion and Museum**. This 1748 country house served as one of George Washington's headquarters while he was in New York. Standing in a preserved rural setting, the Van Cortlandt Mansion has nine rooms open to the public. It includes a cellar kitchen with a Dutch oven, and a parlor with a spinet and excellent Chippendale pieces.

A part of the Bronx that visitors

rarely penetrate into and yet quite safe and hospitable is **City Island**, which is tucked away on Long Island Sound off the eastern shore of the borough and accessible only by car or boat. This very traditional fishing community is an anomaly for New York City, as it hardly shares any of the Big Apple's characteristics and is all the more interesting because of this.

In the 19th century the people here made a living out of extracting salt from sea water. Nowadays, there is a highly specialised boatbuilding trade that has the *Intrepid*, a previous winner of the America's Cup. It is now moored here near a small nautical museum. A causeway connects the island with **Pelham Bay Park** which includes a pleasant stretch of beach and facilities for cycling and tennis.

The Queens

Queens has an image problem – not just for tourists! Residents of Manhattan and the other three outer boroughs share a condescending attitude to Queens and tourists who venture out to Brooklyn, Staten Island and even the Bronx tend to always miss this borough. There are places worth the journey, especially for those with an interest in the subjects covered. If nothing else you will be able to talk about a part of New York that most other travellers only pass through on their journey from John F Kennedy or LaGuardia Airports.

Before Hollywood was a household name, America's movie industry was based in Astoria and this is now where the **American Museum of the Moving Image** is located, at 35th Avenue and 36th Street. Tread in the footsteps of the Marx Brothers, Gary Cooper, Rudolph Valentino, Gloria Swanson – who all began their careers in the studios that now house this excellent little museum

As well as extensive film memorabilia and artefacts there are opportunities to listen to directors explaining some of their famous scenes, a mock 1920s movie theater and a very modern theater showing films. The temporary exhibitions are often enthralling but even without them, the museum puts Queens on the map. Anyone fascinated by the celluloid image will not be disappointed by their visit here.

The neighborhood of **Astoria** contains the largest number of Greeks outside Athens and the streets are full of Greek restaurants and coffee shops.

East of Astoria is **Jackson Heights**, a neighborhood with a different ethnic character which arises from its concentration of South Americans, (Colombians, Ecuadoreans, Argen-tineans and others).

Another neighborhood worth strolling through is **Flushing** – birthplace of the Quaker church. The **Quaker Meeting House** which was built in 1696 is the oldest workship house in Queens. John Bowne, the Quaker leader, bought the land nearby, where **Bowne House** stands, for a song in 1661.

Shea Stadium is where the Mets, a household name in baseball, plays to near-capacity crowds.

A second good reason for visiting Queens is the **Isamu Noguchi Garden Museum**. Isamu Noguchi left Japan for the United States when just a teenager, he later studied under Brancusi in Paris, and created this museum garden to house his sculptures.

Devotees of modern art and anyone familiar with his work, will gladly make the journey here. Buses come here from the Asia Society, at Park Avenue and 70th Street, but a more pleasant journey can be made from Roosevelt Island via the Roosevelt Island Bridge and after a 20-minute walk.

Major attractions for sports fans in Queens are the **Flushing Meadows-Corona Park** and **Shea Stadium**. The former is where the World Fairs were held in 1939 and 1964 and the park is worth wandering through even when there is no special event being staged. Some of the immovable exhibits from the 1964 Fair are still dotted around the place and its easily recognisable landmark is impossible to miss: a huge steel globe lifted 140 feet into the air which is surrounded by fountains and a pond. The **National Tennis Center** is based in the Park and the US Open is held here every year.

Staten Island

Before the Verrazano-Narrows Bridge went up in 1964, Staten Island was a rural backwater whose only significance

The Richmondtown Restoration highlights history from the early colonial period.

for many New Yorkers was that it provided a suitable destination for their daily tons of garbage. The bridge was then the world's longest suspension bridge, surpassed only in 1981 by England's Humber Bridge. Twelve lanes link Staten Island with Brooklyn's Belt Parkway.

After the bridge opened, the island's new importance as a convenient suburb was reflected in the rising price of property. But, do not dream of travelling by bus from Brooklyn across the bridge as the US$0.50 Staten Island ferry not only offers incredibly good value, but also terrific views of Manhattan and the Statue of Liberty.

From the ferry terminal, take the 107 bus to **Staten Island Zoo**. It is a modest zoo, but then again, its reptile collection could rival any in the United States; which includes specimens of every known type of rattlesnake.

While on the island, a trip to the **Richmondtown Restoration** should not be missed. This has been a project for the Staten Island Historical Society for forty years now and the results are showing. This was planned to be a museum village of more than 30 buildings ranging from the early colonial period right up to the 19th-century.

You can step into the **Voorleezer House**, built in 1696, making it the oldest American elementary school, or take a glimpse into Staten Island's past at the **Historic Museum**.

The **Jacques Marchais Center of**

*You'll be impressed by the biggest collection of Tibetan art
in the Jacques Marchais Center.*

Tibetan Art, where the biggest collection of Tibetan art in the Western world is on view, impressed the 14th Dalai Lama who came here in 1991 and most visitors should also not be disappointed. The exhibits are housed in a reproduction of a 1947 Buddhist temple, set amidst a hillside in the middle of a residential district.

Another of the island's treats is the **Alice Austen House Museum & Garden,** which contains a selection of her photographs of Staten Island life and a video that recounts the remarkable ups and down of Austen's life. Austen was born in the lap of luxury, discovered the pleasures of photography at the age of 10, later lost her entire fortune in the Wall Street Crash and would have died in a poorhouse were she not discovered by the editor of *Life* magazine who rescued her.

The **Snug Harbor Cultural Center** is the name given to a group of buildings put up by a charitable foundation, the "Sailor's Snug Harbor" which is dedicated to the provision of shelter for retired merchant sailors. Such a background cannot prepare one for the complex of Greek Revival and Italianate buildings that now house art exhibitions and musical performances.

Close by is the **Staten Island Children's Museum,** an imaginative venture that includes participatory events as well as various heuristic exhibitions. Conceived in 1899, it is the oldest children's museum in the United States.

New York City is the core of the Big Apple but as folks say, "you ain't seen it all!" The appeal of what is beyond the city should not be underestimated. You'll probably discover Long Island and Upstate New York to be the flip side of the coin, quietly complementing the dynamism of the city that never rests.

Begin your journey through museum-rich Long Island, continue up the much-acclaimed Hudson River into the Catskill Mountains, a magnificent portrait of nature's wonders. Next, the capital city of Albany beckons, then, be transported to another realm by the poignant wilderness of the Adirondacks. Down west, the ethereal beauty of the Finger Lakes District makes dreamers of us all. Further west, the mighty Niagara Falls roars its frothy welcome. Savor the bounty that awaits on the other side of the coin.

The Hudson River from Storm King Mount, near Newburgh.

Long Island & Upstate

251

Long Island

Getting from New York City to Long Island is made more convenient by the variety of

Bethpage Village, Long Island.

transportation available. You have the option of the Long Island Railroad which runs from Pennsylvania Station in Manhattan; you could simply hop into a car, travel along any of the four main highways and be refreshed by the greenery and scenic views as you cruise further east.

The boroughs of Brooklyn and Queens take up the western end of Long Island but further east the urban sprawl thins out. The South Shore has a long and smooth stretch of beach and sand. In the summer, it attracts day trippers from the city. **Long Beach** is the closest to the city and is the most crowded. Ferries also ply across to **Fire Island**, a thin spit of land that parallels the shore. New Yorkers that make the trip here

revel on the sandy beaches, with parties that last well into the early morning.

The North Shore has a different appeal, being made up of scraggy cliffs dotted with huge mansions built by the wealthy of yesteryear. Railroad fortune heir Howard Gould once owned **Sands Point Park and Preserve** in Port Washington, on which he built **Castlegould**, a medievally-inspired structure and Tudor-style **Hempstead House**, the estate's main residence.

Stony Brook, located in Suffolk Country, is a restored village of intriguing charm. Rebuilt by Ward Melville in the 1940s, it is aesthetically pleasing with its historic buildings, houses tied in with Revolutionary War activities, and tiny lanes and byways to delve into and explore. Stony Brook and adjacent **Setauket** village would make enough material for any of Tom Clancy's novels, for they are believed to be the cradle of American espionage. Here lived three patriots whose acts of derring-do are documented in the **Emmett Clark Library** in Setauket.

Ward Melville was also the motivating force in the establishment of the **Museums at Stony Brook**. On exhibit here are horse-drawn vehicles, including a handsome hand-painted coach, built in 1771. Also on display is a collection of evocative works of William Sidney Mount, a Long Island native.

The eastern tip of Long Island splits into the sparsely-populated **North Fork** and the trendy **South Fork** that thrives off its image as a playground for the rich. North Fork's residents thrive on farming and visitors are imbued with the contented and relaxed atmosphere when travelling along State 25. Here, fields stretch for as far as the eye could see and at roadside stands, local produce are widely available. Another distinctive feature of North Fork is the more than 20 vineyards that blossomed in the area.

Tours of the **Hargrave Vineyard** in Cutchogue are conducted daily from June to September. Enjoy a glass of complimentary wine in this vineyard that ferments and bottles its own selection of fine wines. Or if time permits, do a **Wine Trail**, that is, take a leisurely tour of some vineyards and wineries that strike your fancy. The oldest on the island,

Palmer Winery in Aquebogue, has designed a thorough self-guided tour where you can acquaint yourself with the entire wine-making process from grapevine to bottled product.

In Cutchogue, two musts are the **Peconic Bay Vineyards** – the vineyards just seem to stretch on forever; and **Bedell Cellars**, which many consider to make the best wines in Long Island. Want to step into the oldest English house in New York State? On the Village Green in Cutchogue, among lush rolling greens, sits the appealing, rather laid-back **Old House** built, yes, in 1649. The **schoolhouse** in the same complex has circa 1840 desks, blackboard and maps.

State 25 ends at **Orient Point**, where the visitor can catch the Cross Sound Ferry to New London, Connecticut.

Museums Galore

Long Island is also home to many museums that chronicle colonial history from three centuries ago. The **Garvies Point Museum and Preserve** in Glen Cove gives visitors insights on the Red Indian's way of life through dioramas and archeology digs.

In Cold Spring Harbor, the **Whaling Museum** stands, a monument to the trade that was once upon a time the mainstay of the island. You'll be impressed with the 400-piece collection of scrimshaw (engravings on teeth and bones of whales). Few can forget the name of Vanderbilt, and a tour of

Cadets on parade at the Military Academy at West Point.

Vanderbilt Museum is one of the highlights of stepping into Long Island. Located on Little Neck Road in Centerport, this museum contains one of the nation's largest planetarium and a 24-room Spanish Revival mansion that William K. Vanderbilt II created. If immersing yourself in the era where the first 'flying machines' were created appeals to you, the **Cradle of Aviation Museum** in Mitchel Field should not be missed. Included in its exhibits is a sister ship of *The Spirit of St Louis*, which took Charles Lindbergh on his legendary transcontinental flight to France.

Walt Whitman, one of America's foremost poets, was born in Long Island in 1816. Today one can visit his birthplace in **Huntingdon** and also the mu-

seum dedicated to him. Definitely a must on the visitor's itinerary is **Sagamore Hill National Historical Site** in **Oyster Bay**. The country home of President Theodore Roosevelt has been painstakingly restored to reflect his taste and its stately ambience will strike the visitor as soon as he enters the house.

Country Air

For ambience of a different kind, spend some time at the **Old Bethpage Village Restoration** to soak in the gentrified 19th-century farmer's lifestyle. Village life then is faithfully recreated in this active working community. Most of the buildings in this village which were

The Women's Rights Movement

If New York State was credited with being the cradle of the Women's Rights Movement, none deserved the credit more than Elizabeth Cady Stanton of Seneca Falls and Susan B. Anthony of Rochester. Their life-long leadership of the movement in the 19th century has earned them a place in American history.

They were two women, working closely together, who insisted on their rights, not despite the fact that they were women, but *because* of it. Both came from different backgrounds: Elizabeth Cady Stanton was from a truly aristocratic family, the Livingstons. After graduation from a prestigious women's college, she read law at her father's office. Susan B. Anthony's father was a liberal Quaker with strong anti-slavery sentiments. Financial crisis forced the young Susan and her sisters to earn a living by teaching. Self-support and personal independence were ideas that developed and became entrenched in her mind.

Both Stanton and Anthony spent their lifetime fighting for the fundamental truth that "men and women are alike" and the remedies they propose to address this oppression are, in the view of the all-male Legislature, fit to be thrown out of the House. Remedies they struggled to implement include the right to vote and sit on juries, equal inheritance rights when their husbands died intestate and a revised marriage code which subjected marriage 'to the laws that controlled all other contracts.'

Stanton is best-remembered for her fiery speech at Seneca Falls, on July 19, 1848. It was her very first lecture, but it was this very speech that, even if read today, would stir the soul of every woman. Six years later, in Albany, in her address to the Legislature of New York on women's rights, she demanded a revision of the state's legal code. This speech caused her father such distress that he threatened to disown her. But she persevered and throughout her entire lifetime (she lived till 87), committed herself to the woman suffrage movement.

Anthony's concern with the woman wage-earner helped propel 19th-century feminism forward. An 'honorable dependence' was what she demanded – a wage adequate to support a respectable life, and work that led to dignity and self-respect. Her ideology of "free labor" became a feminist thrust, just as political democracy was to Stanton. But, like Stanton, she was intensely vocal about women's right to vote. When she was arrested in November 1872 for charges of 'illegal voting,' this arrowed her focus on 'suffrage is the right of citizenship and all persons, including women, were citizens.'

On February 15, 1906, Anthony celebrated her 86th birthday. On hearing the tribute President Roosevelt paid her in his message, this crusader of women's rights commented, "One word from President Roosevelt in his message to Congress, is worth a thousand eulogies of Susan B. Anthony. When will men learn that what we ask is not praise, but justice?"

transported from other areas in Long Island were built in the 18th and 19th centuries. **Powell Farm**, standing where it was built over a century ago, will endear you with its lively stock of farm animals. Bethpage 'villagers' sometimes stage festivities in their attempt to depict 19th-century life.

On South Main Street in **Southampton**, is a 17th-century saltbox colonial house reputed to be the oldest in New York State. It is located in **Halsey Homestead** where the visitor can also catch a glimpse of period furnishings of that era. Also in Southampton, on Meeting House Lane, the grounds of the **Parish Art Museum** come alive with the frenzied activity of craft demonstrations during the summer months. Converted into a simulated village lane,

Sunnyside, home of Washington Irving, Tarrytown.

visitors are treated to a display of techniques of essential trades of the colonial period.

Following the Hudson

The valley of the Hudson River is easily accessed for a day trip from New York, either by car along Route 9 or by train or bus. The further away from the city, the more picturesque the valley becomes, which probably explains the reason for the emergence of the Hudson River school of landscape painters in the 19th century. Painters like Thomas Cole and Frederic Church were particularly enamored with the Catskill Mountains and viewing their canvases in the Met-

ropolitan Museum of Art mentally prepares the visitor for the panoramic views that encompass him. But the exquisite beauty of the mists and mountains has to be encountered firsthand. Not only would it dazzle the imagination but a total exhilaration of the spirits is experienced by many.

"The Most Delicious Bank"

The first place to stop at, about 25 miles out of the city, is **Tarrytown**, where a number of restored buildings make a stopover well worth the time.

The famous chronicler of dear old Rip Van Winkle, none other than writer Washington Irving, was captivated by the beauty of the river that he built his estate here. His *Sleepy Hollow* stories drew much from the region and the site he called "the most delicious bank in the world for Dozing, Dreaming and Reading." Thackeray and Oliver Wendell Holmes must have concurred for they were frequent guests. His country manor, aptly named **Sunnyside**, remains one of the most charming estates on the river. A guided tour would acquaint the visitor with how this first great New Yorker of letters lived. Also consider buying a joint ticket that gives entry to the other restored homes in the vicinity.

A mile away is **Lyndhurst**, an American castle, decorated Gothic style, a complete contrast to the snug and modest Sunnyside. What Lyndhurst commands, however, is a view of the Hudson that one can only dream of. The most extensive of all restoration work around the land of *Sleepy Hollow* is on the **Van Cortland Manor**, with an 17th-century airiness that would definitely please the eye. George Washington was a frequent visitor to the family, who were erstwhile supporters of the Revolution. This stone and wood Dutch manor house was restored in the 1940s by the Rockefellers.

West Point

The name fascinates, sometimes awes. For isn't this the alma mater of the great American heroes – Grant, Lee, MacArthur, Eisenhower and Patton. The United States Military Academy at West Point was *the* place where the top US officers were bred.

West Point is best seen on a self-guided tour. You can pick up a guide at the visitors center which helps to orientate you around the campus. There are about 4,400 cadets enrolled and one activity to catch each day happens at 12.20 p.m. The whole school lines up and you can watch freshmen and sophomores being quizzed by their seniors on, not only military know-how, but surprisingly by, the contents of the *New York Times*.

Poughkeepsie

Located about 10 miles from the Taconic Parkway is **Poughkeepsie**. Derived from *Uppuquipising*, an Indian word meaning "reed-covered hut by a little water place," Poughkeepsie's 'reed-covered hut' has been molded and remolded but recently, urban renewal has given way to preservation of several "historic" centers. One of these is the **Bardavon Opera House**, built in 1869, now restored to its original splendor. You can also pay a visit to **Locust Grove**, home of Samuel Morse, the man who invented the telegraph. Or tour the campus of **Vassar College**, founded in 1881 by local magnate, Matthew Vassar.

Hyde Park

A few miles upriver lies **Hyde Park**,

Vanderbilt Mansion, Hyde Park.

which begins the **16-Mile Historic District**, containing estates which have been home to many of the great names in American history. Foremost among them is **Springwood**, where Franklin D. Roosevelt was born and raised. Springwood is a remarkably evocative place that successfully recreates the sense of domestic bliss that the popular president and his wife Eleanor enjoyed here. Famous personages like Queen Elizabeth and Winston Churchill have been guests at Springwood. Nearby is the **Franklin D. Roosevelt Library Museum** which houses the memorabilia of Franklin and Eleanor Roosevelt. After Franklin Roosevelt's death, his widow retired to **Val-Kil**, a few miles away.

Your entry ticket would also permit you to visit the **Vanderbilt Mansion**, a veritable palace, which commands an unbelievably spectacular view of the Hudson and the Catskills.

Northwards, you'll pass by sleepy **Staatsburg** and then on to **Rhinebeck**. You must definitely reserve for a stay in **Beekman Arms**, America's oldest inn. Yes, it's a rambling old white washed building, with a lobby that looks older that Time itself, but beneath this ambience, you'll find rooms tastefully decorated and interesting fare in its atmospheric dining rooms.

Take River Road, west of the center of Rhinebeck and a few interesting sites greet you as you cruise along. Just before Annandale is **Montgomery Place**, built in 1804 by the widow of Revolu-

The view down form Olana was Federic Church's inspiration.

tionary War hero General Richard Montgomery. Beyond the turnoff for Tivoli, in the town of Clermont is the **Clermont State Historic Site**. Seven generations of the Livingston family have lived in the mansion since 1730, right until 1962 when it turned state property. It was a Livingston who was New York's chancellor before and after the Revolution, a Livingston who was one of the five men who drafted the Declaration of Independence and again a Livingston who negotiated with Napoleon for the Louisiana Purchase.

In **Olana** further north, prepare yourself for an absolutely divine experience. As you look out of Federic Church's mountaintop home, you'll understand what inspired his famous landscape works that hangs in the Metropolitan Museum of Art.

The Catskills

The Indians of yesteryear held these mountains in awe. They called these peaks 'Onteora' which translates to 'The Land in the Sky.' Since then, these picturesque peaks never failed to capture men's imagination.

The city of **Kingston**, on the west bank of the Hudson, serves as a gateway to the Catskills. From there, its only 10 miles to **Woodstock**, a delectable village that is home to **Byrdcliffe**, a 1,500-acre arts colony. You'll also find the nation's oldest chamber music concert

Olympic ski jump at Whiteface Mountain, Lake Placid.

series here, an undertaking that began as early as 1916.

Shandaken, in the heart of the Catskills, tempts many a traveller with its famous local restaurants offering exquisite French burgeois cooking, an experience as satisfying as can be had in Paris or Lyons. Up north, the **Hunter Mountain Ski Area**, in the middle of the village of **Hunter**, is definitely a magnet in winter. Its slopes – a 1,600-foot vertical drop, offers one of the best skiing in the Catskills.

In summer, you can still traipse up Hunter Mountain, in the **Hunter Mountain Skyride**. Prepare yourself for the longest, highest chair lift and if that is not enough, heart-stopping views to render you speechless.

Albany

You'll find **Albany** sophisticated yet endearing, the oldest permanent settlement in the 13 colonies, yet retaining a *joie de vivre* that renders it at once charming and livable. Commanding your attention is the **Empire State Plaza**, a towering office complex solidly planted in the town's center. In the Plaza, the more prominent buildings are **Corning Tower**, with an observation deck on its 42nd floor; the **New York State Museum**, where dramatic audio-visual reconstructions plunge you into the world of an Adirondack windstorm or maybe the New York Metropolis; and the **State Capitol**, with its much talked-about

Thoroughbred racing at Saratoga Springs.

"Million Dollar Staircase." You simply have to climb it to appreciate the intriguing maze of stairs that lend it its name.

Downtown Albany is dotted with graceful 18th-century architectural residences. Some of these private mansions are open for public viewing. Foremost among them is **Cherry Hill**, a pretty name for a comfortable mansion that was held by the descendants of Philip Van Rensselaer for over 200 years after he built it in 1787. The 1761 **Schuyler Mansion** was where the cream of society stepped into, to see and be seen, back in the days of Philip Schuyler, one of the city's earliest leaders and a leading socialite in his time. George Washington and Benjamin Franklin were frequent visitors to his home.

Saratoga Springs

Perhaps one of the factors that contributed to Albany's growth was an old resort 44 miles north of it. Only for a month each year, millions of dollars change hands. August is when high-rolling, cigar-chewing gamblers converge on the stands of the famous racetrack of Saratoga Springs. Built in 1864, The **Saratoga Race Course** has the honor of being the oldest active thoroughbred racetrack in the United States. If reflecting on its glory satisfies you, pay a visit to the **National Museum of Racing**.

But gambling isn't all there is to the Springs. Saratoga Springs is justifiably famous for its spring waters, a secret that the Iroquois Indians guarded until 1767. Then came Sir William Johnson with his lingering war wounds, who had the good fortune of being a close friend to the Native Americans. He resorted to this old-fashioned remedy out of sheer desperation but nevertheless, the spa was born. If you want to sample the spring waters, avail yourself of the visitor's pamphlet, 'The Springs of Saratoga.'

The Adirondacks

It's just a four-hour drive from New York City, but **Adirondack Park**, though not forbidding, compels the visitor with its mighty wilderness. History buffs would be interested to know that the Adirondacks were the last area in New York State to be surveyed (perhaps due to its inaccessibility) and they were originally known as the Peruvians (named by the early French settlers, with visions of probably the lost treasure of the Incas.)

Lost treasure has not been found in the Adirondacks as yet but the area has its own jewels. One of these is **Lake George**, a crystal-clear lake fed entirely by spring water. Many consider this the 'queen' of American lakes. The events that happened here in 1757 formed the basis of the classic of James Fenimore Cooper, the *Last of the Mohicans*. Immediately south of Lake George village, you'll find the entrance to **Prospect**

Mountain. Head up the 5 1/2-mile scenic road to its summit and a spellbinding view awaits you.

Northwards, downhill skiers dot the slopes of **North Creek. Gore Mountain Ski Area** with its 41 downhill trails, is one of the main attractions, the other is the 15-mile stretch of rapids that is rated among the nation's top ten **white water rafting areas**.

About 20 miles west, you'll come across **Blue Mountain Lake**, hometown of a rare jewel, the world-renowned **Adirondack Museum**. Its exhibits as well as its amospheric views have earned it a place as one of the world's best museums.

If being the site of the 1932 and 1980 Winter Olympics is a measure to go by, **Lake Placid** will please any Olympic hopeful. At nearby **Mount Van Hoevenburg**, glide along the same trails used in the 1980 Games.

Lake Placid was also graced with the presence of Dr. Melvil Dewey, the same man who originated the Dewey Decimal System but whose contribution to Lake Placid was his founding of the Lake Placid Club. If not for the club, the nation would be unaware of the joys of winter sports. The village is now official Olympic training center and Dr Dewey has his name firmly entrenched in the history of Lake Placid. Lake Placid was also the grounds of abolitionist James Brown's futile struggle to arm southern slaves. You'll find his farm and grave site two miles south of the town.

Nine miles from Lake Placid lies

Lake Saranac. The author of *Treasure Island* once resided in a cottage here in 1887. Here, he penned most of the *The Master of Ballantrae* when he was recuperating from tuberculosis. Today, if he had visited, Robert Louis Stevenson would not fail to recognise his atmospheric old cottage, preserved in its original condition.

For those keen on experiencing more of what the Adirondack wilderness offer, there is much literature to be gleaned from. Hiking, canoeing, camping, fishing – all these plus a full range of outdoor activities can be enjoyed right within Adirondack Park itself. Perhaps there is treasure awaiting, treasures that free the mind and calm the spirit.

The Finger Lakes

Delectable would be a word to describe this district. You'll find hills and valleys, lakes and waterfalls, in short, views that inspire. Venture first into the town of **Skaneateles**, a delightful community that radiates a comfortable sense of well-being. A few miles west is **Auburn**, named from a line in Goldsmith's poem, "Auburn, loveliest village of the plain."

Fifteen miles westwards, **Seneca Falls** earned a place in American history as the birthplace of the women's rights movement. In 1848, a very brave woman, Elizabeth Cady Stanton, drafted a document, more so a Declaration, that set every women's heart afire and every men's hackles arising. You can view this controversial document in the **Women's Rights National Historical Park.**

North of Lake Seneca is **Geneva**, which holds its own as the world's lake trout capital. A visit to this vintage town would not be complete without a tour of **Rose Hill**. A splendidly restored Greek Revival mansion, its grounds are exquisitely laid.

You'll love the gardens at **Sonnenberg** in **Canandaigua**. Unbelievably luscious, it has been described by the Smithsonian as "one of the most magnificent late Victorian gardens ever created in America." The late-Victorian mansion, though, is worth a miss for the **Granger Homestead** and **Carriage Museum**. It's impressive and visitors are transported to the era of horse-drawn vehicles by the museum's 50 carriage exhibits.

Rochester

Rochester sits adjacent to a waterfall with a 100-foot drop, but that doesn't explain it being called The Lion by the Falls. Of course it's the falls that fuelled early sawmills and nurtured America's first boomtown, but it was the foresight of men like George Eastman that earned the city its title of 'Lion.' Eastman stamped the city with his genius and one could hardly think of Rochester without thinking of Eastman's invention and marketing of roll film and the Kodak camera. But important personages here

The Niagara Falls

Viewing Niagara Falls from the New York side.

On the west of Niagara River is Canada, on the east there is New York State. The River would just be another natural boundary if not for a vast torrent of water that cascades thunderously down. Niagara Falls draws millions of tourists every year and two cities, also called Niagara Falls, one Canadian, the other American, are built around the Falls.

Niagara Falls has two cataracts, the Horseshoe Falls and the American Falls, both joined by Goat Island in the center. Here's a few tips on how to appreciate this 'eighth wonder of the world':

1)   Go to Goat Island. This is where the river approaches the lip of the falls so you can feel the heady excitement on hearing the water pound against the rocks.

2)   An elevator on Goat Island will take you to as near as you can to the foot of the American Falls, where the Cave of the Winds is. Because you'll definitely get wet, admission fees include the loan of a thick yellow slicker.

3)   Take a ride to Prospect Park Observation Tower, go up to the upper-level decks, and see for yourself the panorama that can only be described as 'awesome.'

4)   Or, the most exciting of all, take the elevator down Prospect Park for a boat ride on the *Maid of the Mist*. Getting wet is only half the fun. As the boat nears the base of the Falls, your adrenalin pumps at full speed, you'll feel as if you're just moments away from being sucked into this white misty whirlpool and the boat suddenly turns round. It's as close to the Falls as you can ever get.

would begin a list of Who's Who. Here lived Susan B. Anthony, who together with Elizabeth Cady Stanton in Seneca Falls, worked tirelessly for the women's rights movement. Bausch and Lomb began their optical glass company here. Hiram Sibley started his Western Union here. And escaped slave Frederick Douglass edited his abolitionist newspaper in this very town. The city throbs with life but that doesn't mean historic consciousness is put aside in the name of progress. On the contrary, Rochester has a number of important historical buildings.

Students of photography will find the **International Museum of Photography at George Eastman House** an eye-opener. For the less initiated, studying the displays will help them appreciate why photography is regarded more an art than a skill. Not only is there an

George Eastman's house in Rochester.

elaborate collection of photographic equipment but prints and photographs of famous masters in this 50-room Georgian mansion. Take also a tour of **Kodak Park** where more than 28,000 people work in the 170 buildings in this self-contained city.

Incidentally, the name Kodak was thought of by Eastman himself. He liked the letter 'K', and he wanted an unmistakable, easy to pronounce trademark and after trying out combinations between an opening and concluding 'K,' he hit upon Kodak.

The **Margaret Woodbury Strong Museum** is a draw for its more than 20,000 dolls. This museum, a gift from the Rochester philanthropist, contains artifacts of Victorian family life - right

from the 19th to the early 20th century.

Today, **East Avenue** is Millionaire's Row. Before its era, the west side was where the wealthy built their Victorian and Greek Rovival houses. The **Campbell-Whittlesey House** stood its ground since 1835, complete with original furniture intact.

If you want to soak in more of the 19th-century flavor, south of Rochester is the Genesee Valley, where you'll find **Genesee Country Village and Museum**, a reconstructed version of a mid-western town. You will feel just as if you have stepped into the 19th century as you stroll the streets and watch the village denizens assume roles of their forbears – carpenter, cobbler, blacksmith, even a general store proprietor.

Experience the magical fairyland ambience of the Wintergarden.

Western New York

Western New York isn't only the **Niagara Falls**, which of course, has been bringing in millions of tourists each year, ever since that fateful day in 1678 that Fa-

ther Louis Hennepin cast his eyes upon it and declared that "the Universe does not afford its parallel."

A whole city prospered around it and Niagara Falls, the city that is, attracts its own share of limelight. The **Wintergarden**, a 10-storey tropical

An oasis for art and culture – the Chautauqua Institution.

greenhouse is a must on your itinerary. Stroll beneath 12-meter tall palm trees and savor the glories of over 200 varieties of methodically-labelled plants. If you happen to visit during winter, the 44-day long **Festival of Light** creates a magical fairyland effect when the Wintergarden sparkles in the stark white night.

Mention is also due to **Buffalo**, a town that steered its way through the Civil War. The caricature of the fast-drawing gunslinger probably had its origins right in this town, when 93 saloons and 15 dance halls called the shots in the 19th century. Nowadays it's more sedate in Buffalo, the streets lighting up only during celebrations like the St Patrick's Day Parade and the Polish-originated Pulaski Day Parade.

Buffalo too was the town where President William McKinley was shot while attending the Pan-American Exposition in Delaware Park in 1901. Teddy Roosevelt, at 43, became America's youngest President a week later. He was sworn in as the twenty-sixth president of the United States in the house of Ansley Wilcox, a prominent attorney. Today, the **Wilcox House**, in the **Allentown** district, has been restored and visitors can also tour the museum in the house which recapitulates the dramatic events of September 1901.

South of the Wilcox House on Delaware Avenue is **Trinity Episcopal Church**, a late 19th-century church famous for its Louis Tiffany stained-glass windows. And you might consider strolling over to 472 Delaware Avenue, where the creator of Tom Sawyer and Huckleberry Finn used to keep house. The stable of **Mark Twain's home** is now Cloisters restaurant.

Southwest of Buffalo is **Chautauqua Lake**, home of the **Chautauqua Institution**. In 1874, Methodist minister John Heyl Vincent and industrialist Lewis Miller began a training center to spread culture and the arts, Chautauqua sent bands of performers and artists across the country. As a result, "Chautauqua" came to mean a summer series of lectures and concerts.

Cuisine

New York is a "world city" and the food alone reflects this fact. It is no exaggeration to say that virtually every type of cuisine is available and, while almost every block will have one or two recurring types of eateries, if you know where to go there is nothing that cannot be both tasted and enjoyed. There are more restaurants in New York than anywhere else in the United States and every year an average of 50 places might close – only to be replaced by a greater number of new ones! New Yorkers love food and will discuss the subject with passion and eloquence. They also read with avid interest the food reviews in dailies, magazines and books and as institutionalized in *The New York Times* by Bryan Miller who has been writing about the city's

Stuffed turkey ad cranberry jelly mold.

269

restaurants since 1984. His comments are so influential that a proprietor once offered him US$10,000 to persuade him to visit his restaurant on a certain date and with the assurance that at least two stars would be awarded. Also worth consulting is the *Village Voice* a weekly newspaper that always carries short reviews of new places and old favorites. There is also a well established annual restaurant guide called *Zagat*, which might be too comprehensive for the short stay visitor. More useful, and free, is the restaurant guide booklet put out by the Visitors Bureau. Places are listed by location and type and a price rating accompanies each short description.

Breakfast

Part of the essential New York lifestyle is breakfast at a coffee shop, between 6:00 - 11:00 am, where one is seated at a table or (preferably) at a bar rubbing shoulders with another citizen, oblivious to each other. Virtually every block in the city has at least one coffee shop, run by Greeks in the Midtown area, and Hispanics in Upper Manhattan. The choice is wide enough to try something different each morning. A standard item is two eggs served with bread and beverage but no one actually asks for this without specifying the format. Most basic is how the eggs should be prepared: boiled, poached, scrambled or fried and, if fried, whether "sunny side up" (fried on one side only), "over" (both sides),

"over easy" (both sides fried lightly) or "over hard" (both sides for a longer period). The bread can be plain toast, toasted bagels, or an English muffin – all served with little plastic containers of flavored and fairly unpalatable *jelly* (jam). Even your cup of coffee can be regular or decaf, served with skimmed, semi-skimmed milk, cream or nothing

The epitome of dining – caviar and wine!

at all. While you are eating, keep an ear open for the various requests which more seasoned customers make and try one out the next morning.

Two eggs a day is none too healthy but there you can always order pancakes with lashings of syrup, hash browns (potatoes fried with onions), a smoked mozzarella sandwich.

Fast Food

Hamburgers were invented in Upstate

Sushi bars may be found in many areas in the city.

New York, in a small town called Hamburg. This culinary event occurred when two brothers ran out of meat for the standard pork pattie and improvised with minced meat and flavorings. The hot dog came from nearby Coney Island. However, as both types of fast food can be found the world over, it would be worth giving them a miss in New York and trying something new. Wherever there is an office block, a mobile stall standing on a corner will not be too far away and some of the least expensive fast food is readily available. Try a *falafel* (a vegetarian dish consisting of mashed chick peas served with tahini sauce, salad, mayonnaise or whatever else the vendor happens to have sandwiched in a soft pitta bread). Delicious, it is never priced at more than $3. The same stall, or one nearby, will probably sell pretzels, as well as meat sandwiches.

The Jewish influence accounts for some of the tastiest fast food around, such as *bagels* (rings of hard bread) that are served toasted or served up with embedded cinnamon and fruit and *blintzes* (crepes filled with cheese or fruit and eaten with sour cream).

Fast food is available for lunch or dinner, though a lot of the food served in delis is fresher during the middle of the day. Whatever is on the menu is available *to go* (takeaway) or *to stay* (eating in), the only difference being that a takeaway will be packed with plastic cutlery and napkins. The size of sandwiches will come as a surprise and should not be dismissed as too light to alleviate pangs of hunger. They are about four times bigger than the average European sandwich and packed to overflowing with whatever you chose to have them filled with.

Fast food joints dispensing burgers, tacos, pizzas and chicken are found everywhere. Chinese restaurants often have a takeaway service and, like many of the pizza bars, will deliver free to local hotels.

Brunch

This hybrid of breakfast and lunch has become part of the New York weekend lifestyle. Special menus, usually with fixed prices, are available from just before noon to about 4:00 pm. They are often advertised in restaurant windows and in city newspapers. Apart from lots of food, brunch provides the best opportunity to see New Yorkers relaxing with their families. The food is often standard American steaks or *lox* (smoked salmon) and a mainstay is *eggs benedict* (poached eggs and ham atop a split English muffin, covered with hollandaise sauce). Get an edge on fun with your Sunday brunch by beginning with one or two cocktails.

Ethnic Restaurants

Jewish or Japanese, Afghan or Ethiopian, French, German or Italian, Thai,

Typical shopfront of a Chinese restaurant.

Indian, Pakistani, Chinese – or Ameri can cuisine – has specialist restaurants catering for most budgets ranging from the very reasonable to the heartstopping, expense-account-only-type. Vegetarian cuisine is more difficult to find, although this is not a serious problem if you eat fish. The competition for customers has noticeably increased since the economic depression of the late 1980s and standards of food and service are better than at any time in the past.

Japanese and French restaurants tend to be the most expensive, Chinese and Indian the least pricey, but this is only a generalisation and will vary according to the location, ambience and quality of the food. Restaurants in the financial district around Wall Street are

Pick Of The Best

For excellent Chinese food served amidst the hustle and bustle of Midtown Manhattan, the **China Grill** is hard to beat. It is situated at 60 West 53rd Street (tel: 333 7788) in the lobby of the same towering building that houses CBS. An Oriental atmosphere is evoked by jade-colored walls and a marble floor inlaid with quotations extracted from the journals of Marco Polo. Service is frenzied and erratic but remember that this is Manhattan's business district and the fast pace is all part of the scene. Waiters come rushing out of the kitchen area with dishes of guaranteed quality – grilled shrimp, barbecued salmon, grilled chicken with tempura onion rings, lamb chops with shiitake – all reasonably priced. Main courses cost between $17 and $25 for lunch or dinner. It is necessary to make reservations.

At 214 First Avenue, between 12th and 13th Streets, **Elvie's Turo-Turo** is definitely worth seeking out for an informal Filipino meal en-joyed anytime between 11 am and 9 pm. "Turo-Turo" is a traditional restaurant term in the Philippines that means "point, point" but there is no onus on the customer to do this as explanations of the various dishes are readily provided. There are usually 15 main selections, plus a daily special and typical Filipino dishes like *pork adobo* (meat marinated in soy sauce, vinegar, garlic and bay leaf before being grilled) and *pancit* (stir-fried egg or rice noodles served with bits of chicken and shrimp). The price range in this restaurant is between $4 to $8.

Dining with a view of Manhattan's exciting skyline in the background is one of the highlights of any trip to New York and if you would like the view to change, head for **The View** at the Marriott Marquis Hotel at Times Square (tel: 398 1900). It is the city's only revolving rooftop restaurant and serves an eclectic range of American, French and Italian cuisine. It is a huge and flamboyant and while the food is not exceptional in quality, the atmosphere is. Do not expect a quiet romantic atmosphere because you will be in Times Square in New York. Bring your camera.

The **Union Square Cafe**, in East 16th Street near Fifth Avenue (tel: 243 4020), is a restaurant worth patronising if the previous paragraph describes the sort of place you would rather avoid. It is not advertised in tourist literature and most of its regular diners would be aghast if it ever was. It is currently "in" with knowledgeable New Yorkers who want first class food served with a bit of panache and reasonable prices. It is a fun restaurant for diners; the sort of place where you would not normally mind waiting for the dishes because people or table watching is pure entertainment.

Top class restaurants include **Chanterelle** (tel: 966 6960) at 6 Harrison Street in TriBeCa. While reservations are essential for dinner, the fixed lunch is always good value considering

American fare of grilled barbecued ribs with apricot sauce.

frenetic at lunch time but tend to lack atmosphere at night whereas SoHo and Greenwich Village really come alive at night and their eateries exude energy.

how excellent the food is. Still holding its own as the undisputed home of the finest French food in the city is **Lutece** at 249 East 50th Street. Reservation (tel: 752 2225) are best made weeks in advance if you want to be sure of a table. At **Rao's** (tel: 534 9626) reservations are actually made months in advance because the tables are few in number and the Italian food is simply heavenly. Big names frequent this cozy corner restaurant at 455 East 114th Street.

Equally top-of-the-range, but easier to book a table at, is **The Quilted Giraffe** at 15 East 55th Street close to Madison Avenue (tel: 593 1221). Very expensive and very post-nouvelle cuisine, the food is stylishly served and has won the acclaim of food critics who look for more than mere imagination.

The **Bridge Cafe** (tel: 227 3344), at 279 Walter Street down near the South Street Seaport, is a highly esteemed restaurant that doesn't take reservations despite its popularity among connoisseurs of good food. It goes back to the early 19th century, making it a hundred years older than the respected **Oyster Bar and Restaurant** at the Grand Central Terminal (tel: 490 6650). There is nowhere better in Manhattan for superb seafood served quickly and in a unique setting.

Currently one of the hottest establishments among the rich and famous is **Le Cirque** at 58 East 65th Street (tel: 794 9292). It's a place to spot a celebrity while being assured of excellent food. Reservations, again, have to be made in advance. At **Four Seasons** (tel: 754 9494), at 199 East 52nd Street between Lexington and Park Avenues, the diners may not be instantly recognisable but they will be powerful figures and the food, while not as expensive as Le Cirque is equally good. In the same class, and also requiring formal dress, is **Arcadia** (tel: 223 2900) at 21 East 62nd Street. The food is eclectic but invariably satisfying.

Little Italy, unsurprisingly, has plenty of that country's restaurants but tourists frequently outnumber locals very often which is reflected in the prices. East

Village, by comparison, is pleasantly eclectic in its ethnic range and some of the city's least expensive Japanese and American restaurants can be found there.

With over 15,000 restaurants in Manhattan alone, there is no urgency about visiting the outer boroughs although the various ethnic communities located in these boroughs serve genuine specialities created without the tourist in mind. Caribbean and Italian eateries are common in Brooklyn while Queens has a unique concentration of South American restaurants. Harlem too has its own culinary attractions. The **Jamaican Hot Pot Restaurant** at 2260 Seventh Avenue near 133rd Street (Tel: 491 5270) serves genuine curried goat and other traditional Jamaican dishes while **Sylvia's** at 328 Lennox Avenue, located between 126th and 127th, (Tel: 996 0660), has been tempting customers for a number of years now. The soul food served here has been enjoyed by famous guests such as Jesse Jackson and Winnie Mandela whose photographs adorn the walls. Reservations are essential if you intend to make a special trip to the restaurant.

Drinks

Any decent restaurant will serve wine and quality French establishments will boast impressive wine lists. Native Californian wines are good value for money and can accompany almost any type of

The Tavern on the Green has been a permanent fixture in Central Park since the 1930s.

food. The more expensive wines are known by their label. However, more economically priced bottles are categorised and marked by the kind of European wine they resemble – Chianti or Burgundy for instance. On the other hand, American beer is not to every-body's taste because of its low alcoholic content. This is partly because it is drunk as a thirst quencher. A typical New York home will have cans of American beer in the fridge in the same way that Europeans might keep milk or soft drinks. For a higher alcoholic content you need

The Jockey Club

The **Jockey Club** at the Ritz Carlton is a typical New York hotel restaurant but what makes a visit there distinctive is a cocktail or two sipped in the company of Norman Bukofzer, the chief bartender at the Jockey Club Bar. If he ever decided to leave, the hotel and its restaurant just might follow! Bukofzer is the quintessential fast-talking Manhattanite, with a brand of humor drier than any flinty Chardonnay, and a drink at the bar positioned within earshot of his anecdotes is far better entertainment than some of the stand-up routines performed in comedy clubs.

to ask for an imported brand of beer. Incidentally, whisky will not be Scotch unless specifically asked for, instead you will be served bourbon or American whisky brands. Spirit measures are usually freely poured by the bartender and are generous by comparison to their European equivalents. Cocktails are great fun and come in countless forms that can be experimented with during the Happy Hours that usually operate in bars from between 4 and 7 pm.

Bars are as ubiquitous as eating places and have a very different atmosphere, depending on their location and function. Places in the Upper East and Upper West Side are often singles bars, Greenwich Village and Chelsea abound with gay and lesbian bars. But there are also standard bars where anyone can have an ice-cold beer or cocktail. Committed drinkers take up residence on a bar stool and stack their coins and notes in front of them for the barman to have easy access to as and when is necessary. Irish-style bars are dotted throughout the New York landscape and while many double as decent steak and seafood restaurants, others are basic watering-holes that attract a mainly male clientele. The more common chains are **Blarney Stone** and **McAnn's** which fortunately are not forbiddingly raunchy and often good fun.

W ork hard and play hard" is an unspoken ethic for many New Yorkers and nowhere is this more apparent than in the field of sports, be it as participants or spectators. Take Doc Rivers for instance, one of the key players for the New York *Knickerbockers* basketball team. In a typical season he suffers a broken nose, dislocated shoulders, sprained ankles, bruised ribs and pulled muscles. At the end of a game he will often be loaded down with ice to stifle the pain but when he helps his team to win it is always a case of mind over matter: "Don't need icebags when you win like that. You lose you need a whole lot of icebags." Doc Rivers is definitely an inspiration in his field and the Knicks will need more players of his calibre if they are going to win.

The Knicks play at Madison Square Garden while New York's other professional basketball team, the *Nets*, play at the Meadowlands Sports Complex in New Jersey. Supporters of each team studiously ignore each other and any sports shop worth its salt will ensure a plentiful stock

Yankee Stadium.

Sports & Recreation

279

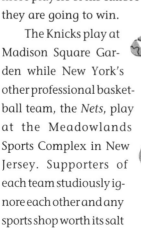

of both sets of supporters' caps. Basketball is an engaging game to watch, with no complicated rules to mystify the non-American and it can be as much fun to watch in a neighborhood park as in one of the stadiums. Amateurs play the game throughout the year but the pros are on show from winter until spring.

Basketball, despite being such a graceful and elegant sport, arouses tremendous passion and many of the injuries that players receive are not accidentally inflicted. Nevertheless, attending a game of basketball as a spectator – or any other sport for that matter – runs none of the risks that sometimes accompany soccer games in Europe. It is part of the American way of life for fathers to take their sons to watch a game of baseball or football and while the atmosphere can get noisy and rowdy, there is always a friendly spirit amongst the crowds.

American Football

American football is the most fun to attend. Big games have big bands which march across the stadium and there is the added "razzmatazz" of enthusiatic cheerleaders. The game itself might seem to the uninitiated to be a brutal battle of muscle against muscle but behind the titan crashes of player against player lies a highly complicated set of rules. When the season is on, between August to the end of December, it is difficult to be in New York and be unaware of this

sport. Most of the games are televised and no one in their right mind would ever suggest changing the channel to watch something else. The season entails a series of play-offs to determine which teams go on to the Superbowl to play the ultimate game of the year on the third Sunday of January. There is no chance of getting a ticket to the Superbowl game and even trying to see one of New York's teams in a play-off can be a daunting task. Of the city's two teams, the *Giants* will remain the most popular as long as they keep their tremendous form, relegating the *Jets* to second although both have devoted sets of fans.

Baseball

American football may be unique to the United States but it resembles the game of rugby in some respects and has a theatricality that makes it instantly spectator-friendly. The same cannot be said of **baseball**. It is the most quintessentially American sport and any visitor with an elementary grasp of the game's arcane rules and mystical appeal will endear himself to the otherwise thick-skinned New Yorker. The season kicks off in April and culminates in October with the misnamed World Series. As a spectator sport, the game is quite different from football or basketball, with a fairly sober audience who often seems to be more interested in their beer and popcorn than the unfolding drama of

American Football at the Giants Stadium.

the game.

However, this is deceptive because the game is closely observed and analyzed and has a complex language code to describe the various shots. As with football, New York's two teams are household names – the *Yankees* and the *Mets* – and aficionados form their allegiances when children. The *Yankees* are the older team, and the legendary Joe Di Maggio once played for them, while the *Mets* only emerged in the 1960s after the famous *Brooklyn Dodgers* and *New York Giants* left New York. The *Mets* have been performing badly in recent years and one hard-nosed columnist has predicted that if they do not improve, then Shakespeare in the Park will attract bigger audiences!

Spectator Sports

Boxing, the sport that first became synonymous with Madison Square Garden, may be leaving its traditional New York base after more than 110 years. The Garden has featured many of the all-time greats such as Jack Dempsey, Joe Louis, Sugar Ray Robinson, Archie Moore and Muhammad Ali, but in recent years competition for bouts has come from Atlantic City and the Garden's administration has become sensitive to recent US Senate hearings which focussed on boxing's alleged control by organised crime. Nowadays, **wrestling** is a more common event at Madison Square Garden and though it hardly counts as a

Rules Of The Game

Baseball

In the top corner of a diamond-shaped field the batter confronts the pitcher positioned 60 feet and six inches away, who hurls a ball towards him at upwards of 90 mph. If the batter swings with his bat but fails to hit, or if the pitcher's ball reaches a designated strike zone (anywhere between the batter's knees and his chest) and the batter fails to swing at it, it is a *strike*. Three strikes and the batter is out. On the other hand, if the pitcher does not reach the strike zone with the ball and the batter does not swing, a *ball* is called. Four balls and the batter is allowed a free *walk* to the first base where he becomes a *runner*. The team that is not batting will position its defenders at each of the bases as well as spread them out across the field. They make up the *fielding team*.

The *batting team* tries to score the maximum number of runs by having their players circle the three bases that make up the other corners of the field. A batter is *played out* if the fielding team catches a ball which has been successfully hit before it touches the ground, if the base is touched before the player reaches it, or if he is tagged between bases. If the batter strikes the ball and circles the bases before being played out, he has scored a *home run*. Any other runners on base when he hits the ball can also score a run each. Passions run high when runners are on all three bases and the maximum four runs are scored which is a *grand slam*.

Each team has nine members and a game is made up of nine innings, divided into a *top* and a *bottom*. The visiting team always plays first – the *top*, and the home team plays last – the *bottom*. The nine innings will take up to three hours to complete.

American Football

The playing field, 300 feet by 160 feet, is divided into five – yard sections which give the pitch its characteristic gridiron appearance. The objective is to score *touchdowns*, similar to a *try* in rugby, but a team's movement towards the touchdown line has to be achieved by a series of *plays*. A team must cover 10 yards of ground within four *plays* or lose possession to the opposing side. One *play* is concluded whenever the player with the ball is tackled to the ground or the ball goes off the pitch. A commentator's summary of the state of play "third and two" for example – means that the game is in its third play and two more yards need to be covered.

If it seems unlikely that the team in possession will cover the 10 yards, at "fourth and eight" for instance, then the team may attempt to kick the ball between the posts and over the crossbar. Known as a *point after*, the team will only gain one point as opposed to six for a touchdown and three points if they score, a *field goal*, which is when they manage to kick the ball between the posts. A team squad has more than 40 members, though only 11 are allowed on the field at any one time. This allows for special teams to specialise in either attacking or defense.

sport it can be tremendously funny to watch the antics of the combatants and the hysteria of the more gullible sections of the audience.

The game of **ice-hockey** is in reality far more violent than the wrestling seen at Madison Square Garden. As a sport it offers a unique combination of speed,

Ice hockey between the Rangers and Pittsburg.

theatricality, skill and brute force and New York has two teams who love to hate each other. The *Rangers* play at Madison Square Garden while their arch enemies the *Islanders* hail from New Jersey.

The premier **tennis** event of the year is the "US Open Tennis Championships," held each September in Queens. Ticket prices are terribly costly and advance booking are not only advisable but often essential. The less prestigious tennis matches are hosted at Madison Square Garden.

Participant Sports

There are plenty of sporting activities available in the city and sometimes you just need to give the shopping excursions and museum trips a break. If you are tempted to imitate those glamorous **roller-skating** daredevils who slide and glide past you and the traffic, there is a safe way to do so. Keep off the traffic

roads unless you want to bring your holiday to a fatal end. Instead roller-skate through the paths in Central Park, Riverside Park, or East River Park. Inexpensive skates can be purchased at any of the Toys-R-Us stores. Central Park is also ideal for **cycling**, especially at weekends when many of the roads are closed to traffic. The **Loeb Boathouse** in the park hires bicycles out by the hour or day and is conveniently situated.

A very popular activity amongst people of different ages and incomes in all five boroughs are the games of **pool** and **billiards**. A pool table is commonly found in bars and the usual pool hall convention is to sign your name on the nearby blackboard or leave your coins on the side of the table. There are also clubs with tables for both games and while some are plush and polished-looking, others are suitably grimy and smoke-filled. The clubs do not have controlled membership but the facilities vary, some are just no-frills pool halls while others serve fresh coffee 24 hours a day.

In winter **ice-skating** appeals to New Yorkers as an exhilarating escape

The New York Marathon

The Marathon is New York's greatest mass spectacle and as an event held in a world city, it is suitably international in character, with representatives from around 100 countries competing. Previous winners of the race have come from Italy, Poland, Tanzania, Kenya, Norway and Mexico and the marathon runners are amazingly diverse in all sorts of way. A man aged 93 finished the 1991 marathon and contestants in wheelchairs, on crutches, or who are blind, also enter.

And being New York, the event attracts both the weird and the wonderful. A man from the Midwest ran wearing an outfit made of pennies; an individual calling himself SuperScot competed in a tartan kilt attached over a Superman costume. An entrant jogged with angel wings attached and a halo over his head; an English runner who played "When the Saints Come Marching In" on his clarinet virtually non-stop for the entire race; a man in a tuxedo carrying a tray with a bottle of water and a glass (who acually passed the finishing line in just over three hours) and a participant who ran the race backwards.

Some fairly unusual groups also participated in what is far more than just a marathon. Two English runners wanted to highlight the plight of the Sumatran rhinoceros so they ran while wearing a rhino costume. The "Centipedes" are a group who are not out to protect the insect world, instead they just stringed themselves together and ran like that for fun.

The New York Marathon began in 1970 with four laps run around Central Park by 127 runners. It attracted little publicity and there were no television cameras to film the 60 or so exhausted athletes who managed to complete the race. The winner crossed the line in two hours and 31 minutes, about 24 minutes slower than the current men's record holder, Juma Ilkangaa of Tanzania. But losers are celebrated just as much as the winners and, for a number of years, there have serious attempts to record the *slowest* possible time to complete the event. One Barry Lee Weisberg went to a lot of trouble to take seven hours and 25 minutes to complete the course, he was dressed as Santa Claus and stopped off whenever possible for tea and bagels, but was sorely disappointed when two other competitors trotted past later than him and behind the race officials!

The most memorable late finisher was a 1986 entrant named Bob Wieland who had lost both his legs in Vietnam but entered the marathon on a board with wheels and his hands to propel himself along. It took him five days to finish but the official finishing line was kept open until he had crossed and collected his medal.

In 1979, the race was expanded to all five boroughs and now the event is a major media event that attracts over 50,000 participants. The idea of a city marathon has spread around the world but New York is where it all started.

from city blues. Central Park has two outdoor rinks and an indoor rink where you can skate at any time of the year. It is located on the 16th storey.

If you are taken by the idea of riding through Manhattan on horseback like the police do, then it is possible to do so, minus the uniform and the threat of traffic. Central Park is one of the better locations but it is also worth traveling out to Brooklyn to watch the

trials which are held around Jamaica Bay.

Despite the popularity of **bowling** in America there is now only one bowling alley left in Manhattan, a fact probably dictated by the astronomical cost of property. However in the other boroughs, alleys are easy to find and the Yellow Pages in the *New York Telephone Book* lists them. The price of real estate definitely explains why there are no golf

Sports Data

Baseball: The *Mets* play at the **Shea Stadium** in Queens (tel: 718 507 8499) while the *Yankees* have their own **Yankee Stadium**, West 161st Street and River Avenue (tel 293 4300).
Basketball: The *Knicks* play at **Madison Square Garden** (tel: 563 8300) and the *Nets* at the **Brendan Byrne Arena** in New Jersey (tel: 201 935 9000).
American Football: Both the *Jets* and the *Giants* play at the **Meadowslands Sports Complex** in New Jersey.
Pool & Billiards: Chelsea Billiards, 54 West 21st Street, located between Fifth and Sixth Avenues (tel: 989 0096). A fairly plush establishment with over 50 tables. The **Julian Billiard Academy**, 138 East 14th Street, between Third and Fourth Avenues (tel: 475 9338), is not as swish as the name might suggest but it has a good atmosphere and newcomers are welcome. The **Billiard Club**, 220 West 19th Street, between Seventh and Eighth Avenues (tel: 206 7665), is fairly sedate and unlike most clubs, there is no alcohol available.
Cycling in Central Park: The **Loeb Boathouse** (tel: 861 4137).
Ice-Skating: The two rinks in Central Park are the **Lasker**, near Fifth Avenue and 110th Street (tel: 397 3106), and the **Wollman**, at 61st Street and Fifth Avenue near the zoo (tel: 517 4800). Both places, from November through April, have a tremendous atmosphere and attract a mix of show-offs, ghetto-blasting teenagers and complete novices. The all-year indoor rink is the **Sky Rink**, at 450 West 33rd Street (tel: 695 6555).
Horse-Riding: The Central Park location is handled by the **Claremont Riding Academy**, 175 West 89th Street and Amsterdam Avenue (tel: 724 5100), with rental by the hour and lessons available for children. The Brooklyn location is managed by the **Jamaica Bay Riding Academy**, 7000 Shore Parkway (tel: 718 531 7000).
Bowling: Bowlmor is in Greenwich Village at 110 University Place (tel: 255 8188) and stays open till the early hours of the morning.
Golf: Courses in the Bronx (tel: 822 4711), Brooklyn (tel: 718 965 6511), Queens (tel: 718 520 53110 and Staten Island (tel: 718 422 7640). The computerised, simulated course is at the **Midtown Golf Course**, 7 West 45th Street (tel: 869 3636).

courses left in Manhattan but this does not mean that you will get no chance to practice.

There are courses all over the outlying boroughs and there is also a simulated course in the city where you can actually tee-off and then watch a microchip calculate its progress on screen. A round of golf for two people will take well over an hour and you can choose your own championship course.

Soccer

The kind of football that is played everywhere else in the world – soccer – has never really caught on in America, although there have been repeated attempts to introduce the game. All the more wonder then if a World Cup tournament will take place in the United States and some of the games will be played the Meadowlands Sports Complex (also known as Giants Stadium). No one is quite sure what the impact of holding a competition in the United States will have on people's attitude to the game. Maybe tickets to a game will be easier to obtain, but on the other hand soccer may gain slow momentum and interest could pick up later.

Nightlife

The nightlife in New York is rich and varied enough to suit all tastes; the problem however is one of making choices from among the multitude of possibilities. Wherever you plan on going for a night out, always call ahead and check on times and prices.

Comedy

Looking down on Times Square.

The sharp one-liner is the quintessential mode of expression for the New Yorker, and comedy in the city is devoted to fine-tuning this elegant and witty art.

Sometimes the lines come so quick and fast that the out-of-towner has a hard time just hearing the words, let alone catching the nuances of meaning or understanding what topical event or personality is providing the butt of the joke. Notwithstanding, the infectious laughter is caught and you find your-

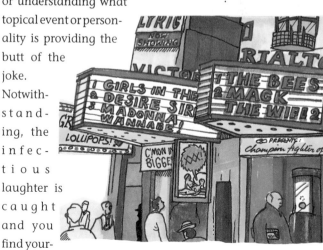

Dusk in the Big City

It is not only surprising what can be seen and done during the hours of dusk but even more pleasant is the enhanced quality of aesthetic enjoyment during the day. A twilight museum visit, for instance, avoids the crowds and allows for a special kind of concentration that arises just from being there at an unexpected time. The **Metropolitan Museum of Art** opens until 8:45pm on Friday and Saturday and offers the bonus of a string quartet and a bar on the balcony overlooking the Grand Hall. The *Iris and Gerald B Cantor Roof Garden* is always worth visiting for its sculptures but viewing Manhattan while in the glow of the setting sun is a rare aesthetic luxury. The uptown **Guggenheim** is open until 8:00 pm every evening (except Thursday) and the museum restaurant stays opens until 9:00 pm so dinner can be enjoyed afterwards.

As a musician's career advances up thescale of recognisiton he will start to perform later and later whereas the dusk hours are associated with the up-and-coming and the plain unknown. This does not make music at dusk intrinsically inferior, just different. The pressure is off the performers and the audience during the traditional happy hour and the result can be a pleasantly relaxed mode. The big bonus is the absence of a stinging cover and minimum drinks charge. Try the **Red Blazer Too**, at 349 West 46th Street (tel: 2623112), that features jazz sessions from around 6 pm to 8 pm at weekends or **CBGB**, at 315 Bowery near Bleecker Street (tel: 982-4052), also during the weekend. CBGB has a reputation to uphold as the place where tomorrow's music will be discovered. New wave and grunge is "old hat" here and only the truly experimental or deeply esoteric will be heard. For something more satisfying familiar, **The Back Fence** is hard to beat and the music starts at 6:00 pm. This Greenwich Village shrine, at 155 Bleecker Street near Thompson Street (tel: 4759221), has been around for 40 years and crowds pack the place later in the night. Turn up early for hassle-free enjoyment of golden oldies and 1960s nostalgia.

Dusk is also the time for good value meals at restaurants that offer special menus between, from 5:00 pm - 6:30 pm. The stylish **Tatou**, at 151 East 50th Street (tel: 7531144) offers a US$20 menu with some very fancy dishes — deviled crab cake with cilantro mayonnaise — and the place turns later into what is currently one of the city's better discos.

For about the same price the Hudson River provides the setting for a meal at the **Hudson River Club** at 250 Vesey Street in the World Financial Center (tel: 7861500). Watch the evening start to unfurl with a glass of wine and a meal enjoyed in the glass-fronted dining room that overlooks the river.

For a genuinely cultural setting the *Book-Friends Cafe* serves a variety of teas with scones and sandwiches from the main room of this quaint Dickensian-looking bookshop. The shop, at 16 West 18th Street in Chelsea (tel: 2557407), specialises in rare editions from 1890 to 1940 and every other Wednesday old-fashioned tea dances are accompanied by live music from 7:00 pm onwards.

---

self laughing anyway and, besides, you quickly acclimatise yourself to the pace and begin to catch the jokes.

Listening to the comedian's anecdotes is even more fun because along the way you pick up precious little insights into how New Yorkers perceive the world, their fears, hopes, aspirations and anxieties.

For instance, anecdotes that involve street crime are a recurrent motif and they reflect the insecurity that is inseparable from living in a city like New York. A typical story tells of a white man walking down the street when a Puerto Rican teenager bumps into him and politely apologises. The man quickly checks his pocket and discovers that his

One of the many Broadway theatres.

wallet is missing. The man runs after the teenager and confronts him angrily, "Wallet! Now!"

The boy hands over a wallet and the man resumes his walk, feeling pleased at his quick reactions. Back home the man finds his wallet on the table where he had left it before he left his house!

One of the well established comedy clubs is **Caroline's** which has only recently moved into a new state-of-the-art club at 1626 Broadway, near 49th Street (tel: 7574100).

The night's program always begins with an up-and-coming but fairly unknown talent, often nervously aware of his or her big chance before a discerning audience, followed by a "hot" headliner

comedian whose reputation is already well established.

Dangerfield's, at 1118 First Avenue (tel: 593 1650), is a very popular East Side comedy club owned by the celebrity comedian Rodney Dangerfield who opened his club in 1971.

The man himself now rarely appears but top contemporary comedians are always featured and there are often surprise appearances of big name guests from film and television programs like Johnny Carson's "Tonight Show" or "Late Night with David Letterman."

On the West Side is **Stand-Up New York** at 236 West 78th Street in Broadway (tel: 595 0850). This club is different in style from both the above.

The stage is deliberately dressed-

An East Village pub.

down and the club feels like the sort of place where Lenny Bruce, the legendary comedian of the late 1950s and early 1960s whose scathing social satire touched a raw nerve in the nation, might have appeared.

An average night will see a mixture of new faces and celebrity stars and at weekends there are often special drop-in guests like Robin Williams or Elayne Boosler. On a weekday the cover charge is only US$7 and a light dinner menu is available.

Cabarets

A night at a cabaret – dinner and a show featuring singers followed by dancing –

is best enjoyed by bringing a hefty dose of nostalgia fuelled by movie images of George Raft, champagne buckets and tragic young singers backed by a swing band. And while you do not have to dress up in a white dinner jacket or know the words to the songs of Cole Porter, this is the kind of atmosphere created at the best of the cabaret clubs.

The **Rainbow Room** on the 65th floor of the Rockefeller Plaza (tel: 632 5100) carries on in the grand tradition of the legendary Art Deco club that first opened here in 1934.

A massive million-dollar renovation has made it the "hot" place to be and it is currently the most ritzy and glossy cabaret club in the city. The dancing starts with the music of the 1940s,

New York's lively disco scene.

progresses to the 1950s and 1960s and ends up with a fast disco pace. Dinner is expensive, ranging from US$35 to US$50, but this is what you pay for the superb atmosphere and quality acts. Reservations are essential.

Be sure to visit the **Rainbow Promenade** for its breathtaking views of Manhattan at night. If this does not convince you that New York is the most exciting city in the world, then nothing else will.

The **Russian Tea Room** (tel: 265 0947) was once famous for the celebrities who turned up for dinner, however, it now enjoys a reputation for staging cabaret shows that are so good that they make up for the mediocre quality of the dinner.

The guests that appear are very varied and range from the occasional stand-up comedian to a star singer or a well known group, so it is best to check if you are choosy about these matters.

In Greenwich Village the **Asti**, (tel: 741 9105) boast a tradition of singing waiters that goes back to its opening in 1925, so it is not just cashing in on a trend! There is no entertainment charge, entrees start at around US$15, and the singing gets going at 6:30 pm – anything goes and diners are invited to sing along in-between bites of pasta.

Nightclubs and Discos

The difference between a cabaret and a

nightclub is not always as clear-cut as more and more nightclubs are offering dinner, although it is not compulsory whereas at a cabaret club it is.

The **Oak Room** at The Algonquin (tel: 840 6800), is a firm favorite that is unlikely to pass out-of-fashion and patrons can definitely be assured of quality performances from whoever is gracing the stage.

In the interests of equality it is only fair to mention **Chippendales**, located 1110 First Avenue near 61st Street (tel: 935 6060).

This is the place where women enjoy the all-male "musical with muscle." Essentially a striptease act, with hints of parody only coming from sections of the audience, the doors of the club open at 6:30 pm with the show beginning 90 minutes later. The admission charge is US$20, with an extra charge for the front row – seating for patrons is always given on a first-come, first-served basis.

Discos are back in fashion in New York and while many of the supper clubs and cabaret shows end the evening by playing disco music, there are also dedicated disco clubs where you can dance till you drop.

The **Limelight** at Sixth Avenue and 20th Street (tel: 807 7850) was once a church, hence the very large dance floor with space enough for three bars. The Limelight boasts of having the very latest sound and laser systems so it attracts a good crowd of ravers.

Another place with an interesting setting is **The Tunnel**, at 220th Street and 12th Avenue (tel: 244 6444), where the acoustics benefit from being heard in a converted old railway tunnel (complete with tracks).

Jazz Clubs

Jazz started in the southern states, developing from ragtime and blues in the 1920s, but its cultural home is now New York and there is nowhere else in the world that effectively provides such an evocative atmosphere.

Whatever the form of jazz – fast tempos, agitated rhythms of bebop, light unforced playing of cool jazz, classic Dixieland, the combination of Western art music with jazz known as third stream, or improvisation – it is best heard at night in a not-too-sophisticated club setting.

To enjoy present day greats as well

The world famous production of A Chorus Line.

as to know that almost every big name from the past has trod the stage here, there is nowhere better than the **Blue Note** at 131 West 3rd Street between Sixth Avenue and MacDougal Street in Greenwich Village (tel: 475 8592).

Shows start at 9:00 and 11:30 pm and the minimum cover charge varies according to the line-up. The audiences here are fervent afficionados of jazz and the musicians here know this. So, expect the best.

Another club with a sense of history is the **Village Vanguard** at 178 Seventh Avenue near 11th Street (tel: 255 4037). It is now into its 60th year and can be relied on for mainstream jazz featuring quintets up to big bands of 20 or even more players.

Monday nights always feature the resident Vanguard Jazz Orchestra and there is flat entrance fee which never exceeds US$15 plus a minimum drinks charge of US$10 at weekends. You'll find the Village Vanguard extremely good value for money.

For jazz enjoyed in comfort, **Bradley's**, at 70 University Place (tel: 228 6440) is hard to beat. The music gets serious after midnight and good news for late, late diners – meals are served until 2:30 am. Another jazz club plus restaurant is **Cajun**, situated in trendy Chelsea at 129 Eighth Avenue near 16th Street (tel: 691 6174). The music is nearly always Dixieland jazz and the name of the club is the same as the type of cuisine served.

Pop/Rock/Soul

Under this category are bands that can appear almost anywhere. International concert tours usually perform their New York gigs at one of these prestigious venues like Carnegie Hall, Radio City Music Hall, the Lincoln Center or Madison Square Garden.

Lots of small clubs open and close within months but in-between they attract post-punk groups ranging from the abysmal to the genuinely creative and the *Village Voice* is the most reliable guide to what's-on and where. One well established club that is unlikely to move from its new premises at 45 West 21st Street, between Fifth and Sixth Avenues, is **Tramps** (tel: 966 4225). Rhythm and blues is the hallmark music of this popular club but folk, rock and even country music, make an appearance.

Creole and cajun food is available at reasonable prices, helping to make Tramps a reliable location for a musical night out.

For something more adventurous, the **Bottom Line**, at 15 West Fourth Street near Washington Square (tel: 228 7880), has a policy of introducing up-and-coming new names (Bruce Springsteen played here as an unknown singer) alongside the eminently successful. A place that is always worth a call to see what's happening is **Sweetwater's** at 170 Amsterdam Avenue (tel 873 4100) which features a mix of salsa, Latin combos, straight rock pop and comedy.

Dining and dancing in the Wintergarden.

Occupying an entire block on West 34th Street at Herald Square is **Macy's**, an excellent place to begin acclimatising oneself with New York's shopping scene. There are 10 floors of merchandise, ranging from household goods and foodstuffs in the basement to serious designer fashion garments at equally serious prices. Macy's is a place to wander around in and become lost – the store directions are hopeless – check prices, assess the range of whatever you are interested in and probably return later after you realise that prices and service at Macy's are as good as anywhere else.

Macy's, the biggest store in the world.

Department Stores & Malls

Just around the corner from Macy's the glitzy facade of **A&S Plaza** beckons. Compared to the shopping malls of Hong Kong and Singapore it is a little disappointing but there is a fair spread of small specialist stores dealing

New York's variety of merchandise range from luxury goods at boutiques....

in computer software, sports gear, clothes and trendy boutiques.

Bloomingdale's, on Third Avenue at 59th Street, is a shopping shrine for New York's consumer pilgrims who come here regularly to see the latest in trendy clothes, jewelry and cosmetics. Flourishing a Bloomingdale bag makes a statement about one's aspirations towards serious and stylish shopping and a visit here can be a lot of fun even if you leave with only US$20 worth of jewelry.

The other major department stores are mostly found along Fifth Avenue but there are important distinctions to be made between them. **Lord & Taylor**, at 39th Street, is the least prestigious but nonetheless worth one's while for the quality of its merchandise. It also sports

a wider range than any of the other Fifth Avenue stores. The sportswear department is renowned but household goods and classy clothes are also available and worth looking over.

More then 10 blocks further up is the inimitable **Saks Fifth Avenue** which has eight storeys of highly desirable items, with the emphasis on top-of-the-range designer clothes for women, men and children. The store has a reputation as *the* place for celebrities to shop but on an average day you are more likely to notice the heavy security than any famous stars.

Assuming you still have money in your account, it is worth walking seven blocks up to 57th Street where **Bergdorf Goodman** successfully manages to

.....to toys at FAO Schwarz.

present itself as the ultimate in gracious shopping. Marble floors and crystal glass provide a suitable setting for all the top designer names – Givenchy; St-Laurent and their ilk. On the other side of the road is an annexe for male consumers of high fashion.

Equally exclusive, but more hip, are two other stores that have cornered the market in trendsetting for the rich and adventurous. **Henri Bendel**, on West 57th Street between Fifth and Sixth Avenues, is a cross between a department store and a very upmarket mall. The building's interior is made up of a series of boutiques dedicated to clothes, cosmetics, shoes and household goodies. **Barney's**, at Seventh Avenue and 17th Street, is nominally a department store but also functions as a highly prestigious clothes store.

For the widest range of fashionable garments it is worth leaving behind the glossy precincts of Fifth Avenue and making it down to Chelsea where Barney's is open late every weekday night, until 9:00 pm on Mondays through Thursday, and until 8:00 pm on Fridays.

Antiques

For fine art, antique furniture and *objets d'art*, there are clusters of treasures waiting to be discovered in shops dotted around Greenwich Village, SoHo and the Flatiron District (Fifth Avenue be-

Cultural Shopping

Serious collectors of art and antiques will head straight for the galleries of SoHo (see the chapter on SoHo) and the specialist antique stores (see the chapter on Shopping) but for more general cultural shopping, the most interesting and reliable shops are those attached to the museums and galleries in the city. It is not necessary to possess a ticket to enter the shops so they can be visited independently of your trips to the museums.

The uptown **Guggenheim** shop, at Fifth Avenue and 89th Street, has a small shop on the top floor but the ground floor shop has a larger selection. Not surprisingly there is a large collection of books on modern art, while all the jewelry and watches – ranging in price from US$20 to US$500 – is as eminently elegant as one would expect from a shop belonging to the Guggenheim. Decorative and functional plates carrying modernistic Miro-type designs are very attractive, as are the Kandinsky-colored scarves, the ultra-smart ties and cuff-links.

The **Metropolitan Museum of Art** shop, located further down Fifth Avenue at East 82nd Street, has a treasure trove of art reproductions for sale. A 9th-century Ibex letter opener (US$35), an early Cycladic figure dating from 2800 BC (US$90), a 5th century mounted archer

from ancient Greece ($150) or – the ultimate fake – a copy of a Roman copy of a Greek original of Aphrodite in cast marble which is priced at US$185 and comes "complete" with the missing head! The shop sports irresistible collection of jewelry that faithfully reproduces pieces from the 12th-century Islamic world and the Spanish Renaissance (the originals are housed within the museum). Books and videos on art, a thousand and one postcards, posters, a whole section on small gift ideas and Tiffany-stained glass are also available. The museum also has a smaller shop outlet in the Rockefeller Center.

The shop at the **Museum of Modern Art (MOMA)**, on West 53rd Street between Fifth and Sixth Avenues, is disappointing by comparison; mostly stocked with books, postcards and obvious items like umbrellas and shopping bags carrying the museum's illustrious name. But, the **MOMA Design Store** next door has items for everyday use which successfully combines functionality with style.

The stretch of Broadway between City Hall and Lafayette Street has a small number of interesting art and antique shops that do not advertise themselves in the tourist literature. There is nothing particularly classy in the shops but the prices are very reasonable.

tween 14th and 23rd Streets). Bargains can be hunted down at the weekend flea markets at 25th Street and 6th Avenue, or Broadway and Grand Street in SoHo.

The **Manhattan Art & Antiques Center**, at 1050 Second Avenue between 55th and 56th Streets, is the best place to head for if you like all your shops under one roof. The Center is a shopping mall with over a hundred antique shops located on three storeys. Prices range from the reasonable to the expensive, but rarely the stratospheric, and there is a wide choice of silver, enamel, china, brassware and crystal.

Serious collectors will be delighted by the number of **specialist antique shops**, many of which will be found between East 70th Street and East 90th Street off Madison Avenue.

Many of these specialise in imported English antiques while others, such as the **Chinese Porcelain Company** at 822 Madison Avenue, are devoted to the East. The Manhattan Art & Antiques Center has its share of specialist shops, like **Flying Cranes** which is dedicated to Oriental arts or **Laura Fisher** which has the largest selection of antique quilts in the city.

Boutique assistant pampering a client.

Jewelry

The big department stores sell jewelry at fixed prices. But, for something more special, there are a number of illustrious shops along Fifth Avenue that may prove irresistible. **Cartier** is located at Fifth Avenue and 52nd Street, **Harry Winston** is further up at 56th Street, and one block higher at 57th Street is **Van Cleef & Arpels** and **Tiffany & Co**. All these stores sport a range that begins with inexpensive costume jewelry and goes right up to extraordinary gold, diamonds and assorted precious gems that only millionaires can afford. Tiffany & Co is especially worth visiting because this famous shop also sells crystal, china, silverware, stationery, toiletries, scarves and handbags. Dedicated jewelry lovers will relish the opportunities afforded by **47th Street**, located between Fifth and Sixth Avenues. Virtually every shop on both sides of the street is packed with trays of every imaginable type of jewelry with two stores in particular specialising in diamonds: **47th Street Diamond Center** and **Diamonds by Rennie Ellen**. Diamonds are cut and polished on the premises and with some gentle negotiation, very competitive prices can be obtained.

Bookshops

The large number of bookshops in the

Casual chic and casual rich — at Tiffany's.

city reflect the fact that New York is the publishing center for the whole of North America. The largest chain of stores belong to **Barnes & Noble**, which now boasts over a dozen outlets and an admirable policy of discounting all their books. Their branch at Fifth Avenue and 18th Street has been designated the world's largest bookshop by the *Guinness Book of Records* but for sheer comfort and elegance it is difficult to beat their new outlet on Broadway and 82nd Street. The store has its own coffee shop and seats are provided near the shelves

million books, that one book you have always wanted is probably here; the problem is whether you have sufficient time to find it! Prices start at under US$1 and almost new books, usually reviewers' copies, sport hefty discounts of 50 percent and more.

Specialist bookshops are tucked away in various corners of the city. Fans of mystery novels will enjoy **Foul Play Books of Mystery and Suspense**, with stores on Eighth Avenue at 12th Street in Greenwich Village, and on Second Avenue at 76th Street. The longstanding **Gotham Book Mart**, at 41 West 47th Street, has a renowned collection of literary books, especially titles not easily found elsewhere and the noticeboard announces literary functions going on in town.

Discount Shopping

New Yorkers love bargains and **Daffy's**, on Fifth Avenue at 18th Street and on Madison Avenue at 44th Street, has been providing this service for many successful years now. The store's clothing and accessories are not the irregulars and seconds that usually fill off-price clothing shops; the outfits which offered at discounts of 50 percent are genuine designer items, just a year or more old. There is also a very helpful refund service for purchases returned within a week.

Just as famous as Daffy's for designer items at budget prices is

on which patrons can relax and read their books before deciding whether to purchase them. It is open until 11:00 pm Monday through Thursday and until midnight from Friday through Sunday.

For secondhand books there is nowhere bigger and more cluttered than the **Strand Book Store** on Broadway at 12th Street. With a stock of over two

Store window, dressed to attract the passersby.

general shopping but on Sundays, vehicle traffic is barred and the street transforms itself into a bustling bazaar. Apart from heavily discounted clothing, there are also bargains to be found in shoewear and accessories.

Speciality Shops

New York has countless speciality shops retailing items that would never find their way into the department store. For example, at the **Grafton Shoppe** at Reidy's, at 22 East 54th Street, it is possible to purchase Irish imports that would otherwise require a trip across the Atlantic. "James Bond" type shops, specialising in high-tech personal security systems, include the **Quark Spy Center** at 537 Third Avenue and the **Counter Spy Shop** at 444 Madison Avenue located between 49th and 50th Streets.

Loehmann's, with outlets in Queens and Brooklyn and the flagship store in the Bronx, Broadway and 236th Street, Riverdale, which can be reached on the 1 subway to 238th Street. It is well worth the trek for anyone determined to return home with something really special bought at an affordable price.

For more designer labels at discount prices and lots more besides, leave a morning free, preferably on a Sunday, for a hectic session at the **Orchard Street Market**, located between Canal and East Houston Streets.

On weekdays the shops are open for

High-tech equipment for the modern New York household, ranging from the bizarre to the functional, is sold at

Shopping Tips

Know your shopping areas: Uptown is pricey and exclusive; Midtown has the major department stores; Downtown has the arty shops, boutiques for the budget-minded, and shops catering for the eccentric and bizarre. Famous streets like Fifth Avenue and Broadway are long enough to offer one different shopping experiences. If for instance you start at 42nd Street, Fifth Avenue is made up of tacky souvenir shops but rapidly progress upmarket as one walks northwards and by the world famous department stores and jewellers are the more typical streetside shops. Between First and Fifth Avenues along 57th Street is another conglomeration of prestigious clothiers and jewellers.

At the bottom end of Broadway, in the Financial District, is a varied collection of stores catering to tourists and city workers alike. But way up at the Columbia University end, from 110th to 115th, bookshops predominate, while 10 blocks to the south, general shops to serve the area's multiracial community are quite safe although rare for tourists to shop in.

Different areas have different shopping hours as well. In Midtown and Uptown, stores tend to open around 10:00 am and close at 6:30 pm. Department stores are likely to be open on Sundays and open until 8:00 or 9:00 pm on Thursdays. In Greenwich Village and SoHo not much opens until after 11:00 am, closing around on average 8:00 pm although some still serve customers at 11:00 pm or later. Chinatown has the most flexible hours of all, being open from early in the morning till late at night every day of the year except for Chinese New Year.

Credit cards are accepted almost everywhere and this is the safest way to shop. Traveller cheques in US dollars will be generally accepted but do not rely on them. Always keep your receipts and remember that most department stores will offer a refund and exchange service, if returned within a week.

When considering electronics, remember that the US voltage is likely to be different from that of your own country and without a transformer or dual voltage capability, the product will not work when you get home. Standard guarantees also only cover the United States. Along 34th Street, near Herald Square, is a cluster of shops selling cameras and electronic items. But, be cautious before purchasing anything from the discount electronic stores: the salespeople here are wily, their opening price is rarely the real one and they will not entertain you if you return dissatisfied. A recommended shop is **47th Street Photo** on West 47th Street. Their competitive prices are fixed and, for a little extra, they offer an extended warranty on everything they sell.

For general souvenirs, there are always shops located around the famous sites and places of interest. Pavement stalls have the least expensive T-shirts and other tourist items and a little sales psychology will usually bring the price down. As a general rule, in any shop or stall where the price is not printed and displayed, there is always the possibility of negotiating a mutually satisfactory price.

the **American Household: Gracious Home Store** on Third Avenue between 70th and 71st Streets.

Record stores are easy to find but for obscure titles and old records, there is nowhere better than **Bleecker Bob's Golden Oldies** on West Third Street near Sixth Avenue. It opens at midday and closes at 1:00 am Monday through Friday and at 3:00 am on weekends.

TRAVEL TIPS

BANKS & EXCHANGE OFFICES

Consult the Yellow Pages for bank branches throughout the city. Not every bank will exchange money or traveller's cheques but branches of Chemical Bank and Citibank will. Outside of banks, currency and traveller's cheques may be exchanged at:

American Express Travel Services
822 Lexington Avenue
Tel. 758-6510

1 World Trade Center
(in the lobby of Building One)
Tel: 775-0370

770 Broadway on 9th St near 4th Avenue
Tel: 598-5000

New York Hilton, 1365 6th Avenue
Tel: 664-7798

Chequepoint USA
551 Madison Avenue, Tel: 960-6443

Deak International
1 Herald Center, at 34th Street and 6th Avenue
Tel: 736-9790.

Freeport Currencies
132 W 45th Street, Tel: 221-2000

Harold Reuter & Co.
Met Life Building., 200 Park Avenue
Tel: 661-0826

Automatic Cash Dispensers accepting Mastercard and Visa 24 hours a day are located at:
Grand Central Terminal on 42nd Street at Park Avenue
100 World Trade Center
11 W 51Street at Rockefeller Center
14th Street and 6th Avenue
59th W 86th Street at Colombus Avenue

CINEMA

Check daily newspapers for current releases and the locations of the various cinema chains across the city. There are many other cinema houses showing films and Village Voice has comprehensive weekly listings. Well-established cinema houses are:
Angelika Film Center
Houston and Mercer Street, Tel: 995-2000

Carnegie Hall Cinema
7th Avenue and 56th Street, Tel: 265-2520

Cinema 3
59th Street near 5th Avenue, Tel: 752-5959

Cinema Village
3rd Avenue between 12th and 13th Street
Tel: 505-7320

Lincoln Plaza
Broadway near 63rd Street, Tel: 757-2280

Quad Cinema
13th Street near 5th Avenue, Tel: 255-8800

Walter Reade
165 W 65th Street (Lincoln Center).
Tel: 875-5600

DEPARTMENT STORES
Bergdorf Goodman
754 5th Avenue between 57th and 58th Streets
Tel: 753-7300

Bloomingdales
1000 3rd Avenue and 59th Street
Tel: 355-5900

Macy's
131 W 34th Street , Tel: 695-4400

Saks Fifth Avenue
611 5th Avenue, Tel: 753-4000

FOREIGN MISSIONS/EMBASSIES/
CONSULATES
Australia: 636 5th Avenue Tel: 245-4000
New Zealand: 630 5th Avenue Tel: 698-4650
Canada: 1251 6th Avenue Tel: 768-2400
Ireland: 515 Madison Avenue. Tel: 319-2555
United Kingdom: 845 3rd Avenue Tel: 752-8400
Japan: 299 Park Avenue Tel: 371-8222

US MISSIONS ABROAD
England
5 Upper Grovenor Street, London W1A 2JB
Tel: 071-7010

Scotland
3 Regent Terrace, Edinburgh EH7 5BW
Tel: 031-556-8315

Ireland
42 Elgin St, Ballsbridge, Dublin
Tel: 01-688777

Australia
Moonhah Place, Canberra
Tel: 62-733-711

New Zealand
29 Fitzherbert Terrace, Thomdon, Wellington.
Tel: 4-722-068.

HOSPITALS
Consult the Yellow Pages under 'Clinics' or 'Physicians and Surgeons' for doctors. In an emergency an ambulance takes patients to the nearest municipal hospital but for private treatment take a taxi to one of the following:
Bellevue Hospital
1st Avenue and E 29th Street
Tel: 561-4141

Mount Sinai Hospital
Madison Avenue and 100th Street
Tel 241-7171

St Vincent's Hospital
7th Avenue and 11th Street
Tel: 790-7000

New York Hospital
E 70th Street and York Avenue.
Tel: 472-5050

Beekman Downtown Hospital
170 Williams Street
Tel 312-5000

New York University Medical Center
1st Avenue at 30th Street
Tel: 340-7300

Roosevelt-St Luke's Hospital.
9th Avenue at 58th Street
Tel: 523-4000

NIGHTSPOTS
Concerts & Opera:
Alice Tully Hall
The Lincoln Center, W 62nd St and Broadway.
Tel: 362-1911

Avery Fisher Hall
Lincoln Center
Tel: 874-2424

Brooklyn Academy of Music
30 Lafayette Avenue and Broadway
Tel: 636-4100

Carnegie Hall
154 W 57th St and 7th Avenue, Tel: 247-7800

Metropolitan Opera
Lincoln Center, Tel: 362-6000

New York City Opera
Lincoln Center, Tel: 870-5570

Night Clubs & Discos:
Au Bar
41 E 58th Street, Tel 308-9455

Catch A Rising Star:
1487 1st Avenue, Tel: 794-1906

The Limelight
660 6th Avenue and 20th Street, Tel: 807-7850

Palladium
126 E 14th Street, Tel: 473-7171

The Tunnel
220 12th Avenue, Tel: 244-6444

USA
218 W 47th Street, Tel: 869-6103

Le Bar Brat
311 W 57th Street, Tel: 307-7228

Sound Factory
530 W 27th Street, Tel: 643-0728

Comeback: (Gay/Lesbian)
507 West St at Jane Street , Tel: 243-0090

Rock Music:
Hard Rock Cafe:
221 W 57th Street between Broadway and 7th
Avenue, Tel 459-9320

Madison Square Garden
7th/8th Avenue at W 31/33 Sts, Tel: 465-6000

Pyramid Club
101 Avenue A, between 6th and 7th Streets,
Tel: 420-1590

Radio City Music Hall
6th Avenue and 50th Street , Tel: 247-4777

CBGB
315 Bowey at Bleecker Street, Tel 677-0455

Tramps
51 W 21st Street, Tel: 727-7788

The Bottom Line
15 W 4th St at Mercer Street, Tel: 228-7880

Lone Star Roadhouse
240 W 52nd Street, Tel: 245-2950

Jazz Clubs:
Birdland
2745 Broadway, Tel: 749-2228

Blue Note
131 W 3rd Street, Tel: 475-8592

Bradley's
70 University Place, Tel: 473-9700

Greene Street Cafe
101 Greene Street, Tel: 925-2415

Sweet Basil
88 7th Avenue , Tel: 242-1785

Village Vanguard
178 7th Avenue, Tel: 255-4037

Fat Tuesday's.
190 3rd Avenue at 17th Street , Tel: 533-7902

Tavern on the Green,Central Park West
67th Street, Tel: 873-3200

The Sign of the Dove
1110 3rd Avenue at 65th Street, Tel: 861-8080

The Five Spot
4 West 31st Street, Tel 631-0100

PLACES OF WORSHIP

Consult the Yellow Pages for details of all 2,500 places of worship in the city. The following all hAvenuee regular services.

Anglican (Episcopal):
Cathedral of St John the Divine.
Amsterdam Avenue, 112th Street, Tel: 678-6888

St Bartholomew's
109 East 50th Street, Tel: 751-1616.

Trinity Church
Broadway and Wall Street, Tel: 602-0872

Catholic:
St Patrick's Cathedral
5th Avenue at 50th Street, Tel: 753-2261.

Jewish:
Temple Emanu-el
5th Avenue at 65th Street ,Tel: 744-1400

Unitarian Church of all Souls: Lexington Avenue 80th Street, Tel: 535-5535.

Baptist:
Calvary Baptist,123 W 57th Street

POLICE

In an emergency phone 911

Phone 374-8000 to establish the location and phone number of the precinct police station nearest to where you are.

POST OFFICES

The main branch is at 8th Avenue and W 33rd St and is open 24 hours a day from Monday to Saturday. Poste Restante should be addressed to the general Post Office, 321 8th Avenue, NY 10001.

SHOPPING CENTERS

A&S Plaza, 100 W 3rd Street and 6th Avenue
Tel 465-0500

Pier 17, South Street Seaport.

Rockefeller Center, 47th to 52nd Streets
Tel: 698-8500

World Financial Center, 200 Liberty Street, on West St, between Liberty and Vesey Streets.
Tel: 945-0505

World Trade Center, between West, Church, Vesey and Liberty streets, Tel: 435-4170.

Manhattan Art and Antique Center, 1050 2nd Avenue and 56th Street, Tel: 355-4400

MUSEUMS

Museums of Art
The Cloisters, Fort Tryon Park, Tel: 923-3700

Cooper-Hewitt Museum, 5th Avenue at 91st Street, Tel: 860-6868

Frick Collection, 1 E 70th Street, Tel: 288-0700

Guggenheim Museum:, 5th Avenue at E 89th Street,Tel: 360-3500

International Center of Photography, 5th Avenue at 94th Street, Tel: 860-1777
Museum of Modern Art, 11 W 53rd Street
Tel: 708-9480

Metropolitan Museum of Art
86th St at Lexington Avenue, Tel: 535-7710

Whitney Museum of American Art
45 Madison Avenue at 75th Street, Tel: 570-3676

Bronx Museum of the Arts
1040 Grand Concourse at 165th Street
Tel: 681-6000

The American Museum of the Moving Image
35th Avenue at 36th Street, Tel: 718-784-0077

Isamu Noguchi Museum
32-7 Vernon Boulevard, Astoria,
Tel: 718-204-7088

Museums of History & Culture
El Museo del Barrio
1230 5th Avenue at 104th Street, Tel: 831-7272

Jewish Museum
5th Avenue at 92nd Street, Tel: 860-1889

Hall of Chinese History
246 Bowery, Tel: 941-7661

Schomburg Center for Research in Black Culture,
515 Lenox Avenue, Tel: 491-2210

Lower East Side Tenement Museum
97 Orchard Street, Tel: 431-0233

Museum of the City of New York
5th Avenue at 103rd Street, Tel: 534-1034

New York Public Library
5th Avenue at 42nd Street, Tel: 930-0501

Police Academy Museum
235 E 20th Street, Tel: 477-97735

South Sea Seaport Museum
Visitors center, 207 Walter Street, Tel: 669-9424

The Ukrainian Museum
203 Second Avenue at 12th Street, Tel: 228-0110

Brooklyn History Museum
128 Pierrepont Street, Brooklyn Heights
Tel: 718-624-0890

Brooklyn Museum
200 Eastern Parkway, Tel: 718-638-5000

American Museum of Natural History
Central Park West, East 79th Street
Tel: 769-5100

Museums of Science
Intrepid Sea-Air-Space Museum.
Pier 86, West 46th Street, Tel: 245-2533

North Wind Undersea Museum:
610 City Island Avenue, City Island,
Tel: 885-0701

Hayden Planetarium
Central Park West, 81 Street Street,
Tel: 769-5920

DIRECTORY

Airlines - International
Air India
400 Park Avenue
Tel: 407-1460

Ana-All Nippon Airways
Tel: 800-235-9262

Cathay Pacific
590 5th Avenue
Tel: 819-0750

China Airlines
635 5th Avenue
Tel: 399-7877

Delta Airlines
120 Broadway
Tel: 239-0700

Garuda Airlines
51 East 42nd Street
Tel: 370-0707

Korean Air
609 5th Avenue
Tel: 371-4820

Pakistan Airlines
551 5th Avenue
Tel: 370-9158

Qantas
542 5th Avenue
Tel: 764-0200

Singapore Airlines
55 East 59th St
Tel: 644-8801 and 800-7422333

Thai Airways
Tel: 800-426-5204

Airlines- Domestic
Alaska Airlines
Tel: 800-426-0333

Aeromexico
37 West 57th St
Tel: 754-2140

America Airlines
Tel: 800-433-7300

American Trans Air
509 Madison Avenue
Tel: 838-4580

America West
Tel: 800-247-5692

Avianca
6 West 49th St
Tel: 399-0844

Continental
Tel: 319-9494

Eastern Airlines
Tel: 800-832-2746

TWA
Tel: 290-2121

USAir
Tel: 800-428-4322

Foreign Missions & Embassies
Argentina
12 West 56th St
Tel: 603-0400

Australia
636 5th Avenue
Tel: 245-4000

Britain
845 3rd Avenue
Tel: 752-8400

Australia
636 5th Avenue
Tel: 245-4000

India
3 East 64th Street
Tel: 879-7800

New Zealand
630 5th Avenue
Tel: 586-0060

Canada
1251 6th Avenue
Tel: 768-2442

France
934 5th Avenue
Tel: 606-3688

Italy
690 Park Avenue
Tel: 737-9100

Japan
299 Park Avenue
Tel: 371-8222

New Zealand
650 5th Avenue
Tel: 698-4650

Tourist Information Offices - Regional
The New York Convention &Visitors Bureau will put visitorsin contact with regional tourist information offices.
2 Columbus Circle.

Tourist Information Offices - Abroad
Australia
King & Castlereagh Streets
Suite 6106, MLC Center,
2000 Sydney
Tel: 233-4666

France
4 Avenue Gabriel
75008 Paris
Tel: 42-60-0066

Germany
Bethmannstrasse 56. 6000
Frankfurt/Main 1
Tel: 92-00-36-17

Hong Kong
26 Garden Road
Central Hong Kong.
Tel: 521-1467

Italy
Via Principe Amedeo, 2/10
20121 Milano
Tel: 2-2900-2657

Japan
Kokusai Building
hi, Chiyoda-ku, Tokyo 100
Tel: 3-3212-242

Korea
82 Sejong-ro, Chongro Ku, Seoul
110-050
Tel: 2-732-2601

Singapore
1 Colombo Court #05-12
Singapore 0617
Tel: 338-9722

Spain
Serrano, 75. 28006 Madrid
Tel: 1-571-4000

United Kingdom
P.O. Box 1EN. London WIA 1EN
Tel: 71-495-4466

US MISSIONS ABROAD
Canada
245 Britannia Road East,
Mississauga, Ontario.
Tel: 685-1930

France
4 Avenue Gabriel
75008 Paris
Tel: 42-60-0066

Germany
Bethmannstrasse 56. 6000
Frankfurt
Tel: 92-00-36-17

Hong Kong
26 Garden Road,
Central Hong Kong
Tel: 521-1467
Fax: 845-9800

Ireland
42 Elgin Road
Ballsbridge, Dublin 4.
Tel: 1-687-122
Fax: 1-682-840

Italy
Via Principe Amedeo, 2/10
20121 Milano.
Tel: 2-2900-2657

Korea
82 Sejong-ro, Chongro Ku, Seoul
110-050
Tel: 2-732-2601

Singapore
1 Colombo Court, #05-12
Singapore 0617
Tel: 338-9722

Spain
Serrano, 75. 28006 Madrid
Tel: 1-571-4000

United Kingdom
5 Upper Grosvenor St
London W1A 2JB
Tel: 71-499-7010

PHOTO CREDITS

314

INDEX

INDEX

319